The Routledge Advanced Language Training Course for K-16 Non-native Chinese Teachers

The Routledge Advanced Language Training Course for K-16 Non-native Chinese Teachers is a content-based and thematically organized textbook designed for non-native in- and pre-service K-16 Chinese language teachers.

Based on five years of field testing, the book offers an innovative approach to advanced language instruction, allowing users to further advance their language proficiency while continuing their professional development in teaching Chinese as a second or foreign language.

The textbook:

- covers a range of up-to-date pedagogical and cultural themes
- provides a variety of engaging activities and exercises, allowing readers for K-16 to explore pedagogical and cultural issues in the target language with best classroom practices in mind
- familiarises users with authentic forms of modern communication in today's China to better engage learners
- is accompanied by a companion website with audio recordings for each lesson as well as supplementary materials and teaching resources

The Routledge Advanced Language Training Course for K-16 Non-native Chinese Teachers is an essential resource for non-native Chinese teachers and for those on TCFL teacher training programs.

Hong Gang Jin is University Chair Professor at the University of Macau.

Lian Xue is Visiting Instructor of East Asian Language and Literature at Hamilton College, New York.

Yusheng Yang is Assistant Teaching Professor at Georgetown University.

Lan Zhao Zhou is Assistant on the Teacher Development Program at the Associated Colleges in China (ACC).

如林K-16非母语中文教师高级培训教程
The Routledge Advanced Language Training Course for K-16 Non-native Chinese Teachers

靳洪刚
薛莲
杨玉笙
周岚钊

Series editor: Yongcan Liu

LONDON AND NEW YORK

First published 2016
by Routledge
2 Park Square, Milton Park, Abingdon, Oxon OX14 4RN

and by Routledge
711 Third Avenue, New York, NY 10017

Routledge is an imprint of the Taylor & Francis Group, an informa business

© 2016 Hong Gang Jin, Lian Xue, Yusheng Yang and Lan Zhao Zhou

The right of Hong Gang Jin, Lian Xue, Yusheng Yang and Lan Zhao Zhou to be identified as authors of this work has been asserted by them in accordance with sections 77 and 78 of the Copyright, Designs and Patents Act 1988.

All rights reserved. No part of this book may be reprinted or reproduced or utilised in any form or by any electronic, mechanical, or other means, now known or hereafter invented, including photocopying and recording, or in any information storage or retrieval system, without permission in writing from the publishers.

Trademark notice: Product or corporate names may be trademarks or registered trademarks, and are used only for identification and explanation without intent to infringe.

British Library Cataloguing-in-Publication Data
A catalogue record for this book is available from the British Library

Library of Congress Cataloging-in-Publication Data
Names: Jin, Honggang, author.
Title: The Routledge advanced language training course for K-16 non-native Chinese teachers / Hong Gang Jin, Lian Xue, Yusheng Yang and Lan Zhao Zhou.
Description: Milton Park, Abingdon, Oxon ; New York, NY : Routledge, [2016]
Identifiers: LCCN 2015027772| ISBN 9781138920927 (hbk. : alk. paper) |
ISBN 9781138920934 (pbk. : alk. paper) | ISBN 9781315686295 (ebk)
Subjects: LCSH: Language teachers–Training of. | Chinese language–Study and teaching–English language. | Chinese language–Sound recordings for English speakers. | Second language education–Study and teaching–English speakers.
Classification: LCC P53.85 .J45 2016 | DDC 495.180071–dc23
LC record available at http://lccn.loc.gov/2015027772

ISBN: 978-1-138-92092-7 (hbk)
ISBN: 978-1-138-92093-4 (pbk)
ISBN: 978-1-315-68629-5 (ebk)

Typeset in Times New Roman, 宋体
by Graphicraft Limited, Hong Kong

目录 (Contents)

Foreword   viii

教学篇 (Pedagogy)

标题 Title	文本形式 Media format	版本 Version	页码 Page
第一课	以标准为本的语言教学 Standards-based Language Instruction	专业讨论 Discussion	全版 CV* 3
	以标准为本的语言教学 Standards-based Language Instruction	专业讨论 Discussion	节选版 AV* 8
第二课	反向课程设计与主题单元 Backward Curricular Design and Thematic Unit Approach	电子邮件 Email	全版 CV 18
	反向课程设计与主题单元 Backward Curricular Design and Thematic Unit Approach	电子邮件 Email	节选版 AV 24
第三课	目标语教学与可理解输入 Teaching in the Target Language and Comprehensible Input	专业讨论 Discussion	全版 CV 49
	目标语教学与可理解输入 Teaching in the Target Language and Comprehensible Input	专业讨论 Discussion	节选版 AV 55
第四课	有效教学策略 Effective Instructional Strategies	教学论坛 Panel discussion	全版 CV 65
	有效教学策略 Effective Instructional Strategies	教学论坛 Panel discussion	节选版 AV 71
第五课	纠错反馈 Corrective Feedback	学术文章 Journal article	全版 CV 81
	纠错反馈 Corrective Feedback	学术文章 Journal article	节选版 AV 87

vi *Contents*

第六课	故事情景教学法 (TPRS) Teaching Proficiency through Reading and Storytelling	专业讨论 Discussion	全版 .... 97 CV
	故事情景教学法 (TPRS) Teaching Proficiency through Reading and Storytelling	专业讨论 Discussion	节选版 .... 102 AV
第七课	任务教学设计 Task-based Instructional Design	面试 Interview	全版 .... 111 CV
	任务教学设计 Task-based Instructional Design	面试 Interview	节选版 .... 116 AV
第八课	汉语语音与声调教学 On Instruction of Chinese Pronunciation and Tones	电子邮件 Email	全版 .... 125 CV
	汉语语音与声调教学 On Instruction of Chinese Pronunciation and Tones	电子邮件 Email	节选版 .... 131 AV
第九课	汉字教学 On Instruction of Chinese Literacy	专业演讲 Lecture	全版 .... 141 CV
	汉字教学 On Instruction of Chinese Literacy	专业演讲 Lecture	节选版 .... 146 CV

文化篇 (Culture)

	标题 Title	文本形式 Media format	版本 Version	页码 Page
第一课	《隐形的翅膀》歌词赏析 A Popular Chinese Song and its Social Impact	博客 Blog	全版 CV	 159
	《隐形的翅膀》歌词赏析 A Popular Chinese Song and its Social Impact	博客 Blog	节选版 AV	 165
第二课	中国教育现状 The Current State of China's Education	报刊文章 Newspaper	全版 CV	 173
	中国教育现状 The Current State of China's Education	报刊文章 Newspaper	节选版 AV	 178
第三课	华人禁忌 Chinese Taboos	杂志文章 Journal article	全版 CV	 186
	华人禁忌 Chinese Taboos	杂志文章 Journal article	节选版 AV	 191

Contents vii

第四课	流行新词 New and Popular Chinese Expressions	社会热点讨论 Discussion	全版 CV	199
	流行新词 New and Popular Chinese Expressions	社会热点讨论 Discussion	节选版 AV	204
第五课	现代科技：微信 Modern Technology: WeChat	科技说明 Instruction	全版 CV	212
	现代科技：微信 Modern Technology: WeChat	科技说明 Instruction	节选版 AV	216
第六课	纪录片讨论《请投我一票》 A Chinese Documentary —Please Vote For Me	影评会 Discussion	全版 CA	225
	纪录片讨论《请投我一票》 A Chinese Documentary —Please Vote For Me	影评会 Discussion	节选版 AV	232

附录 (Appendices)

附录一　教学论坛演讲模板 242
　　　　Panel discussion routines
附录二　讨论会模板 243
　　　　Professional discussion routines
附录三　课堂用语 247
　　　　Classroom expressions
附录四　专业书面表达演说范文 253
　　　　Samples of commonly used Chinese formal and professional
　　　　text format
　　　　推荐专业学术会议（格式：会议介绍与评价）.......................... 253
　　　　Conference recommendation and evaluation
　　　　邀请信（格式：正式书信）.. 253
　　　　Formal invitation letter
　　　　说明语言教学中的纠错反馈（格式：总结要点）...................... 254
　　　　Summary and main points
　　　　讲座总结报告（格式：专业会议信息汇报）.......................... 254
　　　　Lecture summary and conference summary
　　　　课堂观摩反馈（格式：分析与建议）...................................... 255
　　　　Class observation report and feedback
　　　　主持学术会议：介绍来宾（格式：介绍来宾讲稿）.................. 255
　　　　Chair a panel: introduction of the guest speaker
　　　　主持学术会议：主持演讲后的讨论（格式：与听众交流）....... 256
　　　　Chair a panel: moderate discussions after the lecture

Note:
*CV is complete version; AV is abridged version

Foreword

Introduction

The textbook *The Routledge Advanced Language Training Course for K-16 Non-native Chinese Teachers* is a content-based and thematically organized textbook. It is designed for in-service and pre-service K-16 non-native Chinese language teachers, whose needs are twofold: 1. to further advance their language proficiency, and 2. to continue their professional development on teaching Chinese as a second/foreign language. Based on five years of field testing with K-16 in-service and pre-service non-native Chinese teachers, the book strives to offer an innovative approach to advanced language instruction, to cover a variety of up-to-date pedagogical and cultural themes and topics, and to maintain a balance between content-based and language-focused instruction relevant to K-16 Chinese language teachers.

Overarching goal of the book

- to provide continued professional development to K-16 non-native Chinese language teachers in language, pedagogy, and culture

Objectives of the lessons

- to develop professional proficiency in Chinese language so that users can engage in professional activities in the target language
- to expose users to a variety of modern pedagogical theories, contemporary Chinese cultural themes, and effective instructional strategies of teaching Chinese as a foreign/second language
- to familiarize users with a variety of authentic forms and media of communication in China
- to provide a variety of well-designed and engaging activities and exercises for K-16 Chinese teachers to explore pedagogical and cultural issues in the target language and with best classroom practices in mind

Foreword   ix

Content and format of the textbook

This book consists of two major parts: Pedagogy and Culture. The pedagogy section covers 9 language teaching related topics/lessons, including national foreign language standards, backward curricular design, teaching strategies, corrective feedback techniques, task-based language instruction, and instructional strategies specific to Chinese language teaching, such as how to teach Chinese tones, pronunciation, and Chinese characters and reading. The culture section contains 6 topics/lessons, ranging from Chinese arts, education and new cultural phenomena to social taboos, social changes, and technological innovation.

Each lesson replicates a form of modern day authentic communication and social media in China's academia. The examples are professional discussions, panel discussions, academic conference presentations, journal articles, newspaper articles, documentary films, emails, blogs, web publications, etc. In this way, the textbook users will not only be exposed to professional and academic materials in Chinese but are also exposed to authentic communication means and media in Chinese society.

In order to offer differentiated instruction to K-16 teachers with varying language and culture backgrounds, all 15 lessons are presented with two versions: a complete version (CV) with elaboration and an abridged version (AV) with simplification. All of the text content and exercises were field-tested by over 150 non-native teacher participants in our programs during the last five years and have systematically been revised based on participants' feedback, comments, and suggestions.

Each lesson provides a series of usage-based and hands-on activities/tasks covering three types of communicative abilities highlighted by the national foreign language standards: interpretive, interpersonal and presentational communication skills (see the sample lessons). Under this exercise framework, users can engage in group or individual activities and tasks, which helps users map communicative functions with linguistic forms and employ the appropriate professional language to discuss and share teaching and learning experiences.

The textbook will be accompanied by a companion website for supplementary materials and teaching resources.

Organization and structure of each lesson

Each lesson is divided into three parts.

Part 1. Can-do statements and key words

This part of the text clearly states to the user the expected learning outcomes of the lesson. It is expressed in three or four "can-do statements" in terms of communicative functions to be achieved across three communicative modes (interpretive, interpersonal, and presentational). For example, Lesson 1 "can-do statements" state as follows:

x *Foreword*

By the end of the lesson, the learners will be able to:

1. interpret and understand the key concept of standards-based instruction
2. engage in discussions about the key terms involved in this approach
3. present how to design a standards-based lesson plan orally or in writing

In addition, this part also highlights the key terms to be used in the target type of professional discussion.

Part 2. Main text in two versions with vocabulary and key structures

This part provides two versions of the main text: a complete and an abridged version. It is the textbook's intention to accommodate different learners with varying levels of language proficiency and backgrounds (in-service or pre-service). At the end of each text page, the vocabulary is provided with Chinese characters, Pinyin, part of speech, and English meaning. Key structures and grammatical patterns are also listed, each with two examples, at the end of both the complete and abridged text.

Each text is an adapted piece of authentic material, either written by native language professionals, or adapted from professional writings. Each lesson also strives to present the user with authentic and realistic forms of communication in modern day China. For example, 12 different forms of media are used to present different texts so that users are exposed to diverse means of professional interaction and communication. Examples include formal interviews with a professional researcher, informal professional discussions with colleagues, formal panel presentations, email exchanges with colleagues, journal and newspaper articles, PowerPoint presentations, and blogs by Chinese people.

Through its carefully selected text content and format, the textbook meets the dual needs of K-16 teachers: 1. second-language related research issues and pedagogical practices specific to teaching Chinese, and 2. authentic and contextualized professional terms, formulaic expressions, linguistic constructions, and communicative routines necessary to engage in professional discussions in Chinese.

Part 3. Pre-lesson and follow-up activities and tasks

This part consists of six types of pre-lesson and follow-up activities and tasks intended to reinforce what is learned in each lesson. The design focuses on three types of communication in order to help learners map each lesson's communicative functions with linguistic forms in Chinese and to use professional language to communicate with each other.

1. Interpretive task 1: Preview of the text. Using the format of outlining, questions, fill in the blanks, and summary, this activity is intended to familiarize learners with the main topic, sub-topics, text organization, communication routines and key structures of the text prior to class.

Foreword xi

2. Interpretive task 2: Extended reading. Using selected and adapted authentic texts relevant to the main lesson as reading material, this activity functions as a follow-up and supplementary exercise to further learners' comprehension and understanding of the main text and also to extend the knowledge and skills of the lesson. Each extended reading is accompanied by a set of comprehension questions and discussion topics in the format of multiple choice, open-ended discussions, and experience-sharing activities.

3. Interpersonal task 1 (oral): Face-to-face interaction. Using contextualized situations and dialogues, this activity provides opportunities for learners to engage in face-to-face and meaningful conversations with a focus on recycling and practicing target vocabulary and key structures of the lesson. In order to help learners map functions with forms and direct their attention to necessary language nuances in a salient way, each turn of the dialogue is supplied with suggested key structures and fixed patterns to effectively complete the conversation (see the sample lessons).

4. Interpersonal task 2 (written): Online discussion. Using contextualized situations and different forms of social media, such as Facebook, text messages, web discussions, chat rooms, blogs, etc. this activity provides interpersonal communication opportunities in writing to further the understanding of the main topic and to help convert declarative knowledge of the lesson into procedural skills.

5. Presentational task. Using the format of oral and written presentations, this activity provides learners with the opportunity to further consolidate the knowledge and skills learned from the lesson by using the target language in a creative way, such as delivering formal presentations, systematically demonstrating one's professional studies, and sharing one's pedagogical practices with an audience in detail. The examples include a five-minute presentation on a topic, reading response to an article/talk/presentation, PowerPoint presentation on a lesson plan or an exercise/task design, email response, and discussion on a focal topic, etc.

6. Reflective task. With the online teaching resources or research materials as props, this activity uses a three-task cycle—pre-task, core task, and post-task—to help learners reflect on what they have learned from the lesson and how they can apply it to their day-to-day teaching.

Part 4. Companion website

This book comes with a companion website containing different learning and teaching resources.

Short biographies of the four authors

Hong Gang Jin: PhD in second language acquisition (SLA) and teacher education, Jin is currently serving as Chair Professor, Dean of Arts and Humanities at University of Macau. She is a well-established researcher and professor in SLA and Chinese as a foreign language (CFL) fields. With over 25 years of

xii *Foreword*

classroom teaching and program administration experience, Jin has published three sets of Chinese language textbooks in the US and over 30 journal articles on Chinese as a second language. Jin has received eight major grants from federal and private agencies to operate student programs and teacher training programs in China and in the US. She is also a recipient of many national awards for excellence in teaching.

Lian Xue: MA in CFL, Lian is a seasoned language instructor at Hamilton College with an abundance of teaching and coordinating experience. As a result of her excellent teaching experience in two prestigious language programs in the US and China, she was appointed as head teacher and program coordinator of the Chinese Program curriculum in the Department of East Asian Languages and Literatures at Hamilton College. Lian has been directly involved in the K-12 program operation and material development for the past three years.

Yusheng Yang: MA in CFL and a seasoned language instructor at Georgetown University, Yang is currently teaching Chinese language at Georgetown University. Because of her excellent teaching record, she was appointed as coordinator for the Hamilton ACC Fulbright Hays GPA K-16 Teachers Institute in the early years of program establishment. She helped design the K-16 program curriculum and led the program in China for three years. Her experience in K-16 Chinese language teacher development has contributed a great deal to the current textbook.

Lan Zhao Zhou: MA in CFL and an effective language instructor and coordinator at Hamilton's Associated Colleges in China (ACC), Zhou is currently teaching in Beijing, China, at ACC, a study abroad program well known in the US. She has been appointed as coordinator for the Hamilton ACC Fulbright Hays GPA K-16 Teachers Institute for the last three years and has contributed a great deal to the textbook content and revision based on her interviews and interaction with K-16 teacher participants.

Part I
教学篇 (Pedagogy)

第一课　以标准为本的语言教学[1]
Standards-based Language Instruction

（文本形式：专业讨论）

> ➤ 关键词：
> 以标准为本的语言教学、5C、内容标准、能力标准、三种沟通模式、主题单元设计、反向课程设计、能力目标
> ➤ 能力目标：
> 1. 学习者能使用专业术语讨论"以标准为本的语言教学"。
> 2. 学习者能理解并说明如何把"五大教学内容"贯穿在教学中。
> 3. 学习者能讨论如何利用"三种沟通模式"来进行主题单元设计。

---

[1]以标准为本的　yǐbiāozhǔnwéiběnde　NP.　Standards-based Language Instruction
　语言教学　　　yǔyánjiàoxué

课文全版 (Complete Version)

（许老师和孙老师都参加了今年十一月的全美外语教师年会。两个人在会场[2]上认识了。会议休息时，许老师和孙老师决定在楼下咖啡馆喝点儿咖啡，边喝边聊。）

许：孙老师，这是你第一次参加全美外语教师学会[3]的年会吗？

孙：是啊，大会各类报告都有，组织[4]安排也都很棒，不过有意思的主题太多了，没有办法场场都参加。

许：没错。我也有同感[5]。今天早上你听了什么报告？

孙：我听了一场报告，主题是关于"以标准为本的语言教学"。

许：那场报告怎么样？

孙：对我来说很有用。我的项目主任[6]多次提到"以标准为本的语言教学"，这个专业术语[7]我早就听说过了，但是我一直不清楚真正的意思是什么。

许：是吗？现在你明白了吧？报告还提到什么内容？

孙：他们说现在有一本书详细[8]介绍了美国国家外语教学的标准，书名是《二十一世纪的外语教学标准》[9]。报告的一个重点[10]是外语教学的内容标准。报告认为，外语教学应该包括[11]五个以C开头的教学内容。所谓的5C是指：交际沟通[12]、文化学习[13]、文化与语言比较[14]……

许：是不是还有学科联系[15]跟社区应用[16]？

[2]会场	huìchǎng	N.	conference hall
[3]全美外语教师学会	quánměiwàiyǔ jiàoshīxuéhuì	NP.	American Council on the Teaching of Foreign Languages (ACTFL)
[4]组织	zǔzhī	V./N.	to organize; organization
[5]有同感	yǒutónggǎn	VP.	to feel the same way
[6]项目主任	xiàngmùzhǔrèn	NP.	program director
[7]专业术语	zhuānyèshùyǔ	NP.	terminology
[8]详细	xiángxì	Adj.	detailed, in detail
[9]二十一世纪的外语教学标准	èrshíyīshìjidewàiyǔ jiàoxuébiāozhǔn	NP.	Standards for Foreign Language Instruction in the 21st Century
[10]重点	zhòngdiǎn	N.	focal point
[11]包括	bāokuò	V.	to include
[12]交际沟通	jiāojìgōutōng	NP.	Communication
[13]文化学习	wénhuàxuéxí	NP.	Cultures
[14]文化与语言比较	wénhuàyǔyǔyánbǐjiào	NP.	Comparisons
[15]学科联系	xuékēliánxì	NP.	Connections
[16]社区应用	shèqūyìngyòng	NP.	Communities

孙：对对对。这五个方面也是美国外语学习的五大目标。当我们在设计[17]课程时，必须时时刻刻[18]记得把这五个方面的内容都包括进去。

许：除了内容标准以外，报告还讨论了什么？

孙：报告还介绍了语言能力的三个方面，也就是交际的三种沟通模式[19]，包括理解诠释[20]、人际交流[21]和表达演说[22]。这三种沟通模式强调[23]在语言教学中要注重学生的交际能力，而且要从这三个方面培养[24]学生使用语言的能力。

许：报告提到主题单元设计[25]了吗？我对这个题目也很感兴趣。

孙：提到了。主题单元设计非常强调设计课程时利用交际主题[26]把课文串起来[27]。教师可以利用一个主题和几个子题[28]来组织语言教学，让学生使用真实[29]的语言做有意义[30]的沟通。

许：专业教学对教师的要求真的很高，尤其是对新教师来说，要学的东西太多了。

孙：没错。除了主题单元设计外，报告还强调教师要掌握[31]反向课程设计[32]的原则[33]。

许：反向课程设计？反向课程设计的原则是什么？

孙：据我所知，反向课程设计的原则是，首先设定[34]能力目标[35]，也就是教师希望学生在学期末能获得[36]什么语言能力；其次是设计科学的教

[17]设计	shèjì	V./N.	to design; design
[18]时时刻刻	shíshíkèkè	Adv.	constantly, always
[19]三种沟通模式	sānzhǒnggōutōngmóshì	NP.	3 communicative modes
[20]理解诠释	lǐjiěquánshì	NP.	Interpretive Communication
[21]人际交流	rénjìjiāoliú	NP.	Interpersonal Communication
[22]表达演说	biǎodáyǎnshuō	NP.	Presentational Communication
[23]强调	qiángdiào	V.	to emphasize
[24]培养	péiyǎng	V.	to cultivate, to train
[25]主题单元设计	zhǔtídānyuánshèjì	NP.	Thematic Unit Design
[26]交际主题	jiāojìzhǔtí	NP.	communication theme
[27]把…串起来	bǎ … chuànqǐlái	VP.	to string together
[28]子题	zǐtí	N.	sub-theme
[29]真实	zhēnshí	Adj.	authentic, real
[30]有意义	yǒuyìyì	Adj.	meaningful
[31]掌握	zhǎngwò	V.	to master, to know well
[32]反向课程设计	fǎnxiàngkèchéngshèjì	NP.	Backwards Curriculum Design
[33]原则	yuánzé	N.	principle
[34]设定	shèdìng	V.	to establish firmly
[35]能力目标	nénglìmùbiāo	NP.	can-do statement
[36]获得	huòdé	V.	to obtain, to acquire

6 Standards-based Language Instruction

学评估[37]方法，测试[38]学生的学习结果；最后是考虑使用什么样的教学策略[39]和活动帮助学生获得这些能力。

许：　所以反向课程设计的基本原则就是你必须先决定学生应该能做什么，然后才能教学生学什么。听起来非常有道理[40]，你说是不是？

孙：　的确[41]很有道理。

 语言重点：

1. **Subj.参加…（年会/大会/会议/活动/典礼）**

    Subj. takes part in/participates in ... (annual meeting/convention/conference/activity/ceremony)

    - 孙老师，这是你第一次参加全美外语教师学会的年会吗？
    - 为了提高专业教学能力，全国的外语教师都参加了本次以反向课程设计为主题的教学活动。

2. **Subj.以+NP/VP+为本/为主题/为目标/为原则/为重点**

    Subj. uses/takes ... as ... (basis/theme/objective/principle/focal point)

    - 我听了一场很有意思的报告，主题是关于"以标准为本的语言教学"。
    - 在第二语言课程设计中，教师应以内容标准为原则，以三种沟通模式为重点进行设计。

3. **Subj.（在…）多次+VP（提到/强调/重申…）**

    (During/At ...) subj. (raised/emphasized/reaffirmed ...) many times

    - 我的项目主任多次提到"以标准为本的语言教学"。
    - 这位教授在此次以提高第二语言学习者语言能力为目标的会议中多次重申交际的三种沟通模式对培养学习者使用语言能力的重要性。

4. **所谓的NP是指…**

    The so-called NP means ...

    - 所谓的5C是指：交际沟通、文化学习、文化与语言比较、学科联系和社区应用。
    - 报告中多次提到"主题单元设计"这一专业术语，所谓的"主题单元设计"是指设计课程时利用交际主题把课文串起来，教师利用主题跟几个子题组织语言教学。

---

[37]评估	pínggū	V.	to assess, to evaluate
[38]测试	cèshì	V.	to examine, to assess
[39]策略	cèlüè	N.	strategy
[40]有道理	yǒudàolǐ	Adj.	reasonable, rational
[41]的确	díquè	Adv.	indeed

Standards-based Language Instruction 7

5. 当**Sb.**在**VP**（设计课程/设计活动/设计评估方法/设定目标/设定标准/评估）时，必须/应该+**VP**（强调/注意/确立/检测/考虑…）

When/While … (designing curriculum/designing activities/designing assessment methodology/designing objectives/designing standards/assessing), subj. must/should … (emphasize/pay attention to/establish/test/consider …)

- 当我们在设计课程时，必须时时刻刻记得把这五个方面的内容包括进去。
- 当语言教师在设计目标时，必须考虑学生的实际语言能力，同时也应该注意语言目标与能力目标的关系。

6. ① **A**（从…方面）培养**B**的…（语言/交际/专业/教学）能力

  (from … aspects) A cultivates B's … (language/communication/professional/teaching) ability

  ② **A**（从…方面）培养**B**+**VP**（使用语言/与人交流）的能力

  (from … aspects) A cultivates B's ability to … (use language/communicate interpersonally)

  ③ **A**培养**B**对**NP**（音乐/中国文化）的兴趣

  A cultivates B's interest in … (music/Chinese culture)

- 教师在设计课程时，应该注意从理解诠释、人际交流、表达演说这三个方面来培养学生的交际能力。
- 这三种沟通模式强调在语言教学中要注重学生的交际能力，而且要从这三个方面培养学生使用语言的能力。
- 语言教学不仅应以培养学生的语言交际能力为目标，也应以培养学习者对中国文化的兴趣为重点。

7. **Subj.**利用+**NP**来+**VP**（把课文串起来/组织语言教学）…（，让**sb.**+**do sth.**）

Subj. uses NP to … (string together the text/organize language teaching) … (and make/allow sb. to …)

- 主题教学设计非常强调设计课程时利用交际主题把课文串起来。
- 在利用主题与子题来组织语言教学的同时，外语教师也应该利用目标语来进行教学，这样一来，可以让学生获得大量丰富的语言输入。

8. 首先…；其次…；最后…

First … ; then … ; finally …

- 反向课程设计的原则是，首先确立能力目标，也就是教师希望学生在学期末能够获得什么语言能力；其次是设计科学的教学评估方法，测试学生的学习结果；最后是考虑使用什么样的教学策略和活动帮助学生获得这些能力。
- 为了更好地使用目标语教学，在备课时，教师首先应该搞清楚学生对什么内容有困难；其次考虑如何用简单易懂的方法或者例子说明；最后设计好提问内容，以便在课上鼓励学生使用目标语进行语义协商。

第一课　以标准为本的语言教学[1]
Standards-based Language Instruction

（文本形式：专业讨论）

> ➤ 关键词：
> 以标准为本的语言教学、5C、内容标准、能力标准、三种沟通模式、主题单元设计
> ➤ 能力目标：
> 1. 学习者能使用专业术语讨论"以标准为本的语言教学"。
> 2. 学习者能理解并说明如何把"五大教学内容"贯穿在教学中。
> 3. 学习者能讨论如何利用"三种沟通模式"来进行主题单元设计。

---

[1] 以标准为本的语言教学　yǐbiāozhǔnwéiběnde yǔyánjiàoxué　NP.　Standards-based Language Instruction

Standards-based Language Instruction 9

课文节选版 (Abridged Version)

（许老师和孙老师参加了今年十一月的全美外语教师年会。两个人在会场[2]上认识了。会议休息时，许老师和孙老师决定在楼下咖啡馆喝点儿咖啡，边喝边聊。）

许：孙老师，这是你第一次参加全美外语教师学会[3]的年会吗？

孙：是啊，大会各类报告都有，组织[4]安排也都很棒，不过有意思的主题太多了，没有办法场场都参加。

许：没错。我也有同感[5]。今天早上你听了什么报告？

孙：我听了一场报告，主题是关于"以标准为本的语言教学"。

许：那场报告怎么样？

孙：对我来说很有用。我的项目主任[6]多次提到[7]"以标准为本的语言教学"，这个专业术语[8]我早就听说过了，但是我一直不清楚真正的意思是什么。

许：是吗？现在你明白了吧？报告还提到什么内容？

孙：他们说现在有一本书详细[9]介绍了美国国家外语教学的标准，书名是《二十一世纪的外语教学标准》[10]。报告的一个重点[11]是外语教学的内容标准。报告认为，外语教学应该包括[12]五个以C开头[13]的教学内容。所谓的5C是指：交际沟通[14]、文化学习[15]、文化与语言比较[16]……

许：是不是还有学科联系[17]跟社区应用[18]？

[2]会场	huìchǎng	N.	conference hall
[3]全美外语教师学会	quánměiwàiyǔ jiàoshīxuéhuì	NP.	ACTFL
[4]组织	zǔzhī	V./N.	to organize; organization
[5]有同感	yǒutónggǎn	VP.	to feel the same way
[6]项目主任	xiàngmùzhǔrèn	NP.	program director
[7]提到	tídào	V.	to mention
[8]专业术语	zhuānyèshùyǔ	NP.	terminology
[9]详细	xiángxì	Adj.	detailed, in detail
[10]二十一世纪的外语教学标准	èrshíyīshìjìdewàiyǔ jiàoxuébiāozhǔn	NP.	Standards for Foreign Language Instruction in the 21st Century
[11]重点	zhòngdiǎn	N.	focal point
[12]包括	bāokuò	V.	to include
[13]开头	kāitóu	N./V.	beginning, to start
[14]交际沟通	jiāojìgōutōng	NP.	Communication
[15]文化学习	wénhuàxuéxí	NP.	Cultures
[16]文化与语言比较	wénhuàyǔyǔyánbǐjiào	NP.	Comparisons
[17]学科联系	xuékēliánxì	NP.	Connections
[18]社区应用	shèqūyìngyòng	NP.	Communities

孙：对对对。这五个方面也是美国外语学习的五大目标。当我们在设计[19]课程时，必须时时刻刻[20]记得把这五个方面的内容都包括进去。

许：除了内容标准以外，报告还讨论了什么？

孙：报告还介绍了语言能力的三个方面，也就是交际的三种沟通模式[21]，包括理解诠释[22]、人际交流[23]和表达演说[24]。这三种沟通模式强调[25]在语言教学中要注重[26]学生的交际能力，而且要从这三个方面培养[27]学生使用语言的能力。

许：报告提到主题单元设计[28]了吗？我对这个题目也很感兴趣。

孙：提到了。主题单元设计非常强调设计课程时利用[29]交际主题[30]把课文串起来[31]。教师可以利用一个主题和几个子题[32]来组织语言教学，让学生使用真实[33]的语言做有意义[34]的沟通。

许：专业教学对教师的要求真的很高，尤其是对新教师来说，要学的东西太多了。

[19]设计	shèjì	V./N.	to design; design
[20]时时刻刻	shíshíkèkè	Adv.	constantly, always
[21]三种沟通模式	sānzhǒnggōutōngmóshì	NP.	3 communicative modes
[22]理解诠释	lǐjiěquánshì	NP.	Interpretive Communication
[23]人际交流	rénjìjiāoliú	NP.	Interpersonal Communication
[24]表达演说	biǎodáyǎnshuō	NP.	Presentational Communication
[25]强调	qiángdiào	V.	to emphasize
[26]注重	zhùzhòng	V.	to lay stress on; attach importance to
[27]培养	péiyǎng	V.	to cultivate, to train
[28]主题单元设计	zhǔtídānyuánshèjì	NP.	Thematic Unit Design
[29]利用	lìyòng	V.	to use, to utilize
[30]交际主题	jiāojìzhǔtí	NP.	communication theme
[31]把…串起来	bǎ … chuànqǐlái	VP.	to string together
[32]子题	zǐtí	N.	sub-theme
[33]真实	zhēnshí	Adj.	authentic, real
[34]有意义	yǒuyìyì	Adj.	meaningful

语言重点：

1. **Subj.**参加…（年会/大会/会议/活动/典礼）

   Subj. takes part in/participates in … (annual meeting/convention/conference/activity/ceremony)

   - 孙老师，这是你第一次参加全美外语教师学会的年会吗？
   - 为了提高专业教学能力，全国的外语教师都参加了本次以主题单元设计为重点的讨论活动。

2. **Subj.**以+NP/VP+为本/为主题/为目标/为原则/为重点

   Subj. uses/takes … as … (basis/theme/objective/principle/focal point)

   - 我听了一场很有意思的报告，主题是关于"以标准为本的语言教学"。
   - 这次会议以提高全美外语教师的专业教学能力为目标。

3. **Subj.**（在…）多次+VP（提到/强调/重申…）

   (During/At …) subj. (raised/emphasized/reaffirmed …) many times

   - 我的项目主任多次提到"以标准为本的教学"。
   - 这位教授在此次以提高第二语言学习者语言能力为目标的会议中多次重申交际的三种沟通模式对培养学习者使用语言能力的重要性。

4. 所谓的**NP**是指…

   The so-called NP means …

   - 所谓的5C是指：交际沟通、文化学习、文化与语言比较、学科联系和社区应用。
   - 报告中多次提到"主题单元设计"这一专业术语，所谓的"主题单元设计"是指设计课程时利用交际主题把课文串起来，教师利用主题跟几个子题组织语言教学。

5. 当**Sb.**在**VP**（设计课程/设计活动/设计评估方法/设定目标/设定标准/评估）时，必须应该+**VP**（强调/注意/确立/检测/考虑…）

   When/While … (designing curriculum/designing activities/designing assessment methodology/designing objectives/designing standards/assessing), subj. must/should … (emphasize/pay attention to/establish/test/consider …)

   - 当我们在设计课程时，必须时时刻刻记得把这五个方面的内容包括进去。
   - 当语言教师在设计目标时，必须考虑学生的实际语言能力，同时也应该注意语言目标与能力目标的关系。

12 *Standards-based Language Instruction*

6. ① **A（从···方面）培养B的···（语言/交际/专业/教学）能力**

(from ... aspects) A cultivates B's ... (language/communication/professional/teaching) ability

② **A（从···方面）培养B+VP（使用语言/与人交流）的能力**

(from ... aspects) A cultivates B's ability to ... (use language/communicate interpersonally)

③ **A培养B对NP（音乐/中国文化）的兴趣**

A cultivates B's interest in ... (music/Chinese culture)

● 教师在设计课程时，应该注意从理解诠释、人际交流、表达演说这三个方面来培养学生的交际能力。
● 这三种沟通模式强调在语言教学中要注重学生的交际能力，而且要从这三个方面培养学生使用语言的能力。
● 语言教学不仅应以培养学生的语言交际能力为目标，也应以培养学习者对中国文化的兴趣为重点。

7. **Subj.利用+NP来+VP（把课文串起来/组织语言教学）···（，让sb.+do sth.）**

Subj. uses NP to ... (string together the text/organize language teaching), (and make/allow sb. to ...)

● 主题教学设计非常强调设计课程时利用交际主题把课文串起来。
● 在利用主题与子题来组织语言教学的同时，外语教师也应该利用目标语来进行教学，这样一来，可以让学生获得大量丰富的语言输入。

练习活动

理解诠释1：预习单

先看课文，然后完成下面的作业：

一、根据《二十一世纪的外语教学标准》，理解"以标准为本的语言教学"包括的标准、设计原则以及教学方法：

> 内容标准：包括_____大教学内容

> 能力标准：注重培养学生的_____能力

> 设计原则：强调使用_____的原则

> 教学方法：利用_____来组织语言教学

二、所谓的5C是指内容标准还是能力标准？五大教学内容包括哪几个方面的内容标准？

三、当教师设计课程时，应该以培养学生的什么能力为出发点？这种能力目标包括哪几种沟通模式？

四、以标准为本的语言教学强调教师应该利用什么原则来设计课程？这一课程设计包括哪三个具体的原则？

理解诠释2：扩展阅读

　　根据《二十一世纪的外语教学标准》，美国外语学习的五大教学内容包括：交际沟通、文化学习、学科联系、文化与语言比较和社区应用。这五个以C开头的英文词简单明确地提出外语教学应该以什么为主要教学内容。

　　除了5个C以外，作为外语教师还应该时时刻刻注重培养学生的交际能力。外语教学的能力标准应该以交际的三种沟通模式为重点，这三种沟通模式包括：人际交流、理解诠释以及表达演说。首先，所谓的人际交流是指人与人之间进行的语言意义上的协商交流。在交流时，谈话者除了要注意自己的意思是否表达清楚，还要观察、预测对方的反应，根据情况进行调整或者澄清语义。人际交流最常见的例子就是会话，除此以外，沟通交流也是常见的策略，还包括书信或者电子邮件等书面形式。

　　其次，理解诠释并不是以双向交流为重点的沟通模式，而是通过听与读来理解语言意义并且做出恰当的文化诠释。这种听读结合的理解诠释和传统教学中的"听力/阅读理解"有着本质的区别。也就是说，以标准为本的理解诠释除了理解语言形式，了解词、句以外，要更进一步诠释词句之间所包含的文化内涵。一个人对目标语言、文化越了解，就越能做出恰当的文化诠释。

最后，所谓的表达演说是指一种在正式场合中的单向交流模式。表达者通常利用口头呈现与书面写作的方式来传递信息，让不同文化背景的听者和读者获得信息，成功地理解诠释所呈现的交际内容。

1. 这篇文章介绍了"以标准为本的语言教学"的哪两个方面？
   A. 内容标准　　　B. 能力标准　　　C. 设计原则　　　D. 教学方法

2. 下面哪一种形式不属于人际交流的模式？
   A. 面对面的交流　B. 语义协商　C. 听力理解练习　D. 回电子邮件

3. 关于理解诠释的模式，下面哪一种描述是正确的？
   A. 理解诠释是以双向交流为重点的沟通模式。
   B. 理解诠释模式是指人与人之间进行的语言协商。
   C. 所谓的理解诠释与传统教学中的"听力/阅读理解"并没有什么区别。
   D. 理解诠释不但包括对语言形式的理解，而且还包括对词句之间文化内涵的诠释。

4. 下面哪些课堂设计重视培养学生的表达演说能力？（可多选）
   A. 课堂辩论　　　B. 演讲活动　　　C. 会话　　　　　D. 完成书面报告

人际交流1：面对面讨论

在今年全美外语教师学会的年会上，你认识了一位K-12的张老师。在会间休息时，张老师想知道你对外语教学的内容标准与五大教学内容的相关看法：

张老师：　今天上午那场"以标准为本的语言教学"的报告，真是让我受益匪浅。听了那场报告以后，你认为五大教学内容应该以培养学生的什么能力为重点？教师应该如何培养学生的交际能力？

你的回答：【建议词汇和结构：…以培养…为重点/为出发点；在…（设计课程/课堂教学/语言教学）时，sb.应该/必须…；subj.把A跟B联系起来；交际能力】

张老师：　以饭馆为例，在设计课程时，教师应该如何把语言教学与文化学习联系起来呢？

你的回答：【建议词汇和结构：以…为例；subj.把A跟B联系起来；首先…，其次…，最后…】

张老师：　在你看来，利用五大教学内容来设计教学，至少有哪三个好处？

你的回答：【建议词汇和结构：首先…，其次…，最后…；培养sb.的…（交际/语言使用）能力；subj.利用…来进行（语言教学/沟通）；subj.把A跟B联系起来；真实；有意义；实际生活】

人际交流2：电子邮件

下面是一位K-12的新老师写给你的一封电子邮件。请先看电子邮件，然后给他回信。【建议词汇和结构：subj.强调…（教学内容/交际能力/能力标准）的…方面/模式；subj.包括…；…以培养…为重点/为出发点；培养sb.的…（交际/语言使用/人际交流/理解诠释/表达演说）能力；subj.利用…来+V.（进行/完成）…（交际任务/活动）；当…时，sb.应该/必须…；subj.把A和B联系起来；subj.使用…方法+V.（测试/评估/设计）…；真实；有意义；时时刻刻】

XX老师：
　　您好！
　　非常荣幸今天上午听到了您关于"以标准为本的语言教学"的报告。您在报告中提到，当教师在设计课程时，应该时时刻刻注意以培养学生的交际能力为出发点。为了培养学生的人际交流、理解诠释和表达演说能力，您在课堂中使用过什么有效的教学活动呢？麻烦您分别以培养学生的人际交流、理解诠释和表达演说能力为出发点，给我三个具体的例子。
　　谢谢！
　　　　　　　　　　　　　　　　　　　　　　　　　　王小东

 ## 表达演说：分享教案设计

以自己的一课教案为例，具体解释说明在设计课程时，如何把"以标准为本的语言教学"跟实际教学联系起来。分享教案设计时，应该包括：

1. 从内容标准来看，该教案包括了五大教学内容的哪几个方面？你通过什么课堂活动把这些教学内容联系起来？
2. 从能力标准来看，你设计了什么课堂活动来培养学生的交际能力？
3. 在课堂上，你如何把五大教学内容与三种沟通模式联系起来？
4. 你如何评估学生是否获得了交际能力？

建议词汇和结构：所谓的NP（内容标准/能力标准）是指…；subj.包括…；subj.强调…（教学内容/交际能力/能力标准）的…方面/模式；首先…，其次…，然后…；…以培养…为重点/为出发点；培养sb.的…（交际/语言使用/人际交流/理解诠释/表达演说）能力；subj.使用…方法+测试/评估/设计…；subj.利用…来+V.（进行/完成）…（交际任务/活动）；科学的评估方法

反思任务

根据教学视频进行讨论：
http://startalk.umd.edu/teacher-development/videos/2009/OneWorldNow-Chinese

一、前期任务：
从视频上观摩中文课之后，与你的小组成员讨论以下问题：

- 这位教师的教学内容包括了五大教学目标（交际沟通、文化学习、文化与语言比较、学科联系、社区应用）中的哪几项？请举例说明。
- 教师和学生的语言互动是否包括了三种沟通模式（理解诠释、人际交流、表达演说）？请举例说明。

二、核心任务：
根据"二十一世纪外语教学标准"，和你的小组成员设计一份课堂观摩检查单，具体列出课堂观摩的重点，以及怎么呈现该课堂是否符合外语教学标准。

三、后期任务：

- 给其他小组报告你们这份课堂观摩检查单的设计原则、重点。
- 让所有的成员利用这份检查单再次观摩上述的视频，比较两次观摩的结果，讨论你们是否有了新的发现，你们对这堂课的评估是否与以前不同并解释为什么？

 补充材料

二十一世纪的外语教学标准

目标（一）交际沟通：

标准1.1　学生能参与[35]谈话，提供和获得信息[36]，抒发[37]情感[38]和交换意见。
标准1.2　学生理解并能解释有关各种话题的书面信息和口语信息。
标准1.3　学生能向听者或读者呈现[39]有关各种话题的信息、概念[40]和观点。

---

[35]参与　cānyù　　V.　to participate, to engage in
[36]信息　xìnxī　　N.　information
[37]抒发　shūfā　　V.　to express (feelings)
[38]情感　qínggǎn　　N.　feeling, emotion
[39]呈现　chéngxiàn　V.　to present, to show
[40]概念　gàiniàn　　N.　concept

目标（二）文化学习：
标准2.1　学生能够表现出一种对所学文化的行为方式和价值观念[41]之间关系的理解力[42]。
标准2.2　学生能够表现出一种对所学文化的文化表现和文化理念[43]之间关系的理解力。

目标（三）学科联系：
标准3.1　通过学习外语，学生能巩固[44]并加深[45]对其他学科知识的理解。
标准3.2　学生获取信息并能识别[46]那些只有通过学习外语及其文化才能涉及[47]到的独特的观点。

目标（四）文化与语言比较：
标准4.1　通过对所学语言和母语[48]的比较，学生能理解语言的本质特征[49]。
标准4.2　通过对所学文化和母语文化的比较，学生能领会[50]文化的概念。

目标（五）社区应用：能参与国内外多元社区[51]
标准5.1　校园内外，学生都能使用该语言。
标准5.2　为了让自己高兴和充实[52]自己而使用该语言，这表明学生已成为终身[53]学习者。

[1] American Council on the Teaching of Foreign Languages (ACTFL). (2014). World-readiness standards for learning languages. Retrieved from http://www.actfl.org/sites/default/files/pdfs/World-ReadinessStandardsforLearningLanguages.pdf
[2] American Council on the Teaching of Foreign Languages (ACTFL). (2012). ACTFL proficiency guidelines. Retrieved from http://www.actfl.org/sites/default/files/pdfs/public/ACTFLProficiencyGuidelines2012_FINAL.pdf
[3] American Council on the Teaching of Foreign Languages (ACTFL). (2012). Performance descriptors for language learners. Retrieved from http://www.actfl.org/sites/default/files/pdfs/PerformanceDescriptorsLanguageLearners.pdf

[41]价值观念	jiàzhíguānniàn	N.	values
[42]理解力	lǐjiělì	N.	understanding, comprehensibility
[43]文化理念	wénhuàlǐniàn	N.	cultural ideas
[44]巩固	gǒnggù	V.	to reinforce, to consolidate; to strengthen
[45]加深	jiāshēn	V.	to deepen
[46]识别	shíbié	V.	to identify, to recognize
[47]涉及	shèjí	V.	to relate to
[48]母语	mǔyǔ	N.	native language, mother tongue
[49]本质特征	běnzhìtèzhēng	N.	intrinsic characteristic
[50]领会	lǐnghuì	V.	to comprehend
[51]多元社区	duōyuánshèqū	NP.	diverse communities
[52]充实	chōngshí	V./Adj.	to enrich; abundant
[53]终身	zhōngshēn	Adj.	life-long

第二课 反向课程设计与主题单元
Backward Curricular Design and Thematic Unit Approach

（文本形式：电子邮件）

> ➤ 关键词：
> 能力目标、主题、子题、教案设计、应用能力测试、反向课程设计原则
>
> ➤ 能力目标：
> 1. 学习者能使用专业术语说明反向课程设计的步骤。
> 2. 学习者能说明主题单元设计的原则。
> 3. 学习者能介绍自己做过的主题单元设计。
> 4. 学习者能正确使用中文书信格式和书信套语。

课文全版 (Complete Version)

（一）孔哲给竹老师的电子邮件

发件人：孔哲
收件人：竹露茜
主题[1]：　关于主题单元设计的问题

竹老师：

　　您好！

　　很高兴有机会听到您在汉语大会上做的关于设计"主题单元"的讲座[2]。最近我正在为一个为期一周[3]的高中生中文夏令营[4]做准备，我已经决定以"吃饭"为主题，想使用您在会上提到的原则来设计课程。不过，我发现设计主题单元真不简单，除了您提到的几个重点，比方说，利用主题把外语教学标准的五个C贯穿[5]在教学中，强调三个沟通模式，我还有几个问题想请教[6]您：

　　首先，如何把反向课程设计的原则贯穿在主题单元设计中？
　　其次，如何选择主题和子题组织教学活动/任务[7]？
　　第三，如何设定子题和教学时的能力目标？
　　最后，如何评估教学目标是否完成？
　　期待您的回复，谢谢您的指导[8]。
　　敬祝[9]教安[10]！

　　　　　　　　　　　　　　　　　　　　　　　孔哲敬上[11]

---

[1]主题	zhǔtí	N.	subject, theme
[2]讲座	jiǎngzuò	N.	lecture
[3]为期一周	wéiqīyìzhōu	V./Adj.	week-long
[4]夏令营	xiàlìngyíng	N.	summer camp
[5]贯穿	guànchuān	V.	to run through, integrate, penetrate
[6]请教	qǐngjiào	V.	[formal] to consult, to ask for advice
[7]任务	rènwù	N.	task
[8]指导	zhǐdǎo	V.	to instruct, to guide
[9]敬祝	jìngzhù	V.	to respectfully wish
[10]教安	jiào'ān	V.	[lit.] to teach in peace; a polite phrase for ending a letter to a teacher
[11]敬上	jìngshàng	V.	a phrase attached to the signature in a letter to show respect

（二）竹老师的回信

发件人： 竹露茜
收件人： 孔哲
主题：　关于主题单元设计的问题

📎附件一：　主题单元设计.pptx
📎附件二：　教案检查单.docx

孔哲：

你好！谢谢你的来信。你提到的几个问题的确是许多新教师在进行主题单元设计时感到困难的地方。希望以下讨论能帮助你进一步[12]了解"主题单元"设计的原则和步骤[13]。

正像我在报告中提到的那样，主题单元的设计要按照[14]反向课程设计的原则来进行，一般包括四个步骤。首先是设定教学目标。设定主题单元的教学目标要从学生的学习结果出发，也就是说，教师必须清楚地知道学生在学完这个主题单元以后能做什么。英文把这种能力目标叫做Can-Do Statements。能力目标要以外语教学标准的五个C为出发点[15]，决定教学的具体[16]内容。比方说，第一个C要包括什么样的人际交流、理解诠释和表达演说的语言知识和技能[17]。其次是决定采用[18]什么有效的方法测试学生的能力。综合性[19]的应用能力测试(Integrated Performance Assessment-IPA)是最好的方法。第三是决定主题单元的子题和内容。一个单元的主题也好，子题也好，都应该跟学生的学习、生活有关，比方说，如果一个单元的主题是"个人与社会"，子题可以包括"我的生活"、"我的家庭"、"我的学校"、"去饭馆吃饭"等；文化学习也可以包括"中国的家庭结构[20]"和"生活方式"。最后是为每个子题设计有意义、有目的的教学活动和任务。设计时要考虑每课的主要内容、所用的时间、教学材料[21]、教学活动等，一定要强调交际的目的，进行真实的、有趣的交流。完成主题单元的设计以后老师要使用综合性应用能力测试来检查以上能力目标是否完成，学生是否能够完成三种沟通模式的真实任务。

很明显[22]，上面提到的主题设计原则和传统的语言教学有很大的不同。在你设计"吃中国饭"这个子题时，一定要写出清楚的"能力

---

[12]进一步	jìnyíbù	Adv.	further
[13]步骤	bùzhòu	N.	step, procedure
[14]按照	ànzhào	Prep.	according to
[15]出发点	chūfādiǎn	N.	[lit.] point of departure, start point
[16]具体	jùtǐ	Adj.	specific, concrete
[17]技能	jìnéng	N.	skill
[18]采用	cǎiyòng	V.	to adopt, to use
[19]综合性	zōnghéxìng	N.	integrated, comprehensive
[20]家庭结构	jiātíngjiégòu	NP.	family structure
[21]材料	cáiliào	N.	material
[22]明显	míngxiǎn	Adj.	obvious, distinct

目标"，也就是我们所说的Can-Do Statements。除了包括跟吃饭有关的词汇、语法以外，还需要考虑语言功能[23]，比方说，"选择饭馆"、"订位[24]"、"点菜"、"付钱"等交际能力。此外，教师要学会设计教案[25]，（请参考[26]附件[27]"教案检查单[28]"），特别是考虑什么样的任务能帮助学生获得语言使用能力。学生学完这个单元以后，教师可以利用真实任务来测试学生的能力，让他们自己上网找中国饭馆、订位，然后去饭馆点菜、吃饭、付钱。这样一来，教师就能清楚地知道学生能利用语言做什么了。

希望上面的回答对你的课程设计有所帮助，如果有任何其他问题，欢迎你随时[29]和我联系[30]。随信附上[31]我在汉语大会报告"主题单元"时使用的投影片[32]以及教案检查单，供[33]你参考。

祝教学顺利[34]！

竹露茜

 语言重点：

1. **Subj.为…做+准备/安排/设计**

   Subj. for the purpose of/on behalf of ... make(s) preparations/arrangements/plans

   - 最近我正在为一个为期一周的高中生中文夏令营做准备。
   - 竹老师在参加汉语大会时多次提到主题单元设计与反向课程设计，她还现场要求在场教师为"问路"这一主题做教学设计。

2. **把…贯穿在…（教学/课程设计/任务/生活）中**

   to run/to link ... throughout/from beginning to end

   - 不过，我发现设计主题单元真不简单，除了您提到的几个重点，比方说，利用主题把外语教学标准的五个C贯穿在教学中，强调三个沟通模式，我还有几个问题想请教您。
   - 为了培养学生对中国文化的兴趣，教师可以把一些文化知识贯穿在课程设计中。

---

[23]语言功能	yǔyángōngnéng	NP.	language function
[24]订位	dìngwèi	V.	to reserve seats
[25]教案	jiào'àn	N.	lesson plan
[26]参考	cānkǎo	V./N.	to refer to; reference
[27]附件	fùjiàn	N.	attachment
[28]检查单	jiǎnchádān	N.	checklist
[29]随时	suíshí	Adv.	at any time
[30]联系	liánxì	V.	to contact
[31]随信附上	suíxìnfùshàng	VP.	enclosed
[32]投影片	tóuyǐngpiān	N.	slides; a PowerPoint file
[33]供	gōng	V.	to offer, to provide
[34]顺利	shùnlì	Adj.	smoothly; without a hitch

3. （…，）**Subj.进一步+VP**（了解/表达/强调/测试）…

   (… ,) Subj. moves a step further in (understanding/expressing/emphasizing) …

   - 希望以下讨论能帮助你进一步了解"主题单元"设计的原则与步骤。
   - 所谓的"能力目标"就是指学生能利用语言做什么，清楚地写出"能力目标"可以让教师进一步强调交际能力的重要性。

4. ① **Obj.应该/要/可以+按照…来+V(P)**（进行…/调整/设计）

   Obj. should be/needs to be/can be (implemented/revised/designed …) according to …

   ② **Subj.应该+按照…来+V(P)**（设计/调整语言输入的难度）

   Subj. … should (design/adjust the difficulty of language input) according to …

   - 主题单元的设计要按照反向设计原则来进行。
   - 使用目标语教学时，教师应该按照学生的理解情况来调整语言输入的难度。

5. **A也好，B也好，都必须/应该+VP**（考虑/强调/跟…有关/按照…来设计）

   No matter whether A or B, both need to be/must be (considered/emphasized/related to … /designed according to …)

   - 一个单元的主题也好，子题也好，都应该跟学生的学习、生活有关。
   - 教学材料也好，课堂活动也好，都应该考虑其趣味性，并按照真实、有意义的原则来设计。

6. **…也就是sb.所说的…**

   … is/are precisely what sb. calls …

   - 在你设计"吃中国饭"的子题时，一定要写出清楚的"能力目标"，也就是我们所说的Can-Do Statements。
   - 教师应该让学生把学到的词汇、语法应用在不同的沟通模式中，也就是外语学习标准中所说的理解诠释、人际交流跟表达演说。

7. …，这样一来，subj.就能…，（而不是只…）

   Then/By doing so, subj. can … , (and not merely …)

   - 学生学完这个单元以后，教师可以利用真实任务来测试学生的能力，让他们自己上网找中国饭馆、订位，然后去饭馆点菜、吃饭、付钱。这样一来，教师就能清楚地知道学生能利用语言做什么了。
   - 除了竹老师的回答以外，你也应该参考随信附上的投影片中真实的例子，这样一来，你就能了解设计主题单元的具体步骤，而不是只知道教学设计的原则。

8. ① …以…为出发点

   to take … as a starting point

   ② …从…出发

   to start out/set off from …

   - 设定主题单元的教学目标要以学生的学习结果为出发点。
   - 设定主题单元的教学目标要从学生的学习结果出发。

第二课　反向课程设计与主题单元
Backward Curricular Design and Thematic Unit Approach

（文本形式：电子邮件）

> 关键词：
> 能力目标、主题、子题、教案设计、应用能力测试、反向课程设计原则
> 能力目标：
> 1. 学习者能使用专业术语说明反向课程设计的步骤。
> 2. 学习者能说明主题单元设计的原则。
> 3. 学习者能介绍自己做过的主题单元设计。
> 4. 学习者能正确使用中文书信格式和书信套语。

课文节选版 (Abridged Version)

（一）孔哲给竹老师的电子邮件

From: Kong Zhe
To: Zhu Luxi
Subject: Some Questions about Thematic Unit Design

Dear Professor Zhu,

How are you? I am so glad to have the opportunity to listen to your lecture on "Thematic Unit Design" in the Mandarin Conference. I am making preparations for a one-week Chinese summer camp for high school students. The theme will be "Dining" and I would like to use the principles you mentioned in the conference to design the curriculum.

However, I realize that designing a thematic unit is by no means an easy task. I have a couple of questions to ask you about the focal points you mentioned, such as how to run the 5Cs of the Standards of Foreign Language Learning through teaching using common themes, as well as how to emphasize the three modes of communication:

First, how does one run the principles of Backwards Curriculum Design through the Thematic Unit Design?

Second, how does one choose the themes and sub-themes to organize the teaching activities and tasks?

Third, how does one set up the can-do statements of each sub-theme unit?

Last, what is the best way to evaluate whether the goals of can-do statements have been achieved?

Thanks in advance for your answer.

Sincerely,

Kong Zhe

26　Backward Curricular Design, Thematic Units

（二）竹老师的回信

发件人： 竹露茜
收件人： 孔哲
主题[1]： 关于主题单元[2]设计的问题

📎附件一： 主题单元设计.pptx
📎附件二： 教案检查单.docx

孔哲：

你好！

谢谢你的来信。你提到的几个问题的确是许多新教师在进行主题单元设计时感到困难的地方。希望以下讨论能帮助你进一步[3]了解"主题单元"设计的原则[4]和步骤[5]。

正像我在报告中提到的那样，主题单元的设计要按照[6]反向课程设计的原则来进行，一般包括四个步骤。首先是设定教学目标。设定[7]主题单元的教学目标要从学生的学习结果出发，也就是说，教师必须清楚地知道学生在学完这个主题单元以后能做什么。英文把这种能力目标叫做Can-Do Statements。能力目标要以外语教学标准的五个C为出发点[8]，决定教学的具体[9]内容。比方说，第一个C要包括什么样的人际交流、理解诠释和表达演说的语言知识和技能[10]。其次是决定采用[11]什么有效[12]的方法测试[13]学生的能力。综合性[14]的应用能力测试 (Integrated Performance Assessment-IPA)是最好的方法。第三是决定主题单元的子题和内容。一个单元的主题也好，子题也好，都应该跟学生的学习、生活有关，比方说，如果一个单元的主题是"个人与社会"，子题可以包括"我的生活"，"我的家庭"，"我的学校"，"去饭馆吃饭"等；文化学习也可以包括"中国的家庭结构[15]"和"生活方式"。最后是为每个子题设计有意义、有目的的教学活动和

---

[1]主题	zhǔtí	N.	subject, theme
[2]单元	dānyuán	N.	unit
[3]进一步	jìnyíbù	Adv.	further
[4]原则	yuánzé	N.	principle
[5]步骤	bùzhòu	N.	step, procedure
[6]按照	ànzhào	Prep.	according to
[7]设定	shèdìng	V.	to set
[8]出发点	chūfādiǎn	N.	[lit.] point of departure, start point
[9]具体	jùtǐ	Adj.	specific, concrete
[10]技能	jìnéng	N.	skill
[11]采用	cǎiyòng	V.	to adopt, to use
[12]有效	yǒuxiào	Adj.	effective, valid
[13]测试	cèshì	V.	to test
[14]综合性	zōnghéxìng	N.	integrated, comprehensive
[15]家庭结构	jiātíngjiégòu	NP.	family structure

任务。设计时要考虑每课的主要内容、所用的时间、教学材料[16]、教学活动等，一定要强调交际的目的，进行真实的、有趣[17]的交流。完成主题单元的设计以后老师要使用综合性应用能力测试来检查以上能力目标是否完成，学生是否能够完成三种沟通模式的真实任务。

很明显[18]，上面提到的主题设计原则和传统的语言教学有很大的不同。在你设计"吃中国饭"这个子题时，一定要写出清楚的"能力目标"，也就是我们所说的Can-Do Statements。除了包括跟吃饭有关的词汇、语法以外，还需要考虑语言功能[19]，比方说，"选择饭馆"、"订位"、"点菜"、"付钱"等交际能力。此外，教师要学会设计教案[20]，（请参考[21]附件[22]"教案检查单[23]"），特别是考虑什么样的任务能帮助学生获得语言使用能力。学生学完这个单元以后，教师可以利用真实任务来测试学生的能力，让他们自己上网找中国饭馆、订位，然后去饭馆点菜、吃饭、付钱。这样一来，教师就能清楚地知道学生能利用语言做什么了。

希望上面的回答对你的课程设计有所帮助，如果有任何其他问题，欢迎你随时[24]和我联系[25]。随信附上[26]我在汉语大会报告"主题单元"时使用的投影片[27]和教案检查单，供[28]你参考。

祝教学顺利[29]！

竹露茜

 语言重点：

1. **Subj. 为…做+准备/安排/设计**

    Subj. for the purpose of/on behalf of ... make(s) preparations/arrangements/plans

    - 最近我正在为一个为期一周的高中生中文夏令营做准备。
    - 竹老师在参加汉语大会时多次提到主题单元设计与反向课程设计，她还现场要求在场教师为"问路"这一主题做教学设计。

---

[16]材料	cáiliào	N.	material
[17]有趣	yǒuqù	Adj.	interesting
[18]明显	míngxiǎn	Adj.	obvious, distinct
[19]语言功能	yǔyángōngnéng	NP.	language function
[20]教案	jiào'àn	N.	lesson plan
[21]参考	cānkǎo	V./N.	to refer to; reference
[22]附件	fùjiàn	N.	attachment
[23]检查单	jiǎnchádān	N.	checklist
[24]随时	suíshí	Adv.	at any time
[25]联系	liánxì	V.	to contact
[26]随信附上	suíxìnfùshàng	VP.	enclosed
[27]投影片	tóuyǐngpiān	N.	slides; a PowerPoint file
[28]供	gōng	V.	to offer, to provide
[29]顺利	shùnlì	Adj.	smoothly; without a hitch

2. ① **Obj.**应该/要/可以+按照⋯来+V(P)（进行⋯/调整/设计）

   Obj. should be/needs to be/can be (implemented/revised/designed ...) according to ...

   ② **Subj.**应该+按照⋯来+V(P)（设计/调整语言输入的难度）

   Subj. ... should (design/adjust the difficulty of language input) according to ...

   - 主题单元的设计要按照反向设计原则来进行。
   - 使用目标语教学时，教师应该按照学生的理解情况来调整语言输入的难度。

3. **A也好，B也好，都必须/应该+VP**（考虑/强调/跟⋯有关/按照⋯来设计）

   No matter whether A or B, both need to be/must be (considered/emphasized/related to ... /designed according to ...)

   - 一个单元的主题也好，子题也好，都应该跟学生的学习、生活有关。
   - 教学材料也好，课堂活动也好，都应该考虑其趣味性，并按照真实、有意义的原则来设计。

4. ⋯**也就是sb.所说的**⋯

   ... is/are precisely what sb. calls ...

   - 在你设计"吃中国饭"的子题时，一定要写出清楚的"能力目标"，也就是我们所说的Can-Do Statements。
   - 教师应该让学生把学到的词汇、语法应用在不同的沟通模式中，也就是外语学习标准中所说的理解诠释、人际交流跟表达演说。

5. ⋯**，这样一来，subj.就能**⋯**，（而不是只**⋯**）**

   Then/By doing so, subj. can ... , (and not merely ...)

   - 学生学完这个单元以后，教师可以利用真实任务来测试学生的能力，让他们自己上网找中国饭馆、订位，然后去饭馆点菜、吃饭、付钱。这样一来，教师就能清楚地知道学生能利用语言做什么了。
   - 除了竹老师的回答以外，你也应该参考随信附上的投影片中真实的例子，这样一来，你就能了解设计主题单元的具体步骤，而不是只知道教学设计的原则。

练习活动

 理解诠释1：预习单

先看课文，然后完成下面的作业：

一、按照反向课程设计原则来进行的主题单元设计包括的四个步骤分别是什么？

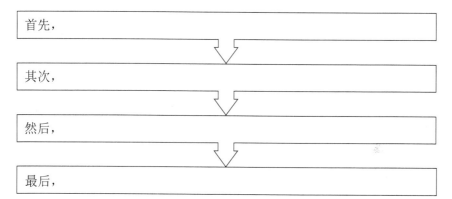

首先，

其次，

然后，

最后，

二、请指出下面的活动分别属于主题单元设计的哪个步骤。

①教师设计"图片展示"、"小组讨论"、"角色扮演"等课堂活动，让学生通过课堂任务学习如何运用与"吃饭"有关的词汇和句型。

这个活动属于第（　　）个步骤

②教师确定学生学完"吃饭"这个主题单元之后能够用课堂上所学的词汇、句型以及文化知识去中国饭馆订位、点菜以及付钱。

这个活动属于第（　　）个步骤

③教师确定"吃饭"的主题单元包括三个方面的内容：订位、点菜、付钱。

这个活动属于第（　　）个步骤

④教师设计情景模拟的检测方式来评估学生是否能够运用所学生词和句型在中国饭馆点菜。

这个活动属于第（　　）个步骤

三、根据课文进行填空。

在进行主题单元设计时，应该遵循＿＿＿＿＿＿＿＿＿＿原则。首先，设定教学目标时要以＿＿＿＿＿＿＿＿＿为出发点。在设定目标时除了要包括语言知识，也应该考虑＿＿＿＿＿＿＿＿。其次，要决定采用什么有效的方法来＿＿＿＿＿学生的学习结果。然后，决定＿＿＿＿＿和＿＿＿＿＿的内容，为了培养学生的学习兴趣，无论是主题还是子题的选择，都应该跟学生的＿＿＿＿＿＿＿＿＿有关，以＿＿＿＿＿＿＿为中心。最后，为每个子题设计＿＿＿＿＿、＿＿＿＿＿的教学活动和任务，这样一来，能让学习者进行＿＿＿＿＿、＿＿＿＿＿的交流。

四、每个主题单元教学目标的设定都应该包括两个方面：语言知识（知道什么）和语言技能（能做什么），下面的项目中哪些属于语言知识，哪些属于语言技能？请在相应的项目里画"×"

项目	语言知识	语言技能
例：学生学习五个生词	×	
学生能用中文介绍他的家人		
学生知道如何称呼家人		
学生掌握表达爱好的词汇和句型		
学生能用聊爱好的方式交新朋友		
学生看得懂菜单		
学生能阅读中文菜单并点菜		
学生能运用方位词问路或指路		
学生能听懂方位词		

扩展阅读

改编自2013ACC-K12项目学员何明乐教案：
Lesson Plan

			老师：何明乐
Unit:	饮食（次单元3）	Lesson Number:	5 of 12

Stage 1: What will students know and be able to do at the end of this lesson?

语言知识KNOW：
- 您要吃/喝点儿什么？
- 请来一classifier（盘/份）＋N（春卷/宫保鸡丁）
- Sb.（不）喜欢，（因为……）
- 买单/结账！
- 酸、甜、苦、辣、风味、口味

语言技能DO：
- 学生能看懂菜单，认识一些常见的中国菜。
- 学生能表达自己想喝、吃什么东西。
- 学生能掌握用餐礼仪，包括请客、点菜和结账等。

Stage 2: How will you know that students can do that?

- 教师可以通过以下的活动来测试学生是否达到了以上的教学目标。第6节课集中于学生的角色扮演，这些表演要证明他们是否掌握了用餐的词汇和句型、而且是否能够符合中国的用餐礼仪。最后有一个单元考试，学生可以通过考试展示他们的知识。

Stage 3: What instructional activities will be used? (Use as many as necessary to achieve your learning targets.)

Opening/Activity 1: "你要不要喝茶？"
1. 上课之前，教师把学生的桌子分为四人一组，安排如下。这样可以模拟饭店的餐桌。

2. 在每位学生的小桌子上有以下的材料：
   - 一个杯子（一次性的）
   - 一本词典
   - 一张卡，上面印着一种中国菜的图片和名字（比如：春卷），卡上的菜没有拼音。
3. 教师要求学生看自己的卡，把菜名的拼音写下来。如果不知道拼音，可以用词典来查字。
4. 在学生写拼音的同时，老师给每个学生倒茶，先问"你要不要喝茶？"。学生可以回答"要"或"不要"，然后"谢谢"。

Activity 2: 菜单的分类

1. 教师把菜的种类名称写在黑板上。
2. 教师要求学生把自己的菜贴在合适的分类下面。
3. 教师检查学生是否把自己的卡贴在合适的位置，然后简单解释不熟悉的菜应该放在哪里。
4. 教师让学生讨论怎么猜想一种菜的分类（比如：月字旁与肉有关、草字头与蔬菜有关等）。

Activity 3: 角色扮演

1. 教师提前准备一段小对话，分给每一位学生。教师先和一位学生一起来做角色扮演。
2. 角色扮演以后，教师跟不同的学生小组再次模拟对话的不同部分。比如说，在某个桌子问学生"几位？"学生回答。然后到其他桌子问学生"你要喝什么？"等等。
3. 教师要求学生自己做角色扮演。每一个小组有三个顾客和一个服务员。学生看黑板点菜，然后服务员从黑板上把卡拿下来给他们。

```
                         在饭店
fúwùyuán:   huānyíngguānglín! jǐ wèi?
服务员：     "欢迎光临！几位？"
gùkè:       ... wèi.
顾客：       "……位"
fúwùyuán:   nǐ yào chī shénme? nǐ yào hē shénme?
服务员：     "你要吃什么？你要喝什么？"
gùkè:       wǒ yào/wǒ lái yí fèn ... (yì wǎn fàn, yì bēi chá, yì píng kělè)
顾客：       "我要/我来一份……"（一碗饭、一杯茶、一瓶可乐）
fúwùyuán:   háiyǒu shénme?
服务员：     "还有什么？"
gùkè:       méiyǒu or "wǒ hái yào"
顾客：       "没有"（或"我还要"）
fúwùyuán:   hǎo, nín diǎn de shì ...
服务员：     "好，您点的是……"
gùkè:       fúwùyuán! zài lái ...
顾客：       "服务员！再来……"
                         ***
gùkè:       mǎi dān!/jié zhàng!
顾客：       "买单/结账！"
```

Activity 4: 问答游戏

教师提前准备一些有关中国用餐礼仪的多选题。最好的问题是一些有幽默答案的问题。问题的内容包括：
- 怎么请客（"做东"、"AA制"等）
- 倒茶
- 夹菜
- 结账（怎么买单、给小费的礼仪）

1. 例题：If your friend says "我请你吃饭", what is the best way to respond?
   a. 谢谢！我们几点见？　　　　b. 你太客气了！
   c. 你为什么请我吃饭？　　　　d. 不好意思。

   Correct Response: **b.** "你太客气了" means "You're being too polite!" This is a way to indirectly thank your friend and verify whether they really mean to invite you. If they insist on treating you, you should thank them ("谢谢！") and then set a time to eat.
2. 学生分小组讨论每一个问题，把答案写在纸上。如果小组有正确答案，他们得一分，如果不正确就得零分。
3. 得分最多的小组赢得一个小奖品（比如：糖、饼干等）。

Closing/Activity 5:
1. 教师给学生展示一份菜单模板，最好菜单上有不同风味和口味的菜（例如：麻婆豆腐、北京烤鸭、鱼香茄子等）。
2. 学生可以看看菜单然后表达是否喜欢某种菜，例如"我很喜欢烤鸭！"或"我不喜欢臭豆腐！"
3. 教师布置作业：
   - 每一个小组要制作一个自己的菜单。
   - 学生要从每一个菜品分类中选三个有代表性的菜，然后设计自己的菜单。
   - 学生要研究他们选的菜：名字叫什么（拼音）？有什么口味？属于什么风味的菜？
   - 下一节课，小组要做小报告来解释他们的菜单。

Materials needed for this lesson:
- 杯子（见第一个活动）
- 卡
- 榜样菜单
- 茶叶、茶壶、开水
- 有关用餐礼仪的PPT（问答游戏）
- 小奖品

Performance Tasks:

Interpretive tasks:
- 学生看有关饮食文化的材料和电影，能够回答问题。
- 学生看卡片，把菜分成不同类。学生也能猜想不熟悉的菜属于哪些分类。
- 单元考试：学生展示所掌握的和饮食有关的语言知识。学生能够表达是否喜欢或想要XX东西，能够看菜单、点菜，能够回答有关饮食文化和用餐礼仪的问题。

Interpersonal tasks:
角色扮演：学生能模拟在饭店吃饭的全过程，比如怎么点菜、结账等。

Presentational tasks:
- 学生设计自己的菜单，做小报告解释某种菜的特点、来源等。
- 单元考试：学生要写小短文或句子来表达为什么喜欢或不喜欢某种菜（比如，用表示口味的词汇："我喜欢宫保鸡丁，因为很辣！"）或为什么要买某种东西（例如："因为我要做沙拉，所以我买西红柿、黄瓜和生菜。"）。

1. 你认为该教案中的课堂任务设计是否以外语教学标准的5个C为出发点？如果是，请具体举例说明。

2. 该教案中第二个课堂活动"菜单的分类"体现了哪几种沟通模式？
   A. 理解诠释　　B. 人际交流　　　　　　C. 表达演说

3. 通过该教案中第四个课堂活动"问答游戏"，学生能获得哪种语言技能？
   A. 看懂菜单　B. 表达自己想吃、想喝的东西　C. 掌握用餐礼仪

4. 下面哪些课堂活动属于综合性应用能力测试？（可多选）
   A. 活动1"你要不要喝茶"中"教师要求学生看自己的卡，把菜名的拼音写下来"。
   B. 活动2"菜单的分类"中"教师要求学生把自己的菜贴在合适的分类下面"。
   C. 活动3"角色扮演"中"学生分小组扮演顾客和服务员"。
   D. 活动5"设计菜单"中"学生分小组制作菜单、做报告"。

人际交流1：会后讨论

在今年的星谈(Startalk)大会上有一个关于"主题单元设计"的讲座，讲座之后你和一位参加会议的何老师就讲座的具体内容展开了讨论。

何老师：　我个人觉得这个讲座提到的"主题单元设计原则"对于中文教学非常有指导意义。在你看来，所谓的"反向课程设计"与"传统教学设计"最大的不同之处是什么？

你的回答：【建议词汇和结构：明显；具体；注重；强调；所谓的…是指…；…以…（学习结果）为出发点；把…贯穿在…（教学/课程设计）中】

何老师：　哦，也就是说我们老师在进行主题单元设计的时候应该先设定教学目标，对吗？那你认为，在设定教学目标的时候应该注意哪些方面呢？

你的回答：【建议词汇和结构：真实；有意义；原则；当Sb.在VP（设定教学目标）时，必须+VP（考虑）；进一步+VP；按照…来+VP】

何老师：　我如果用这种教学法来教授"交通"这个主题的话，你觉得应该设定什么样的能力目标呢？

你的回答：

Backward Curricular Design, Thematic Units 35

 人际交流2：电子邮件交流

下面是在星谈大会上跟你交流过的何老师写给你的一封电子邮件。请先看电子邮件，然后给他回信。【建议词汇和结构：注重；强调；真实；包括；时时刻刻；采用；三种沟通模式；所谓…是指…；以…为本/出发点；…，这样一来，subj.就能…】

XX老师：

　　您好！

　　最近怎么样？工作还顺利吗？上次星谈会议上跟您一起讨论"主题单元设计"让我受益良多。可是我还不太清楚如何设计一个综合性应用能力测试来评估学生的学习结果。首先，我不了解所谓的"综合性应用能力测试"到底是指什么，它和普通的测试有什么不同。其次，我也不知道在具体实践中如何操作。就拿这个星期来说吧，这个星期我尝试用主题单元设计的方法来教"交通"这一主题。今天我教的子题是"方向"，我设定的教学目标是：让学生掌握和方向有关的词汇；能用方位词来问路和指路。针对这个教学目标，我到底应该设计什么样的测试呢？我相信您一定有很好的方法，还请您不吝赐教！期待您的回复。

　　祝您工作顺利！

　　　　　　　　　　　　　　　　　　　　　　　　　　　　　何明乐

 表达演说：

你现在要做一个以"交通"为主题的教学演示，在进行教学演示前，你需要针对你的演示做一个5分钟的介绍。你的介绍应该包括以下几点：

1. 该主题单元的能力目标是什么？
2. 你设计了什么样的子题？
3. 如何评估学生的学习结果？

建议词汇和结构：设定；原则；按照…（主题）来VP；把…（主题）贯穿在…（课堂教学）中；以…为主题/重点；当sb.在VP时，应该…；（从…方面）培养…的能力

 反思任务

利用反向课程设计的原则进行教案设计。

一、前期任务：
四位成员为一组，每组分配一个主题，如："生病了"、"去饭馆"、"去商店"、"买东西"…。根据反向课程设计的原则，进行教案设计。

二、核心任务：
完成前期任务以后，四位小组成员分别去不同的组做报告，介绍本组设计的教案。报告时，其他小组的成员利用教案检查单（附件二）进行点评，提出意见。

三、后期任务：
以前期任务时的小组为单位，汇总在核心任务中其他小组的成员提出的意见，并对本组设计的教案进行修改，完成最终的教案设计。

 补充材料

能力目标 (Can-Do Statements) 制定模板 (Template)

学完"我的家庭"以后，学生可以获得什么语言知识和技能？
What key *knowledge* and *skills* will learners acquire as a result of this lesson?

学生知道什么？ 也就是你要教的内容 **Learners will know:** **(Content Standards)**	内容: Enter the Content Standards for your unit (i.e., what you want your students to know). 语言形式 Language forms 1. 2. 3. 4. 语言功能 Language functions 1. 2. 3. 交际策略 Communicative strategies 1. 2. 文化策略 Cultural strategies (concepts, practices, and product) 1. 2.
学生会做什么？ 也就是你要教的技能 **Learners will be able to: (Performance Standards)**	技能 Enter the Performance Standards for your unit (i.e., what you want your students to do). 任务 Tasks 1. 2. 3. 4.

补充材料

附件一：竹露茜老师的演讲稿：主题单元设计.pptx

Slide 1

Standards...

- 针对教学重点 *WHAT is important to teach*
- 提供了一个教学大纲 *A FRAMEWORK for teaching and learning a language*
- 指出教学和评估所应改变的方向 *CHANGE in focus, teaching, and in assessment*

Slide 2

Standards clarify that language acquisition is...

强调要让学生不断地

- 用实际生活中的真实的语言
  做有意义的沟通

- *USING LANGUAGE IN REAL-LIFE SITUATIONS*
  - Meaningful, purposeful communication

Slide 3

美国中小学生中文学习目标
Standards for Chinese Language Learners
五大学习目标

- Communication　　运用语言交际沟通
- Cultures　　　　　体认文化和习俗
- Connections　　　 与其他学科贯连
- Comparisons　　　 比较语言文化特性
- Communities　　　 参与社会实践
　　　　　　　　　　享受学习乐趣

Slide 4

美国中小学生中文学习目标

学生能在实际生活中
运用语言沟通的能力
透过文化的了解和比较
与其它学科贯连
享受学习中文乐趣

Slide 5

What are goals and standards?

- 学习标准 Content Standards 学什么
  WHAT students should know and be able to do
  学生应该学什么，能学会什么
- 能力标准 Performance Standards
  会什么
  HOW students show what they are able to do
  怎么样让学生能够实际操作表现实践能力

Slide 6

美国中小学生学习中文的最终目的

能够了解和分辨（the reason why）
在不同时态情况下（to know how and when）
如何得体地使用中文（what should be said）
跟不同的对象（人或事务 to whom）进行有意义的交际沟通（meaningful communication）。

For ALL students to learn how, when and why to say what to whom in Chinese

Slide 7

What are the three modes of communication?

- Standard 1.1 人际沟通 Interpersonal
- Standard 1.2 理解诠释 Interpretive
- Standard 1.3 表达演示 Presentational

Slide 8

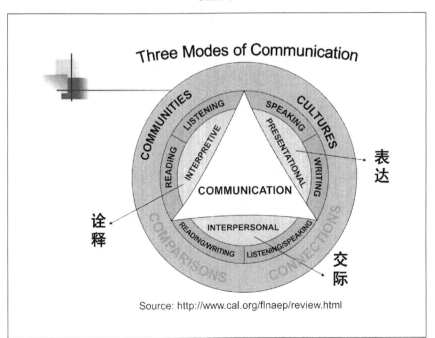

Slide 9

老师们，别忘了………．

- 明确你的教学目的
  - Purposeful, intentional lessons targeting specific outcomes
- 教学的题材要能吸引学生的兴趣，
  进行有意义的沟通
  - Students engaged in meaningful, authentic communication about important topics that interest them
- 老师要少说，学生要多说
  - More Student Talk than Teacher Talk

Slide 10

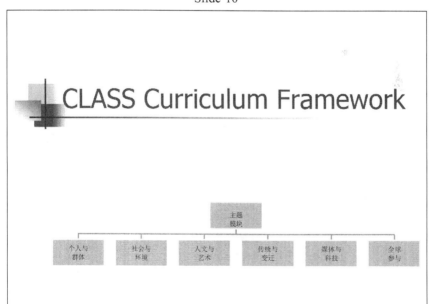

Slide 11

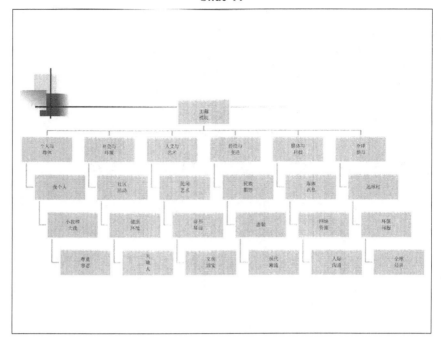

Slide 12

Integrated Thematic Planning
主题教学单元

- brings content to the language lesson 充实语言学习的内容
- connects four skills in more meaning-based communicative ways 有意义的交际沟通
- links the language class to the outside world
  将语言学习从校内延伸到校外
- creates activities that are task-based, relevant, personalized and accomplished in cooperative settings
  教学活动是有任务性的而且互相相关联

Slide 13

Integrated Thematic Planning
主题教学单元

- creates a meaningful context
  提供有意义有目的的语言学习情境
- makes instruction more comprehensible
- 让学生容易了解所教的内容和题材

Slide 14

Integrated Thematic Planning
主题教学单元

- places focus on using the language to communicate something related to a theme
  着重与主题有关的语言沟通和使用
  ✓ *students no longer repeating words in isolation with no connection to them or the classroom*
  ✓ *学生有意义地学习的单字词汇*

Slide 15

Process of designing a thematic unit

1. **Identify sources of outcomes**
   - Standards, local and state curriculum frameworks
   - List of language functions

2. **Choose a thematic center/unit focus**
   - Consider a curriculum concept, a book, a poem, a story, a school, a piece of art or music...
   - Sample topics out of which themes can grow: Celebrations, Daily activities, Family and friends, Solar system, My house of the future, the Haunted house, Olympics...

Slide 16

Process of designing a thematic unit

3. **Brainstorm/develop a web of potential outcomes, content and activities for the theme**

4. **Choose outcomes and possible assessments**
   - Culminating in performance assessment or task
   - Subject content outcomes/assessments

Slide 17

Unit Plan Inventory:	Unit Title: Language Level:					Carlo Ann Dahlberg/Helena Curtain.2006
Scenario/Unit Overview:						
Enduring Understanding(s) (Students will understand that...) Essential Question(s): Targeted Standards: Outcomes/Objectives/Progress Indicators:						[1]
Performance Assessment:						[2]
Interpersonal Task and Rubric		Interpersonal Task and Rubric			Interpersonal Task and Rubric	
Language (Language Functions)	Grammatical Structures/ Literacy	Vocabulary	Culture(s)	Subject Content (Connections)	Essential Materials	Learning Activities, Performances (Assessments) [3]
						Beginning
						Middle
						End
Comparisons						
Communities						

Slide 18

Template for a Standards-based Lesson Plan (—)

- **Overview:** How does this lesson connect to student's previous knowledge?
- **Level / Grade:**
- **Targeted Standards:** (Check all that apply)
    - Communications:
        ___ 1.1 Interpersonal ___ 1.2 Interpretive ___ 1.3 Presentational
    - Cultures:
        ___ 2.1 Products of Culture ___ 2.2 Practice of Culture
    - Connections:
        ___ 3.1 Making Connections ___ 3.2 Acquiring New Information
    - Comparisons:
        ___ 4.1 Linguistic Comparison ___ 4.2 Cultural Comparison
    - Communities:
        ___ 5.1 School and Community ___ 5.2 Personal Enjoyment

Slide 19

Template for a Standards-based Lesson Plan (二)

- **Functional Objectives** (Learning Outcomes): — What should students be able to do at the end of this lesson? (SWBD)
- **Content Objectives:** — What skills and knowledge will students gain from this lesson?
- **Materials/Resources Needed:**
- **Time Allotment:** — Time management and pacing of the lesson

Slide 20

Template for a Standards-based Lesson Plan (三)

- **Instructional Procedures:**
    - How will you activate prior knowledge?
    - How will you connect that with the new information/concept?
    - How will you conduct guided practice?
    - What strategies can you use for different learning styles?
    - How will you reinforce learned materials?
    - How will you provide a new context in which knowledge/skills learned can be applied to that new setting?
    - How will you find out if students really "got it?"
    - How will you do a closure for the class?
- **Assessment:** formative and/or summative; holistic or analytic

[1] American Council on the Teaching of Foreign Languages (ACTFL). (2013). NCCSFL-ACTFL can-do statements: Progress indicators for language learners. Retrieved from http://www.actfl.org/sites/default/files/pdfs/Can-Do_Statements.pdf
[2] STARTALK OneWorld Now! (2009). STARTALK Classroom Video- OneWorld Now! (Chinese). Segment 15:42–17:19. STARTALK classroom video collection. (Video file). Retrieved from https://startalk.umd.edu/teacher-development/videos/2009/OneWorldNow-Chinese
[3] Annenberg Foundation. (n.d.). Teaching foreign languages K-12: Communicating about sports (Chinese). Segment 20:26–21:52. (Video file). Retrieved from http://www.learner.org/libraries/tfl/chinese/gao/index.html
[4] 主题词卡 网络链接 http://cop.yes-chinese.com/cnpic/index_en.html

附件二：教案检查单 （根据星谈项目总部资料翻译）.docx

Lesson Planning Checklist
教案检查单

✓	检查项目 Item
Stage 1 第一步	
	I have identified what I want students to be able to do (the learning targets) by the end of the lesson. 学生在课程结束时应达到什么学习目标？
	I have determined what students need to know (vocabulary and structures) in order to reach the learning targets. 学生应获得什么语言知识(knowledge)和技能(skills)？
Stage 2 第二步	
	I know how students will show me that they have achieved the learning targets by the end of the lesson. 在课程结束时，能否利用最科学的测试衡量学生的学习结果？
Stage 3 第三步	
	I have thought about various activities that could be used to achieve the learning targets. 设计什么活动可以让学生达到预期的学习目标？
	From the activities I have thought about, I have carefully chosen these activities because they hold the greatest promise for reaching the learning targets. 所设计、选择的活动，是否经过深思熟虑，效果是否最佳，是否保证达到教学目标？

The activities I have selected do the following: 教学设计及活动应该有以下作用：	
	Give students a reason for needing to pay attention, wanting to pay attention, and being on-task 让学生清楚了解活动的意义，主动集中注意力
	Provide students with an authentic (real-world) purpose for using the language 让学生真实、有目的地使用语言
	Make the learner – not the teacher – the active participant 让学生，而不是老师做积极的参与者
	Engage all students, as opposed to just one or two at a time 让所有学生，而不是个别学生参与活动
	Provide sufficient opportunities for input before expecting output 首先提供输入，然后要求输出
	Provide multiple, varied opportunities for students to hear new words and expressions in contexts that make meaning transparent 为学生提供各种机会，让学生在语境丰富的情况下，多次反复地学习新词汇及新的表达方法
	Represent the best use of instructional time 有效利用课上时间
	Take an appropriate amount of time considering the age of the learner 根据学生的年龄安排课堂活动时间
	Include enough variety to enable a lively pace for the lesson 利用各种活动活跃课堂气氛，调节课堂节奏
	Vary in level of intensity and physical movement from one to the next 调整课堂强度，及时变换课堂活动位置

第三课　目标语[1]教学与可理解输入[2]
Teaching in the Target Language and Comprehensible Input

（文本形式：专业讨论）

> ➢ 关键词：
>   目标语、可理解输入、控制词汇量、语义协商、语言定式、肢体语言、音调变化、语境
> ➢ 能力目标：
>   1. 学习者能理解使用目标语教学与提供可理解输入的重要性与挑战。
>   2. 学习者能使用专业术语讨论使用目标语教学与提供可理解语言输入的策略。
>   3. 学习者能利用教学实例讨论并演示如何在课堂上利用目标语提供可理解输入，如何通过提问进行语义协商。

---

[1] 目标语　　mùbiāoyǔ　　N.　target language
[2] 可理解输入　kělǐjiěshūrù　NP.　comprehensible input

课文全版 (Complete Version)

（在今年的汉语大会上，孙老师、常老师、许老师又见面了。午餐时，他们边吃边谈，一会儿，讨论的话题转到了在课上使用目标语和提供可理解输入的挑战[3]。）

孙：我今年一直在尝试[4]使用目标语进行教学。我发现这种教法不但能为学生提供大量[5]、丰富[6]的语言输入，而且对提高教师自己的语言水平也大有好处，就是操作[7]起来并不容易。

常：我完全同意。我自己的问题是，中文水平还不够高，无法[8]一堂五十分钟的课都说中文。

孙：没错，我也认为完全使用目标语来教学对非母语教师来说是一个很大的挑战。

常：在我们学校的双语项目[9]中，我注意到有几位教师采取[10]控制[11]词汇量[12]的做法。上课使用的都是学生听得懂的词汇。

孙：许老师，根据你的经验，第二语言教学的关键[13]是什么？

许：我认为有两点非常重要，第一，教师在课上应该尽量[14]使用目标语，最好达到[15]百分之九十以上[16]；第二是为学生提供可理解输入，也就是comprehensible input，这两个因素[17]是密切相关[18]的。

[3]挑战	tiǎozhàn	V./N.	to challenge; challenge
[4]尝试	chángshì	V./N.	to attempt, to try
[5]大量	dàliàng	Adj.	a great quantity
[6]丰富	fēngfù	Adj.	abundant, plentiful, rich
[7]操作	cāozuò	V.	to operate, to manipulate (machinery, etc.), to work, to handle, to carry out the proper procedures (in manufacturing, testing, etc.)
[8]无法	wúfǎ	V.	to be unable to, to have no way to
[9]双语项目	shuāngyǔxiàngmù	NP.	bilingual language program
[10]采取	cǎiqǔ	V.	to adopt, to use
[11]控制	kòngzhì	V.	to control, to bring sth. under control
[12]词汇量	cíhuìliàng	NP.	amount of vocabulary, number of words and phrases
[13]关键	guānjiàn	N./Adj.	the key (to sth.), key point; crucial
[14]尽量	jìnliàng	Adv.	as much as possible, to the greatest extent
[15]达到	dádào	V.	to reach (a figure), to achieve an objective
[16]以上	yǐshàng	N.	more than (for example, more than 90%)
[17]因素	yīnsù	N.	factor
[18]密切相关	mìqièxiāngguān	Idiom	be closely related

孙：可理解输入……，是不是只要说得慢一点，让学生听得懂就行了？
许：是的，不过这只是其中的一点，并不代表[19]全部。在课上提供有效的可理解输入，表面上看起来很容易，其实是非常复杂[20]的。
孙：您的意思是……？
许：我的意思是说，提供可理解输入有很多策略，比方说，控制课上使用的语言，上课的时候教师说话语速[21]不要过快，用举例[22]的方法说明生词的意思，不要翻译，还要重复[23]强调课文中的关键词。
常：要做到这几点，还需要大量的实际[24]教学经验，而且还要做大量的课前准备。
许：是的，教师的课前准备十分重要。只有在课前准备好了，才能在课上有效使用目标语。这也就是说教师必须备课[25]。比方说：你得考虑到学生对什么内容有困难；你如何用简单易懂[26]的方法或者例子说明。我总是在上课前一天设计好提问[27]内容，在上课的时候，我还会鼓励[28]学生使用目标语进行语义协商[29]。
常：语义协商是什么意思呢？
许：语义协商就是让学生对自己不理解的语言进行提问，比方说："老师，你说什么，我没听懂。""……是什么意思？"或者"你的意思是不是……？"
孙：原来这就是语义协商啊。没想到提这些问题也是一种可理解输入。
许：常老师，听说你有些同事也在尝试使用目标语教学，他们用了一些什么好的策略呢？
常：让我想想。我看过他们在课堂上用很多语言定式[30]，比方说，"好久不见"，"今天我们就到这儿吧，明天再谈"，等等。并且让学生不断[31]重复。此外，也让学生常常采用公式化语言[32]来回答问题，比方说，"对啊，好久不见，最近怎么样？"对了，教师还应该使用大量的肢体语言[33]或者音调变化[34]。

[19]代表	dàibiǎo	V./N.	to represent, stand for; representative
[20]复杂	fùzá	Adj.	complicated, complex
[21]语速	yǔsù	N.	rate of speech
[22]举例	jǔlì	V.	to give an example
[23]重复	chóngfù	V.	to repeat
[24]实际	shíjì	N./Adj.	practice, reality, actuality; real, actual
[25]备课	bèikè	V.	(of a teacher) to prepare lessons
[26]易懂	yìdǒng	Adj.	easy to understand
[27]提问	tíwèn	V.	to ask questions
[28]鼓励	gǔlì	V.	to encourage
[29]语义协商	yǔyìxiéshāng	N.	negotiation of meaning
[30]语言定式	yǔyándìngshì	NP.	set word or grammar patterns
[31]不断	búduàn	Adv.	continuously
[32]公式化语言	gōngshìhuàyǔyán	NP.	formulaic speech or language
[33]肢体语言	zhītǐyǔyán	NP.	body language
[34]音调变化	yīndiàobiànhuà	NP.	inflection

52　*Teaching in the Target Language*

许：　这些策略都很有用。还有一个很重要的策略，就是利用语境[35]。语境包括提供与课文话题相关的背景知识[36]，多种媒体[37]的教材等。当语境很清楚时，就不需要做太多的解释了。

孙：　可理解输入真可以说是包括了教学的方方面面[38]，但是实际操作起来并不容易。

常：　根据我的经验，这种方法值得一试[39]。不但能增强[40]学生的信心，而且学生学完后有很高的成就感[41]。哎呀，已经一点四十五分了。下午的报告就要开始了，我们四点半在大厅见吧！

孙/许：　好啊！

语言重点：

1. **Do sth. 对 sb.（来说）是一种/一个+挑战**

   Doing sth. is a challenge for sb.

   - 一会儿，讨论的话题转到了在课上使用目标语和提供可理解输入的挑战。
   - 在课堂中，完全使用目标语来教学对非母语教师来说是一个很大的挑战。

2. **Subj.（一直/不断/努力）尝试+do sth.（使用目标语/控制词汇量/利用语境/提供可理解输入/采取…）**

   Subj. (consistently/without stopping/diligently) tries to (use the target language/control vocabulary/use language context/provide comprehensible input/adopt …)

   - 我今年一直在尝试使用目标语进行教学。
   - 在课上，教师鼓励学生不断尝试使用目标语进行语言协商，如此一来，为学生提供了大量丰富的可理解输入。

3. **A为/给B提供+NP（输入/语境/教材/背景知识）**

   A provides B with (input/(language) context/teaching material/background knowledge)

   - 我发现这种教法不但为学生提供大量、丰富的语言输入，而且对提高教师自己的语言水平也大有好处，就是操作起来并不容易。
   - 语境包括为学生提供与课文话题相关的背景知识，多种媒体的教材等。

---

[35]语境	yǔjìng	N.	(language) context
[36]背景知识	bèijǐngzhīshi	NP.	background knowledge
[37]媒体	méitǐ	N.	media
[38]方方面面	fāngfāngmiànmiàn	NP.	each and every aspect
[39]值得一试	zhídéyíshì	VP.	worth trying
[40]增强	zēngqiáng	V.	to strengthen, to reinforce, to enhance
[41]成就感	chéngjiùgǎn	N.	sense of achievement, sense of accomplishment

Teaching in the Target Language 53

4. **(Subj.)无法+VP**

    (Subj.) is incapable of doing sth./unable to do sth.

    - 我的中文水平还不够高,无法一堂五十分钟的课都说中文。
    - 在使用目标语教学时,如果教师不提供可理解输入,学习者便无法达到学习目标。

5. **(为了…,) subj.采取+…(控制词汇量/利用语境/提供可理解性输入/使用目标语教学)的做法/策略/方法/措施**

    (For the purpose of … ,) subj. chooses the strategy of … (controlling vocabulary/using language context/providing comprehensible input/using the target language)

    - 在我们学校的双语项目中,我注意到有几位老师采取控制词汇量的做法。
    - 为了给学生提供大量、丰富的语言输入,教师应采取使用目标语教学的方法。

6. **Subj.尽量+do sth.(使用目标语/尝试…/控制词汇量/采用…的策略/利用语境/提供…输入/进行语义协商)**

    Subj. does his/her/their best to … (use the target language/attempt to … / control the amount of vocabulary/adopt strategies of … /use language context/provide … input/negotiate meaning)

    - 教师在课上应该尽量使用目标语,最好达到百分之九十以上。
    - 在提供可理解输入时,教师应该尽量利用多种语境,否则使用目标语教学对学习者来说将是一个挑战。

7. **A和B是密切相关的**

    A and B are closely related.

    - 这两个因素是密切相关的。
    - 教师是否能在课上有效地使用目标语和课前的准备是否充分是密切相关的。

8. **Subj.表面上…,其实…**

    On the surface/on the face of it … , but actually/in reality …

    - 表面上看来很容易,其实有效地提供可理解输入是非常复杂的。
    - 采取使用目标语教学的方法表面上并不复杂,其实在教学前教师应该提前考虑课堂中的方方面面。

9. **A鼓励B+do sth.**（使用…/采用…的策略/进行语义协商/利用语境/尝试…）

    A encourages B to ... (use ... /adopt ... strategies/negotiate meaning/use language context/attempt to ...)

    - 我总是在上课前一天设计好提问内容，在上课的时候，我还会鼓励学生使用目标语进行语义协商。
    - 在汉语大会上，竹老师鼓励外语教师努力尝试利用主题把外语教学标准的五个C贯穿在教学中。

10. ① …（主题教学设计/反向课程设计/使用目标语教学/提供可理解输入）的方法/做法/策略+值得一试

    The method/strategy of ... (Thematic Unit Design/Backwards Curriculum Design/using target language/providing comprehensible input) is worth a try.

    ② **…值得sb.+V**（讨论/强调/介绍/采用）

    It is worth ... (discussing/emphasizing/introducing/adopting)

    - 根据我的经验，这种方法值得一试。
    - 使用目标语教学不但能增强学生的信心，而且学生学完以后有很高的成就感，因此这种策略值得采用。

第三课　目标语[1]教学与可理解输入[2]
Teaching in the Target Language and Comprehensible Input

（文本形式：专业讨论）

> ➢ 关键词：
> 目标语、可理解输入、控制词汇量、语义协商、语言定式、肢体语言、音调变化、语境
> ➢ 能力目标：
> 1. 学习者能理解使用目标语教学与提供可理解输入的重要性与挑战。
> 2. 学习者能使用专业术语讨论使用目标语教学与提供可理解输入的策略。
> 3. 学习者能利用教学实例讨论并演示如何在课堂上利用目标语提供可理解输入，如何通过提问进行语义协商。

---

[1]目标语　　mùbiāoyǔ　　N.　　target language
[2]可理解输入　kělǐjiěshūrù　NP.　comprehensible input

课文节选版 (Abridged Version)

（在今年的汉语大会上，孙老师、常老师、许老师又见面了。午餐时，他们边吃边谈，一会儿，讨论的话题转[3]到了在课上使用目标语和提供可理解输入的挑战[4]。）

孙：我今年一直在尝试[5]使用目标语进行教学。我发现这种教法不但能为学生提供大量[6]、丰富[7]的语言输入，而且对提高教师自己的语言水平也大有好处，就是操作[8]起来并不容易。

常：我完全同意。我自己的问题是，中文水平还不够高，无法[9]一堂五十分钟的课都说中文。

孙：许老师，根据你的经验，第二语言教学的关键[10]是什么？

许：我认为有两点非常重要，第一，教师在课上应该尽量[11]使用目标语，最好达到[12]百分之九十以上[13]；第二是为学生提供可理解输入，也就是comprehensible input。

孙：可理解输入……，是不是只要说得慢一点，让学生听得懂就行了？

许：是的，不过这只是其中的一点，并不代表[14]全部。提供可理解输入有很多策略[15]，比方说，控制课上使用的语言，上课的时候教师说话语速[16]不要过快，用例子说明生词的意思，不要翻译[17]，还要重复[18]强调课文中的关键词。

[3]转	zhuǎn	V.	to transfer, to switch
[4]挑战	tiǎozhàn	V./N.	to challenge; challenge
[5]尝试	chángshì	V./N.	to attempt, to try
[6]大量	dàliàng	Adj.	a great quantity
[7]丰富	fēngfù	Adj.	abundant, plentiful, rich
[8]操作	cāozuò	V.	to operate, to manipulate (machinery, etc.), to work, to handle, to carry out the proper procedures (in manufacturing, testing, etc.)
[9]无法	wúfǎ	V.	to be unable to, to have no way to
[10]关键	guānjiàn	N./Adj.	the key (to sth.), key point; crucial
[11]尽量	jìnliàng	Adv.	as much as possible, to the greatest extent
[12]达到	dádào	V.	to reach (a figure), to achieve an objective
[13]以上	yǐshàng	N.	more than (for example, more than 90%)
[14]代表	dàibiǎo	V./N.	to represent, stand for; representative
[15]策略	cèlüè	N.	strategy, tactics
[16]语速	yǔsù	N.	rate of speech
[17]翻译	fānyì	V.	to translate
[18]重复	chóngfù	V.	to repeat

常： 对，我同意。
许： 还有，我认为教师必须备课[19]。比方说：你得考虑到学生对什么内容有困难；你如何用不同的方法或者例子说明。我总是在上课前一天设计好提问[20]内容，在上课的时候，我还会鼓励[21]学生使用目标语进行语义协商[22]。
常： 语义协商是什么意思呢？
许： 语义协商就是让学生对自己不理解的语言进行提问，比方说："老师，你说什么，我没听懂。""……是什么意思？"或者"你的意思是不是……？"
孙： 原来这就是语义协商啊。没想到提这些问题也是一种可理解输入。
许： 常老师，听说你有些同事也在尝试使用目标语教学，他们用了一些什么好的策略呢？
常： 让我想想。我看过他们在课堂上用很多语言定式[23]，比方说，"好久不见"，"今天我们就到这儿吧，明天再谈"，等等。并且让学生不断[24]重复。此外，也让学生常常采用公式化语言[25]来回答问题，比方说，"对啊，好久不见，最近怎么样？"对了，教师还应该使用大量的肢体语言[26]或者音调变化[27]。
许： 这些策略都很有用。还有一个很重要的策略，就是利用语境[28]。语境包括提供与课文话题有关的背景知识[29]，多种媒体[30]的教材[31]。当语境很清楚时，就不需要做太多的解释[32]了。
常： 根据我的经验，这种方法不但能增强[33]学生的信心，而且学生学完后有很高的成就感[34]。哎呀，已经一点四十五分了。下午的报告就要开始了，我们四点半在大厅见吧！
孙/许： 好啊！

[19]备课	bèikè	V.	(of a teacher) to prepare lessons
[20]提问	tíwèn	V.	to ask questions
[21]鼓励	gǔlì	V.	to encourage
[22]语义协商	yǔyìxiéshāng	N.	negotiation of meaning
[23]语言定式	yǔyándìngshì	NP.	set word or grammar patterns
[24]不断	búduàn	Adv.	continuously
[25]公式化语言	gōngshìhuàyǔyán	NP.	formulaic speech or language
[26]肢体语言	zhītǐyǔyán	NP.	body language
[27]音调变化	yīndiàobiànhuà	NP.	inflection
[28]语境	yǔjìng	N.	(language) context
[29]背景知识	bèijǐngzhīshi	NP.	background knowledge
[30]媒体	méitǐ	N.	media
[31]教材	jiàocái	N.	teaching material
[32]解释	jiěshì	V.	to explain
[33]增强	zēngqiáng	V.	to strengthen, to reinforce, to enhance
[34]成就感	chéngjiùgǎn	N.	sense of achievement, sense of accomplishment

语言重点：

1. **Do sth.对sb.（来说）是一种/一个+挑战**

   Doing sth. is a challenge for sb.

   - 一会儿，讨论的话题转到了在课上使用目标语和提供可理解输入的挑战。
   - 在课堂中，完全使用目标语来教学对非母语教师来说是一个很大的挑战。

2. **Subj.（一直/不断/努力）尝试+do sth.（使用目标语/控制词汇量/利用语境/提供可理解输入/采取…）**

   Subj. (consistently/without stopping/diligently) tries to … (use the target language/control vocabulary/use language context/provide comprehensible input/adopt …)

   - 我今年一直在尝试使用目标语进行教学。
   - 在课上，教师鼓励学生不断尝试使用目标语进行语言协商，如此一来，为学生提供了大量丰富的可理解输入。

3. **A为/给B提供+NP（输入/语境/教材/背景知识）**

   A provides B with (input/(language) context/teaching material/background knowledge)

   - 我发现这种教法不但为学生提供大量、丰富的语言输入，而且对提高教师自己的语言水平也大有好处，就是操作起来并不容易。
   - 语境包括为学生提供与课文话题相关的背景知识，多种媒体的教材等。

4. **(Subj.)无法+VP**

   (Subj.) is incapable of doing sth./unable to do sth.

   - 我的中文水平还不够高，无法一堂五十分钟的课都说中文。
   - 在使用目标语教学时，如果教师不提供可理解输入，学习者便无法达到学习目标。

5. **Subj.尽量+do sth.（使用目标语/尝试…/控制词汇量/采用…的策略/利用语境/提供…输入/进行语义协商）**

   Subj. does his/her/their best to … (use the target language/attempt to … / control the amount of vocabulary/adopt strategies of … /use language context/provide … input/negotiate meaning)

   - 教师在课上应该尽量使用目标语，最好达到百分之九十以上。
   - 在提供可理解输入时，教师应该尽量利用多种语境，否则使用目标语教学对学习者来说将是一个挑战。

6. **A鼓励B+do sth.**（使用…/采用…的策略/进行语义协商/利用语境/尝试…）

   A encourages B to … (use … /adopt … strategies/negotiate meaning/use language context/attempt to …)

   - 我总是在上课前一天设计好提问内容，在上课的时候，我还会鼓励学生使用目标语进行语义协商。
   - 在汉语大会上，竹老师鼓励外语教师努力尝试利用主题把外语教学标准的五个C贯穿在教学中。

练习活动

理解诠释1：预习单

先看课文，然后完成下面的作业：

一、现在有越来越多教师尝试使用目标语教学，这样做有哪些好处？
1. 对学生来说：

2. 对老师来说：

二、根据课文进行填空。
  在课上尽量使用目标语的意思是_____以上的时间用目标语进行教学。要做到这一点，就得为学生提供可理解输入。
  许多教师以为提供可理解输入就是放慢语速，其实可理解输入包括了教学的方方面面，操作起来并不容易。教师在课前必须_____，按照学生的语言水平设计提问内容，考虑到什么内容会让学生感到困难，需要用什么_____来说明，或者利用清楚的语境，比方说给学生提供_____等，就不需要做太多的解释了。另外，在课堂上用很多_____，比方说"好久不见"，或者让学生采用_____回答问题，不断重复，最重要的是控制课上使用的语言、在学生听不懂时鼓励学生_____，都是值得尝试的方法。

三、根据你对课文的理解，判断下面哪些做法属于提供有效可理解输入的策略，请在相应的栏目里画"√"

项目	有效的可理解输入策略
教师大量重复学生不熟悉的关键词	
教师通过图片、表演让学生了解意思	
教师利用翻译让学生很快就了解意思	
教师控制词汇量，使用学生听得懂的生词	
教师将学生分组，自由讨论课上不能理解的内容	

四、根据你的汉语教学/学习经验，在进行语义协商时，常用的话有哪些？（至少五句）

理解诠释2：扩展阅读 根据靳洪刚教授（2012）原文改编

根据互动假设理论，第二语言习得的研究除了应探讨学习者所经历的内在学习过程外，更重要的是研究学习者跟他人交际时所产生的互动对语言习得的作用。换句话说，学习者与他人之间的交流互动是第二语言习得研究的中心课题之一。互动假设理论认为：第二语言学习者必须依赖一种既听得懂，又有挑战性的课堂语言，也就是可理解输入，方能学会第二语言。而可理解输入不但来自各种形式的课堂语言，更重要的是来自互动中的互动调整(modified interaction)。除了像重新叙述(paraphrase)、句子调整(repair)外，常见的例子还有：确定对方的理解度(comprehension check)，如，"我去吃了一顿年夜饭，'年夜饭'你知道吧，就是大年三十晚上全家吃的饭。"请求对方澄清事实(clarification request)，以及进行语义协商。

语义协商是一种常见的、多功能的加强语言结构的课堂技巧。主要的课堂技巧是采用各种回应性提问(echoic questions)。按照Long and Sato (1983)的研究，回应性提问可以分为三种：一是理解检测类提(comprehension check)。这类提问通常是为了确定对方的理解而提出的，例如："我去吃了一顿年夜饭。'年夜饭'你知道吧，就是大年三十晚上全家吃的饭。"这里"'年夜饭'你知道吧"就是一种确定对方是否理解"年夜饭"一词的方法。二是要求说明类提问(clarification check)。这类提问是要求对方进一步说明，或进一步澄清没有听清楚或没有理解的信息，如："你说什么？我不太明白你的意思。""什么，什么？"等都属于要求说明类提问。三是确定理解类提问(confirmation check)。这类提问是说话者通过提问，确定自己是否已准确理解对方所表达的意思，如："你是不是说……？"

1. 互动假设理论认为，可理解输入的来源包括哪些？（可多选）
   A. 各种形式的课堂语言
   B. 人际交流中的互动调整
   C. 学习者的内在学习过程

2. 下面哪些方法是常见的"互动调整"？　（可多选）
   A. 句子调整　　B. 语义协商　　C. 重新叙述　　D. 澄清事实

3. 语义协商可以有效加强语言结构。主要的课堂技巧是采用各种回应性提问(echoic questions)。回应性提问可分为哪三类？

4. 请你分析一下，在下列对话中，一共使用了哪些<u>回应性提问</u>？
   孙老师：上个周末您做什么了？
   许老师：我去吃尾牙了。
   孙老师："尾牙"是什么？这道菜好吃吗？
   许老师：尾牙不是一道菜，是一个台湾传统习俗。就是在年底的时候，公司、学校、公家机关请员工吃饭，有些公司甚至还会发奖金、进行抽奖活动呢！
   孙老师：哦，所以是老板请客，对吗？听起来真有意思。
   许老师：有机会你也应该去参加，边吃边玩，有趣极了。

人际交流1：面对面讨论

开学以前，一位同事想在新的学期尝试使用目标语教学，于是来请教你：

王老师：　我不久前参加了一个教学会议，听了一场关于使用目标语教学的报告，觉得值得一试。不知道您对使用目标语教学有什么看法？您认为课堂多少时间应该用目标语教学才够呢？
你的回答：【建议词汇和结构：可理解输入；A为B提供+NP；大量；丰富；成就感；尽量+VP；…以上】
王老师：　我是个非母语教师，担心自己的语言水平不够高，无法一堂课都说中文。您有什么建议吗？
你的回答：【建议词汇和结构：Do sth.对sb.（来说）是一种挑战；为了…，subj.采取…的方法/策略；控制；提问；A鼓励B+do sth.；尝试；语境；语义协商】
王老师：　这不但需要大量的实际教学经验，而且还要做大量的课前准备。虽然是个挑战，不过好处很多，我一定会好好准备的，谢谢。

人际交流2：在脸书(Facebook)上征求意见

下面是一位老师在脸书上发布的一则近况。请你读了之后给他至少三个建议。【建议词汇和结构：subj.表面上…，其实…；大量；肢体语言；尽量+VP；重复；公式化语言；举例；语速；语境；背景知识；音调变化；媒体；subj.采取…的方法/策略；控制；A鼓励B+do sth.；尝试；备课；提问；词汇量；关键词；可理解输入】

> 📰 近况　📷 相片/影片　▶ 生活要事
>
> 各位朋友，我这个学期教一年级中文，学生的词汇量很小。如果要在课上使用目标语进行教学真的很难！求好方法。

表达演说：分享教学经验

请你准备一个5分钟的演讲，跟同学分享一下自己使用目标语教学的经验（若没有教学经验，请分享学习中文时，老师使用目标语教学的情况），并且举例说明。分享教学/学习经验时，应该包括：

1. 你的课堂，百分之多少的时间是使用目标语进行教学的？你认为应该增加还是减少，为什么？
2. 你/老师设计了什么课堂活动来鼓励学生进行语义协商？请举例说明。
3. 你/老师如何检测课堂语言是"可理解输入"？
4. 在你看来，学生的语言能力是否因此而提高，自信心也增强了？

建议词汇和结构：无法+VP；可理解输入；A为B提供+NP；大量；丰富；成就感；因素；A尽量+VP；…以上；Do sth.对sb.（来说）是一种挑战；subj.采取…的方法/策略；控制；提问；A鼓励B+do sth.；尝试；语境；复杂；肢体语言；音调变化；重复；公式化语言；语速；语境；媒体；不断+VP；词汇量；关键；A和B是密切相关的

❓ 反思任务

根据教学视频进行讨论：
http://startalk.umd.edu/teacher-development/videos/2009/OneWorldNow-Chinese

一、前期任务：
从视频上观摩中文课之后，和小组成员一起设计一份课堂观摩检查单。设计检查单时应注意如何涵盖到三位老师在交流中提到的使用目标语教学与可理解输入的关键内容及有效策略。

二、核心任务：
根据检查单里列出的内容，与小组成员一起对老师的教学加以讨论。讨论时应该包括：

- 这位老师在教学过程中用到了哪些教学策略，具体做法是什么？
- 这位老师在哪些方面还需要加以调整？说明理由和建议。

三、后期任务：
报告自己小组讨论的结果。

补充材料

Comprehensible Input Checklist
可理解性输入检查单
（根据星谈项目有关文件翻译）

Category I: <u>Creating Comprehensible LANGUAGE</u> 第一项：使用可理解的语言 ☐ The teacher paraphrases new words and expressions. 　　使用简单的目标语解释新的生词、短语。 ☐ The teacher slows down the rate of speech for the level of the students. 　　根据学生水平，调整放慢语速。 ☐ The teacher defines new words with examples rather than translation. 　　举例解释说明生词，不做词对词直译。 ☐ The teacher uses vocabulary and structures that the students know and builds on them over time. 　　使用学生熟悉的词汇及结构，并在此基础上扩展学生的词汇量。 ☐ The teacher uses new words and expressions more than once or twice and enters and re-enters these language elements frequently in the input. 　　新词汇及短语在输入中应反复出现并反复使用，不能只用一次就不再重复。 ☐ The teacher signals new words and structures using tone and voice. 　　利用语调来强调或标注新词汇及结构的特点。
Category II: <u>Creating comprehensible INTERACTIONS with students</u> 第二项：鼓励学生进行可理解性互动 ☐ The teacher involves the students in several ways and does not just lecture to the class (e.g., signaling, responding, completing a sentence after meaning has been established). 　　不采用课堂演讲，但使用不同方法鼓励学生参与。（如，在语义理解的基础上回答问题，完成句子、示意答案等） ☐ The teacher uses question sequences that begin with "yes/no questions," move to "forced-choice questions," and end with "open-ended, personalized questions." 　　使用教师提问引发互动。提问由"是否问句"开始，到"选择问句"，最后到"开放式个人化问题"。 ☐ The teacher provides useful phrases to help students negotiate meaning, such as asking for repetition, asking for clarification (Can you say more?), checking comprehension (Do you mean … ?), and confirming understanding (I think you are saying … Am I right?). 　　教学生一些实用的语义协商策略。如，要求重复（请再说一次），语义澄清（……是什么意思）；理解检测，确定理解（你是说……；明白了，你的意思是不是……）。

Category III: Creating CONTEXTS for comprehension 第三项：利用语境促进语言理解 ☐ The teacher uses gestures to make new language clear. 利用肢体语言让学生清楚了解新的语言形式。 ☐ The teacher uses videos and props to enhance students' comprehension. 使用视听辅助材料促进理解。 ☐ The teacher focuses student attention on the input by making sure students know the topic and objective of the lesson in advance of the input activity. 让学生先了解课堂主题及课程目标，然后让学生将注意力集中在要学的语言材料或输入材料上。 ☐ The teacher creates a lesson with a meaningful and purposeful context that is relevant to the students. 为学生提供与其个人相关、有意义、有目的的交际语境。 注：以上检查单根据美国星谈项目(STARTALK)编发的英文版翻译改写

[1] STARTALK Concordia Language Villages. (2009). Talking with Dr. Carol Ann Dahlberg. Module 2, Segment 5: Language and culture. *STARTALK Multimedia Workshop: Staying in the Target Language.* [Video file]. Retrieved from https://startalk.umd.edu/teacher-development/workshops/2009/Concordia/content/

[2] STARTALK Concordia Language Villages. (2009). Talking with Dr. Carol Ann Dahlberg. Module 2, Segment 6: Magic. *STARTALK Multimedia Workshop: Staying in the Target Language.* [Video file]. Retrieved from https://startalk.umd.edu/teacher-development/workshops/2009/Concordia/content/

[3] Laine, C. (2013). Comprehensible Input as Foundation for Language Output and Interaction. Retrieved from http://www.youtube.com/watch?v=s8dbxEzJ9to

[4] Myers, Aaron G. (2011). 25 Ways to Find or Create Comprehensible Input. Retrieved from http://www.everydaylanguagelearner.com/2011/06/02/24-ways-to-find-or-create-comprehensible-input/

第四课　有效教学策略
Effective Instructional Strategies

（文本形式：教学论坛[1]）

> ➢ 关键词：
>   目标语教学、以学生为中心、文化教学、真实语料、任务、应用能力测试
> ➢ 能力目标：
>   1. 学习者能理解专业论坛讨论、说明各种有效汉语教学策略。
>   2. 学习者能就一、两个教学策略阐述、演示其在课上的具体做法。
>   3. 学习者能介绍、分析自己使用过的不同教学策略。
>   4. 学习者能使用正式套语主持讨论会。

---
[1]论坛　lùntán　N.　forum

课文全版 (Complete Version)

主持人[2]： 欢迎大家来参加汉语教学论坛，今天我们就汉语教学的策略进行讨论。讨论的方式是首先由主讲人[3]总结[4]每个教学策略的要点[5]，然后分四个小组进行讨论，最后请每个小组代表[6]发言[7]。下面我们有请主讲人张教授。

主讲人： 谢谢主持人，各位好。我们知道，在外语教学时，每个教师都应该利用反向课程设计原则为学生制定[8]能力目标，设计课堂活动，进行能力测试。在设计课堂活动时，教师应该了解各种有效的教学策略，让学生在课堂上进行有效互动[9]，最终学会使用语言。美国的星谈项目是由美国政府资助的暑期外语培训项目。为了培养更多的外语教师，星谈项目制定了六条有效教学策略，并提出每个策略的具体做法。今天我们组织这个论坛，就是为了让大家熟悉、了解不同的教学策略，并且进一步讨论如何在课堂上实施[10]这些策略。

第一个有效教学策略是：**课程设计以外语标准为本，用文化主题贯穿教学内容**。对于这个教学策略，具体的做法有三点：

- 每课课文都应该以外语教学标准为本，设定清楚的单元文化主题，让学生学会在真实语境下进行有主题、有意义的交流。
- 每堂课的教学都要有清楚的能力目标(Can-Do Statements)，也就是说，在每课结束以前，学生就知道自己能获得哪些语言知识，能利用语言做什么事情。
- 教师应该知道语法是交际的工具，并不是每个课程、单元、课文的中心。要避免[11]没有意义的句型操练[12]，保证[13]有意义、有目的的交流。

小组讨论：
1. 你认为让学生了解自己的能力目标对他们的语言学习有什么帮助？你认为使用什么方法最容易让学生了解自己的能力目标？请举例说明。
2. 让学生了解能力目标的方法有哪些？好处是什么？

[2]主持人	zhǔchírén	N.	host
[3]主讲人	zhǔjiǎngrén	N.	speaker, lecturer
[4]总结	zǒngjié	V./N.	to sum up, to summarize; summary
[5]要点	yàodiǎn	N.	key point
[6]小组代表	xiǎozǔdàibiǎo	NP.	group representative
[7]发言	fāyán	V.	to make a statement/speech
[8]制定	zhìdìng	V.	to draw up, to formulate
[9]互动	hùdòng	V./N.	to interact; interaction
[10]实施	shíshī	V.	to implement, to carry out, to operate
[11]避免	bìmiǎn	V.	to avoid
[12]句型操练	jùxíngcāoliàn	NP.	sentence pattern drill
[13]保证	bǎozhèng	V.	to ensure, to assure

3. 你认为什么样的活动/任务可以让学生在课上进行有意义、有目的的交流？在你的课堂上，或你所经历的课堂上，什么样的活动，让学生觉得最有趣，最愿意参与？请举例说明。

第二个有效教学策略是：**利用目标语进行教学**。具体做法有三点：
- 教师在课堂上使用的目标语应占全部课堂交流的百分之九十以上。
- 教师应采取不同的策略给学生提供有效的可理解输入，不断检测[14]学生的理解度[15]，并且根据学生的水平调整[16]课上使用的语言。
- 教师应使用举例的方式或利用肢体语言说明生词的意思，不要翻译。

小组讨论：
1. 什么是可理解输入？为什么可理解输入对学生的语言学习很重要？
2. 在课上你会采用什么策略有效地使用目标语进行教学？
3. 你通常采用什么方法给学生讲解[17]生词及语法，你用什么方法鼓励学生使用目标语进行课上互动？

第三个有效教学策略是：**创造[18]以学生为中心[19]的课堂**。具体做法有三点：
- 采用多种教学方式让学生学习语言，如利用故事情节[20]、动手活动[21]、图片说明[22]或专题讨论[23]等活动为学生提供大量、丰富的语言输入及合适的语境。
- 在课堂上，教师应提供各种机会让学生进行真实、有意义的交流。
- 教师在课上要以分组的方式组织教学活动让学生进行交流。

小组讨论：
1. 什么是以学生为中心的课堂？这种课堂有什么特点[24]？请你从学生需求[25]、能力目标、课堂活动、说话机会、教材及测试等方面进行讨论。
2. 组织分组活动时，应该考虑哪些方面的因素？比方说，学生的语言水平、文化背景、个性等。
3. 举例说明一个最有效的分组活动，讨论它的能力目标、活动内容、方法、结果等。

---

[14]检测	jiǎncè	V.	to check, to examine
[15]理解度	lǐjiědù	N.	degree of comprehension
[16]调整	tiáozhěng	V.	to adjust
[17]讲解	jiǎngjiě	V.	to explain
[18]创造	chuàngzào	V.	to create
[19]以学生为中心	yǐxuéshēngwéizhōngxīn	VP./Adj.	learner-centered
[20]故事情节	gùshìqíngjié	NP.	story plot
[21]动手活动	dòngshǒuhuódòng	NP.	hands-on activity
[22]图片说明	túpiànshuōmíng	NP.	picture description
[23]专题讨论	zhuāntítǎolùn	NP.	seminar
[24]特点	tèdiǎn	N.	characteristic, feature
[25]学生需求	xuéshēngxūqiú	NP.	learner's needs

第四个有效教学策略是：**把文化、学科知识[26]融入[27]语言课堂**。在结合文化教学时，教师不但要重视文化产物[28]（如筷子）及文化习俗[29]（如结婚时穿红色的衣服的习俗），也应该把文化教学的重点放在文化观念（如孝敬父母的观念）[30]及文化比较上。

小组讨论：
1. 在课堂上，你是如何把文化产物、习俗、观念和语言结合起来进行教学的？
2. 你使用过哪些有效的文化活动或跟其他学科相关的课堂活动？学生认为这样的活动对他们的语言学习有什么帮助？

第五个有效教学策略是：**使用适合学生年龄及认知发展[31]阶段[32]的真实语料[33]**。具体做法有两点：
- 教师利用真实语料设计符合学生兴趣，适合学生年龄及语言水平的真实任务。
- 教师利用像报刊[34]、视频[35]这样的真实材料组织教学。

小组讨论：
1. 你认为什么是"真实语料"？
2. 教师在上语言课的时候为什么要使用"真实语料"？
3. 你认为选择"真实语料"的标准是什么？在课上你是如何使用"真实语料"进行教学的？

第六个有效教学策略是：**进行任务式[36]应用能力测试[37]**。
- 教师在平常的课程教学中应利用教学活动、真实任务，多次进行不同能力的测试及评估，根据测试结果调整教学。
- 学生在完成学习目标及任务的过程中，教师提供不同的反馈[38]，帮助学生提高语言水平。

小组讨论：
1. 什么是应用能力测试？这种测试的目的是什么？要达到这个目的最好采取什么形式？打分标准[39]是如何设定的？
2. 反馈对学生的作用是什么？为什么教师应该为学生提供反馈？

---

[26]学科知识	xuékēzhīshi	N.	knowledge of a discipline
[27]融入	róngrù	V.	to blend in, to assimilate
[28]文化产物	wénhuàchǎnwù	NP.	cultural product
[29]文化习俗	wénhuàxísú	NP.	cultural practice
[30]观念	guānniàn	N.	idea, concept
[31]认知发展	rènzhīfāzhǎn	NP.	cognitive development
[32]阶段	jiēduàn	N.	stage, phase
[33]语料	yǔliào	N.	language data, language material
[34]报刊	bàokān	N.	newspaper
[35]视频	shìpín	N.	video
[36]任务式	rènwùshì	Adj.	task-based
[37]应用能力测试	yìngyòngnénglìcèshì	NP.	performance assessment
[38]反馈	fǎnkuì	V.	to give feedback
[39]打分标准	dǎfēnbiāozhǔn	NP.	grading criteria

语言重点：

1. **Subj.就+NP/VP进行+V**（讨论/讲解/说明/解释/比较）

   Subj. conducts discussion/explanation/comparison on the topic of …

   - 欢迎大家来参加今天的汉语教学论坛，今天我们就汉语教学策略进行讨论。
   - 竹老师在电子邮件中就如何设计主题单元进行了说明和解释。

2. **避免+NP**（句型操练/…的发生）

   avoid … (sentence pattern drills/the occurrence of …)

   - 要避免没有意义的句型操练，保证有意义、有目的的交流。
   - 为了避免学生在课堂中不能理解教师语言现象的发生，教师应采取不同的策略给学生提供有效的可理解输入，不断检测学生的理解度，并且根据学生的水平调整课上使用的语言。

3. **（据+VP/根据+NP，）A占B的百分之…（，这反映出…）**

   (According to …), A makes up … percent of B (, and this reflects the fact that …)

   - 教师在课堂上使用的目标语应占全部课堂交流的百分之九十以上。
   - 根据全美外语教师学会的统计，2007–2008学年学习中文的学生人数虽然只占学习语言的学生总数的百分之零点六七，但是学习中文的人数比2004–2005学年增加了近两倍，已达六万人，这反映出美国开始出现了学中文热。

4. **（随着…/为了…，）subj.不断+VP**（进行语义协商/调整教学/重复语言定式）

   (Along with … /For the purpose of …), subj. continuously … (carries out negotiation of meaning/adjusts teaching/repeats formulaic speech)

   - 教师应利用不同的策略给学生提供可理解性输入，不断检测学生的理解度，并且根据学生的水平调整课上使用的语言。
   - 在教学中，教师应该多次对学生进行不同能力的测试及评估。随着测试结果的变化，教师应不断调整教学。

5. **Subj.（通过…的方法/方式）检测…（学生的理解度/学生是否理解）**

   Subj. evaluates … (students' level of comprehension/whether or not students have understood) by means of …

   - 教师应利用不同的策略给学生提供可理解输入，不断检测学生的理解度。
   - 在以主题单元设计为本的课堂中，教师可以通过不断提问检测学生是否理解课文内容，并通过提问的上升与加强检测学生对语言知识的理解度。

6. **Subj.**（通过…）创造…的课堂/机会/环境（，以便…）

    Subj. creates a class/opportunity/environment of … (by means of …), (so that … /in order for …)

    - 创造以学生为中心的课堂。
    - 在课堂上，教师要创造各种机会，以便让学生最大限度地进行有真实意义的思想交流。

7. **Subj.**把…重点放在…上/方面（，如此一来…）

    Subj. places emphasis on … , (so that …)

    - 在结合文化教学时，教师不但要重视文化产物及文化习俗，也应该把文化教学的重点放在文化观点及文化比较上。
    - 在设计课程时，教师应该把重点放在以外语教学标准为本，建立清楚的单元主题上，如此一来，学生可以学会在真实语境下进行自发、即兴的交流。

第四课　有效教学策略
Effective Instructional Strategies

（文本形式：教学论坛[1]）

> ➤ 关键词：
>   目标语教学、以学生为中心、文化教学、真实语料、任务
> ➤ 能力目标：
>   1. 学习者能理解专业论坛讨论、说明各种有效汉语教学策略。
>   2. 学习者能就一、两个教学策略阐述、演示其在课上的具体做法。
>   3. 学习者能介绍、分析自己使用过的不同教学策略。
>   4. 学习者能使用正式套语主持讨论会。

---

[1] 论坛　lùntán　N.　forum

72 *Effective Instructional Strategies*

课文节选版 (Abridged Version)

主持人[2]：欢迎大家来参加汉语教学论坛，今天我们就汉语教学策略进行讨论。讨论的方式是首先由主讲人[3]总结[4]每个教学策略的要点[5]，然后分四个小组进行讨论，最后请每个小组代表[6]发言[7]。下面我们有请主讲人张教授。

主讲人：谢谢主持人，各位好。我们知道，在外语教学时，每个教师都应该利用反向课程设计原则为学生制定[8]学习能力目标，设计课堂活动，进行能力测试。在设计课堂活动时，教师应该了解各种有效的教学策略，让学生在课堂上进行有效互动[9]，最终[10]学会使用语言。美国的星谈项目是由美国政府资助的暑期外语培训项目。为了培养更多的外语教师，星谈项目制定了六条有效教学策略，并提出了每个策略的具体做法。今天我们组织这个论坛，就是为了让大家熟悉、了解其中的三个策略，并且进一步讨论如何在课堂上实施[11]这些策略。

第一个有效教学策略是：**课程设计以外语标准为本，用文化主题贯穿**[12]**教学内容**。对于这个教学策略，具体的做法有三点：

- 每课课文都应该以外语教学标准为本，设定清楚的单元文化主题，让学生学会在真实语境下进行有主题、有意义的交流。
- 每堂课的教学都要有清楚的能力目标(Can-Do Statements)，也就是说，在每课结束以前，学生就知道自己能获得哪些语言知识，能利用语言做什么事情。
- 教师应该知道语法是交际的工具[13]，并不是每个课程、单元、课文的中心。要避免[14]没有意义的句型操练[15]，保证[16]有意义、有目的的交流。

小组讨论：
1. 你认为让学生了解能力目标对他们的语言学习有什么帮助？你认为使用什么方法最容易让学生了解自己的能力目标？请举例[17]说明。

[2]主持人	zhǔchírén	N.	host
[3]主讲人	zhǔjiǎngrén	N.	speaker, lecturer
[4]总结	zǒngjié	V./N.	to sum up, to summarize; summary
[5]要点	yàodiǎn	N.	key point
[6]小组代表	xiǎozǔdàibiǎo	NP.	group representative
[7]发言	fāyán	V.	to make a statement/speech
[8]制定	zhìdìng	V.	to draw up, to formulate
[9]互动	hùdòng	V./N.	to interact; interaction
[10]最终	zuìzhōng	Adv.	finally
[11]实施	shíshī	V.	to implement, to carry out, to operate
[12]贯穿	guànchuān	V.	to run through
[13]工具	gōngjù	N.	tool
[14]避免	bìmiǎn	V.	to avoid
[15]句型操练	jùxíngcāoliàn	NP.	sentence pattern drill
[16]保证	bǎozhèng	V.	to ensure, to assure
[17]举例	jǔlì	V.	to give an example

2. 让学生了解能力目标的方法有哪些？好处是什么？
3. 你认为什么样的活动/任务可以让学生在课上进行有意义、有目的的交流？在你的课堂上，或你所经历的课堂上，什么样的活动，让学生觉得最有趣，最愿意参与？请举例说明。

第二个有效教学策略是：**利用目标语进行教学**。具体做法有三点：
- 教师在课堂上使用的目标语应占全部课堂交流的百分之九十以上。
- 教师应采取不同的策略给学生提供有效的可理解输入，不断检测[18]学生的理解度[19]，并且根据学生的水平调整[20]课上使用的语言。
- 教师应使用举例的方式或利用肢体语言说明生词的意思，不要翻译。

小组讨论：
1. 什么是可理解输入？为什么可理解输入对学生的语言学习很重要？
2. 在课上你会采用什么策略有效地使用目标语进行教学？
3. 你通常采用什么方法给学生讲解生词及语法，你用什么方法鼓励学生使用目标语进行课上互动？

第三个有效教学策略是：**创造[21]以学生为中心[22]的课堂**。具体做法有三点：
- 采用多种教学方式让学生学习语言，如利用故事情节[23]、动手活动[24]、图片说明[25]、或专题讨论[26]等活动为学生提供大量、丰富的语言输入及合适的语境。
- 在课堂上，教师应提供各种机会，让学生进行真实、有意义的交流。
- 教师在课上要以分组的方式组织教学活动让学生进行交流。

小组讨论：
1. 什么是以学生为中心的课堂？这种课堂有什么特点[27]？请你从学生需求[28]、能力目标、课堂活动、说话机会、教材及课本、测试等方面进行讨论。
2. 组织分组活动时，应该考虑哪些方面的因素？比方说，学生的语言水平、文化背景、个性等。
3. 举例说明一个最有效的分组活动，讨论它的能力目标、活动内容、方法、结果等。

---

[18]检测	jiǎncè	V.	to check, to examine
[19]理解度	lǐjiědù	N.	degree of comprehension
[20]调整	tiáozhěng	V.	to adjust
[21]创造	chuàngzào	V.	to create
[22]以学生为中心	yǐxuéshēngwéizhōngxīn	VP./Adj.	learner-centered
[23]故事情节	gùshìqíngjié	NP.	story plot
[24]动手活动	dòngshǒuhuódòng	NP.	hands-on activity
[25]图片说明	túpiànshuōmíng	NP.	picture description
[26]专题讨论	zhuāntítǎolùn	NP.	seminar
[27]特点	tèdiǎn	N.	characteristic, feature
[28]学生需求	xuéshēngxūqiú	NP.	learner's needs

语言重点：

1. **Subj.就+NP/VP进行+V**（讨论/讲解/说明/解释/比较）

   Subj. conducts discussion/explanation/comparison on the topic of …

   - 欢迎大家来参加今天的汉语教学论坛，今天我们就汉语教学策略进行讨论。
   - 竹老师在电子邮件中就如何设计主题单元进行了说明和解释。

2. **避免+NP**（句型操练/…的发生）

   avoid … (sentence pattern drills/the occurrence of …)

   - 要避免没有意义的句型操练，保证有意义、有目的的交流。
   - 为了避免学生在课堂中不能理解教师语言现象的发生，教师应采取不同的策略给学生提供有效的可理解输入，不断检测学生的理解度，并且根据学生的水平调整课上使用的语言。

3. **（据+VP/根据+NP，）A占B的百分之…（，这反映出…）**

   (According to …), A makes up … percent of B (, and this reflects the fact that …)

   - 教师在课堂上使用的目标语应占全部课堂交流的百分之九十以上。
   - 根据全美外语教师学会的统计，2007–2008学年学习中文的学生人数虽然只占学习语言的学生总数的百分之零点六七，但是学习中文的人数比2004–2005学年增加了近两倍，已达六万人，这反映出美国开始出现了学中文热。

4. **（随着…/为了…，）subj.不断+VP**（进行语义协商/调整教学/重复语言定式）

   (Along with … /For the purpose of …), subj. continuously … (carries out negotiation of meaning/adjusts teaching/repeats formulaic speech)

   - 教师应利用不同的策略给学生提供可理解性输入，不断检测学生的理解度，并且根据学生的水平调整课上使用的语言。
   - 在教学中，教师应该多次对学生进行不同能力的测试及评估。随着测试结果的变化，教师应不断调整教学。

5. **Subj.（通过…的方法/方式）检测…（学生的理解度/学生是否理解）**

   Subj. evaluates … (students' level of comprehension/whether or not students have understood) by means of …

   - 教师应利用不同的策略给学生提供可理解输入，不断检测学生的理解度。
   - 在以主题单元设计为本的课堂中，教师可以通过不断提问检测学生是否理解课文内容，并通过提问的上升与加强检测学生对语言知识的理解度。

6. **Subj.**（通过…）创造…的课堂/机会/环境（，以便…）

   Subj. creates a class/opportunity/environment of … (by means of …), (so that … /in order for …)

   - 创造以学生为中心的课堂。
   - 在课堂上，教师要创造各种机会，以便让学生最大限度地进行有真实意义的思想交流。

练习活动

理解诠释1：预习单

先看课文，然后完成下面的作业：

一、根据课文进行填空。

　　在外语教学时，教师应该利用_____原则为学生制定_____，设计课堂活动，进行_____测试。在设计课堂活动时，教师应该了解各种_____，让学生在课堂上进行_____，最终学会语言使用。

二、此次教学论坛就哪些汉语教学的策略进行了讨论？（课文全版包括六个有效教学策略；课文节选版包括三个有效教学策略）

```
                    ┌── 有效策略一：
                    │
                    ├── 有效策略二：
                    │
   有效教学          ├── 有效策略三：
   策略             │
                    ├── 有效策略四：
                    │
                    ├── 有效策略五：
                    │
                    └── 有效策略六：
```

三、所谓的"真实语料"是指什么？教师应该如何使用"真实语料"进行教学？请举例说明。

理解诠释2：扩展阅读　　　节选自《语言教学与研究》（2010年第6期）

以下内容是南京某大学就对外汉语教师的有效教学行为进行的一次问卷调查：

本次调查的目的在于了解对外汉语教师和留学生对多媒体技术运用、语法教学、学习评估、文化教学、错误纠正、目标语使用、交际性语言教学策略等七类24项教师行为的有效性评价，考察教师和学生评价的实际情况，分析两组评价是否存在差异，并与Brown (2009)的调查结果进行对比，尝试对得出的结果进行分析并提出相应的教学建议。

表1　"有效对外汉语教师行为"调查表中的24个问题：

序号	内容
Q1	在对外汉语教学中经常使用多媒体技术
Q2	学生的成绩至少有一部分是根据完成指定的小组任务的情况来评估
Q3	在文化教学上花费的时间不少于语言教学
Q4	要求学生在课堂外使用目标语同别人交流
Q5	当学生说话出现错误时，不立即纠正
Q6	允许学生使用非目标语来回答听力与阅读测试题
Q7	不在对外汉语课堂上使用非目标语
Q8	当学生说话出现错误时，只是间接而非直接地纠正学生的错误（例如，向他们重复正确的说法而不是直接指出他们的错误）
Q9	不只目标语掌握得很好，而且对目标语国家的文化知识渊博
Q10	不把语法的准确性作为评价学生语言产出（比如说话、写作）水平的主要依据
Q11	主要通过让学生完成具体任务的方式（例如，找出房间的价格和酒店的费用），而不是强调通过语法的练习来教语言
Q12	用目标语发出指令让学生用身体动作做出反应（例如"起立"，"把书捡起来"等）
Q13	通过马上解释学生回答不正确的原因来处理错误
Q14	从上课的第一天起就要求学生在课堂上说目标语
Q15	完成课堂活动时不是主要采用小组练习的方式
Q16	上课大多采用练习特定语法点的活动，而不是采用仅仅是为了交换信息的活动
Q17	只有当学生感到已经做好准备时，才要求他们开始说目标语
Q18	介绍某个语法点时，需要说明该语法结构在具体、真实的情境中的运用情况
Q19	（非母语教师）说目标语时在语法和口音上都应控制得像母语者一样
Q20	教授语法时，在解释语法规则前，应先提供关于这种语法结构的例句
Q21	在教授语言和文化时主要使用真实的生活材料（比如音乐、图片、食物、衣服等），而非课本
Q22	不简化或改变说法，以便使学生能听懂所说的每一个词语
Q23	评估学生的成绩至少有一部分是依据他们在课堂上用目标语跟同学成功互动的能力
Q24	在采用的活动中让学生必须用目标语从同学那里发现未知的信息

根据内容上的联系和考察的目的，问卷中的24项教师行为总体上可以划分为七类，其中有些教师行为同时属于两种或多种类型，具体情况见表2。

表2　调查表中24项教师行为的分类：

考察的类型	问题
多媒体技术	Q1
语法教学	Q10，Q16，Q18，Q20
学习评估	Q2，Q6，Q10，Q23
文化教学	Q3，Q9，Q21
错误纠正	Q5，Q8，Q13
目标语使用	Q7，Q14，Q17，Q19，Q22，Q23
交际性语言教学策略	Q2，Q4，Q11，Q12，Q15，Q21，Q23，Q24

总体来看，学生对在课堂上使用目标语的评价很高，并且非常重视学习和使用标准目标语，希望教师对他们的要求更加严格及时，为他们的学习提供可靠的帮助。教师对学生的语法错误则表现出较强的容忍性。调查结果显示，教师和学生都很重视目标语在日常交际中的使用。在教学过程中，采取增加交际练习的行为和策略很受欢迎。在课堂上多采用分组练习或小组活动，要求学生在课内与课外使用目标语与别人进行互动交流是大家普遍接受的"有效行为"。

1. 此次问卷调查的目的是什么？

2. "评估学生的成绩至少有一部分是依据他们在课堂上用目标语跟同学成功互动的能力"，这个问题属于考察哪些教师行为？（可多选）
   A. 目标语使用　B. 错误纠正　C. 交际性语言教学策略　D. 学习评估

3. 调查结果显示，学生和教师对哪一类教师行为的评价有较大的差异？
   A. 错误纠正　B. 学习评估　C. 交际性语言教学策略　D. 语法教学

4. 根据调查结果，下面哪些做法是学生和教师都接受的"有效行为"？（可多选）
   A. 要求学生在课堂上使用目标语进行信息交换。
   B. 只有当学生感到已经做好准备时，才要求他们开始说目标语。
   C. 在课堂上进行分组练习。
   D. 学生在课堂上使用目标语，课外可以使用自己的母语。

78　*Effective Instructional Strategies*

 人际交流1：教学工作坊 (workshop)

你被邀请在一场关于"以学生为中心"的工作坊上担任主讲人：

主持人：　　各位老师、各位学员，欢迎大家参加今天的教学工作坊，在此请允许我为大家介绍今天的主讲人刘教授。刘教授有多年汉语教学的经验，目前就职于美国纽约州汉明顿大学，主要负责中文系一年级的教学工作。今天，她将就"以学生为中心"这一话题跟我们分享她的教学心得，请大家热烈欢迎。

主持人：　　刘教授您认为什么是以学生为中心的课堂？这种课堂有什么特点？

你的回答：　【建议词汇和结构：所谓的N是指…；避免+NP（句型操练/…的发生）；subj.（通过…）创造…的课堂/机会/环境（，以便…）；学生需求】

主持人：　　哪些教学策略能体现以学生为中心的课堂呢？

你的回答：　【建议词汇和结构：subj.利用NP为sb.提供sth.（语言输入/语境）；subj.把…重点放在…上/方面（，如此一来…）；A鼓励B+do sth.；大量；丰富】

主持人：　　根据您的经验，组织分组活动时，应该考虑哪些方面的因素？

你的回答：　【建议词汇和结构：subj.采取…的方法/策略；避免+NP（…的发生）；A鼓励B+do sth.；尽量+VP；控制】

主持人：　　刘教授今天的经验分享给了我们很大的启发，让我们再次以热烈的掌声感谢她！

✉ 人际交流2：回复博客(Blog)留言

在工作坊之后，一位老师在你的博客上留言，请给他回复。【建议词汇和结构：subj.就+NP/VP进行+V（讨论/比较/解释）；subj.利用NP为sb.提供sth.（语言输入/语境）；A鼓励B+do sth.；尽量+VP；尝试；subj.把…重点放在…上/方面（，如此一来…）；subj.不断+VP（进行语义协商/调整教学/检测）】

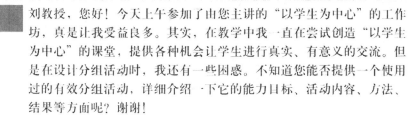

2楼 xhrrongshuai 2013-04-30 19:59发表

刘教授，您好！今天上午参加了由您主讲的"以学生为中心"的工作坊，真是让我受益良多。其实，在教学中我一直在尝试创造"以学生为中心"的课堂，提供各种机会让学生进行真实、有意义的交流。但是在设计分组活动时，我还有一些困惑。不知道您能否提供一个使用过的有效分组活动，详细介绍一下它的能力目标、活动内容、方法、结果等方面呢？谢谢！

1楼 maas 2013-03-25 21:05发表

表达演说：教学心得分享

请你准备一个5分钟演讲，分享你在教学中所使用的某一个有效教学策略（若没有教学经验，请分享学习外语时，你的老师使用过的某一个有效教学策略），并且举例说明。分享教学/学习经验时，请包括以下内容：

1. 你/你的老师为什么使用这个有效教学策略？使用的效果如何？
2. 你/你的老师是如何使用这个有效教学策略的？以课堂活动为例，说明具体的做法。
3. 在使用这个有效教学策略时，你遇到的困难与困惑是什么？你是如何解决的？（你的老师在使用这个有效教学策略时，是否有不足之处或者出现了什么问题？如果你来尝试，你会怎么解决？）

建议词汇和结构：…以…为例/为出发点；subj.采取…的方法/策略；subj.利用NP为sb.提供sth.（语言输入/语境）；subj.把A跟B联系起来； subj.表面上…，其实…；A为B提供+NP；大量；丰富；subj.不断+VP（进行语义协商/调整教学/检测）；关键；避免+NP（句型操练/…的发生）；subj.（通过…的方式）检测…（学生的理解度/学生是否理解）；A和B是密切相关的；反馈

反思任务

一、前期任务：
将所有学员按照四人一组的方法分成若干小组，每一个小组将选择一个有效策略（不重复）。

- 小组成员之间对课文中"小组讨论"中所涉及的问题进行讨论。
- 各个小组将对一个主题，如："生病了"、"去饭馆"、"去商店"、"买东西"……，设计一个任务，其任务必须体现本组所讨论的教学策略的要求。

二、核心任务：
对学员进行重新分组(A1B1C1，A2B2C2 …)，分组之后，每个学员向新小组成员报告第一次分组时小组所设计的任务，其他成员一方面要理解其设计的原则，另一方面要看这个设计是否体现了自己组所讨论的教学策略。

三、后期任务：
每个学员通过前两个任务，修改或者重新设计任务，其结果应该尽可能满足六条有效教学策略，并形成书面文字。

补充材料

[1] Couet, R. (n.d.). Authentic materials: Where to find them, how to use them [PowerPoint slides]. Retrieved from https://ed.sc.gov/agency/se/Instructional-Practices-and-Evaluations/documents/AuthenticMaterials.pdf

[2] Martinez, A. G. (2002, February). Authentic materials: An overview. Retrieved from http://www3.telus.net/linguisticsissues/authenticmaterials.html

[3] Ramirez, L. (n.d.). *Keeping it real! Culturally authentic materials in the language classroom.* [PowerPoint slides]. Retrieved from http://www.miscositas.com/Keeping%20it%20Real.ppt

[4] National Capital Language Resource Center (NCLRC). (2009). *Authentic materials.* Retrieved from http://nclrc.org/teaching_materials/links_to_fl_materials/authentic.html

[5] American Council on the Teaching of Foreign Languages (ACTFL). (2006). *Standards for foreign language learning: Preparing for the 21st century* (pp. 47–52). Alexandria, VA: ACTFL.

第五课　纠错[1]反馈
Corrective Feedback

（文本形式：学术文章）

（选自靳洪刚发表[2]于《世界汉语教学》杂志
2011 Vol. 25:1, pp. 78–98 的论文：《现代语言教学的十大原则》）

> ➢ 关键词：
>   直接纠错、间接纠错、计划性纠错、随机纠错、自发性纠错、重述性纠错
> ➢ 能力目标：
>   1. 学习者能理解诠释关于纠错反馈的学术文章。
>   2. 学习者能讨论纠错反馈研究的重点及方向。
>   3. 学习者能说明纠错反馈对学习第二语言的积极作用。
>   4. 学习者能举例说明纠错原则以及各类纠错技巧。
>   5. 学习者能举例说明每种纠错技巧的特点和功能。

---

[1] 纠错　jiūcuò　V.　to correct
[2] 发表　fābiǎo　V.　to publish

课文全版 (Complete Version)

《世界汉语教学》第25卷 2011年第1期　　　靳洪刚，《现代语言教学的十大原则》

"纠错反馈"(corrective feedback)原则强调通过直接[3](direct/explicit)或间接[4](indirect/implicit)的纠错反馈方法，让学习者意识到自己的第二语言与目标语的差异，并提高自我纠错[5]意识，最终促进第二语言系统的重新建立(Ellis, 2001)。

从八十年代到现在，对于纠错反馈的实验研究证实[6](White, 1989; DeKeyser, 1993; Gass, 1997; Long, 1999)：课堂纠错可以为学习者提供必要的[7]语言"差异"。这种"差异"为学生提供三个方面的语言信息：(1)目标结构有什么限定性[8]；(2)学习者的母语与目标语之间的差异；(3)学习者的表达与母语者或教师之间的差异。因此，纠错反馈有助于[9]第二语言的学习。

纠错原则可以通过两种形式在课堂中完成：一种为计划性纠错[10]，大多采取课堂讲解、直接改错等方式；另一种为自然交际中随机纠错[11]，多采用直接或间接反馈、自我纠错、重述[12]等方式。

计划性纠错技巧[13]最常用的有两种(Ellis, 1994)：一是直接纠错。如就学生的错在课上举例(problem illustration)纠正，其目的是让学生意识到目标结构的语言规则[14]；二是导出[15]错误法(garden path technique) (Tomasello and Herron, 1988, 1989)。这种方法是把学生带到容易出错的语言点[16]，导出学生可能出现的语言表达错误后，马上根据情况进行纠正。比方说，在讲解中文形容词[17]和名词[18]搭配[19]时，教师可以从"单音节[20]形容词+名词"开始，如，"好人"、"大房子"、"小桌子"，然后到双音节[21]形容词，如，"好看"、"奇怪"。先让学生组词[22]，导出错误"好看人"，

[3]直接	zhíjiē	Adj.	explicit, direct
[4]间接	jiànjiē	Adj.	implicit, indirect
[5]自我纠错	zìwǒjiūcuò	NP.	self-correction
[6]证实	zhèngshí	V.	to confirm, to verify
[7]必要的	bìyàode	Adj.	essential
[8]限定性	xiàndìngxìng	N.	restriction
[9]有助于	yǒuzhùyú	V.	to help, to contribute to
[10]计划性纠错	jìhuàxìngjiūcuò	NP.	planned error correction
[11]随机纠错	suíjījiūcuò	NP.	spontaneous error correction
[12]重述	chóngshù	V.	to recast
[13]技巧	jìqiǎo	N.	skill, technique
[14]规则	guīzé	N.	rule
[15]导出	dǎochū	V.	to induce, to guide out
[16]语言点	yǔyándiǎn	N.	grammar point
[17]形容词	xíngróngcí	N.	adjective
[18]名词	míngcí	N.	noun
[19]搭配	dāpèi	V.	to collocate
[20]单音节	dānyīnjié	N.	monosyllable
[21]双音节	shuāngyīnjié	N.	disyllable
[22]组词	zǔcí	V.	to combine words, to form words into phrases

然后马上指出[23],"好看+人"不符合搭配规则,需要在"好看"和"人"之间加上"的"("好看的人"),让学生明白这个语言规则。这种方法的好处是可以在导出错误的同时引起学习者对语言规则的注意。

自然交际中随机纠错可以分为三种:一是自发性纠错[24](self-initiated error correction)。这一方法是引导[25]学习者自己找错,如教师说"不对","再试试",或"你说什么?"等,但不提供正确的答案,以便让学生自己完成纠错过程;二是交际中,在不打断[26]交流的前提下直接改正学习者的错误。如:

(1)　教师:　今天怎么样?
　　　学生:　*我一点儿累。
　　　教师:　我**有**一点儿累。(强调"有"字)
　　　学生:　啊,对,我有一点儿累。

三是重述性纠错[27](recast),可以有四种方式。第一是用升调[28]重复学生的错句;第二是用升调重复错句,紧接着[29]提供一个对句;第三是先回答错句的问题再进行纠错;第四是典型[30]的"重述"。方法是接着学生的错句,用疑问句[31]来提醒学生,暗示[32]前边所说的句子中有错误。如例(2)与例(1)几乎[33]一样,但是例(2)中重述部分的代词[34]是"你"而不是例(1)的"我":

(2)　教师:　今天怎么样?
　　　学生:　*我一点儿累。
　　　教师:　你**有**一点儿累吗?(强调"有"字)
　　　学生:　啊,对,我有一点儿累。

重述是最近几年第一语言及第二语言习得研究[35]的一个重要课题[36]。这种纠错方法采用间接的重复法,根据学习者所说的话一边交流,一边纠错。如例(3):

[23]指出	zhǐchū	V.	to point out
[24]自发性纠错	zìfāxìngjiūcuò	NP.	self-initiated error correction
[25]引导	yǐndǎo	V.	to guide
[26]打断	dǎduàn	V.	to interrupt
[27]重述性纠错	chóngshùxìngjiūcuò	NP.	recasting
[28]升调	shēngdiào	N.	rising (vocal) tone
[29]紧接着	jǐnjiēzhe	Adv.	immediately, subsequently
[30]典型	diǎnxíng	Adj.	typical, representative
[31]疑问句	yíwènjù	N.	interrogative sentence
[32]暗示	ànshì	V./N.	to imply; implication
[33]几乎	jīhū	Adv.	almost, nearly, practically
[34]代词	dàicí	N.	pronoun
[35]第二语言习得研究	dì èryǔyánxídéyánjiū	NP.	study of Second Language Acquisition
[36]课题	kètí	N.	issue, project

(3) 学生：*这件衣服比我的不舒服。
老师：*比我的不舒服？（语调提高，语速放慢，句尾加疑问声调）
学生：噢，这件衣服不……
老师：这件衣服**没有**你的舒服吗？（突出"没有"）
学生：对，对，这件衣服没有我的舒服。
老师：那你买了吗？

相对于直接纠错，间接纠错技巧对教师的挑战较大，要求丰富的教学经验。在纠错过程中，教师要学会利用各种暗示，如声调[37]、停顿[38]、手势[39]、板书[40]、眼神[41]等清楚地指出交流中的错误。没有一定的经验或训练[42]，教师很难做得完美。因此，系统训练[43]十分必要。

参考文献：

DeKeyser, R. (1993). The effect of error correction on L2 grammar knowledge and oral proficiency. *Modern Language Journal*, vol. 77:4, pp. 501–514.

Ellis, N. (2001). Memory for language. In P. Robinson (Ed.), *Cognition and Second Language Instruction* (pp. 33–68). Cambridge, England: Cambridge University Press.

Ellis, R. (1994). A theory of instructed second language acquisition. In N. Ellis (Ed.), *Implicit and Explicit Language Learning*. London: Academic.

Gass, S. (1997). *Input, Interaction, and the Second Language Learner*. Lawrence Erlbaum Associates, Publishers. New Jersey: Mahwah.

Jin, Hong Gang. (2011). 10 Methodological principles of modern language teaching. *Journal of Chinese Teaching in the World (SJHYJX)*, vol. 25:1, pp. 78–98.

Long, M. (1999). *Task-based Language Teaching*. Oxford, England: Blackwell.

Tomasello, M. and Herron, C. (1988). Down the garden path: inducing and correcting overgeneralization errors in the foreign language classroom. *Applied Psycholinguistics*, vol. 9, pp. 237–46.

Tomasello, M. and Herron, C. (1989). Feedback for language transfer errors: the garden path technique. *Studies in Second Language Acquisition*, vol. 13, pp. 513–17.

White, L. (1989). *Universal Grammar and Second Language Acquisition*. Philadelphia, PA: John Benjamins.

[37]声调	shēngdiào	N.	tone, intonation
[38]停顿	tíngdùn	V./N.	to pause; pause
[39]手势	shǒushì	N.	gesture
[40]板书	bǎnshū	N.	words written on the blackboard
[41]眼神	yǎnshén	N.	expression in one's eyes
[42]训练	xùnliàn	V./N.	to train; training
[43]系统训练	xìtǒngxùnliàn	NP.	systematic training

语言重点：

1. 促进+NP（…的建立/…的发展）

   to promote the establishment/development of …

   - "纠错反馈"原则强调通过直接或间接的纠错反馈方法，让学习者意识到自己的第二语言与母语的差异，并提高自我纠错意识，最终促进第二语言系统的重新建立。
   - 课堂中教师的计划性纠错可以促进学习者语法知识体系的发展以及语言输出准确度的提高。

2. 直接/间接+VP

   to directly/indirectly …

   - 计划性纠错大多采取课堂讲解、直接改错等方式。
   - 相对于直接纠错，间接纠错技巧对教师的挑战较大，要求丰富的教学经验。

3. 引导sb.+do sth.

   to guide sb. to …

   - 自发性纠错是一种引导学习者自己找错的纠错方法。
   - 除了讲解语言点以外，教师也应引导学生提高独立思考、分析归纳和灵活运用基础知识的能力。

4. 在…的前提下，subj.+do sth.

   under the premise of … , subj. does …

   - 二是交际中，在不打断交流的前提下直接改正学习者的错误。
   - 重述纠错时，在给出正确的目标结构的前提下，教师也要利用各种暗示，如声调、停顿、手势、板书、眼神等清楚地指出交流中的错误。

5. …，紧接着，…

   … , immediately/subsequently, …

   - 第二是用升调重复错句，紧接着提供一个对句。
   - 使用导出错误法纠错时，教师把学生带到容易出错的语言点，导出学生可能出现的语言表达错误后，紧接着，马上根据情况进行纠正。

6. 相对于+NP，subj. …

   with respect to … , subj. …

   - 相对于直接纠错，间接纠错技巧对教师的挑战较大，要求丰富的教学经验。
   - 相对于自然交际中随机纠错，计划性纠错能够使学习者对目标语言的限定性更加清楚。

7. ① …（十分/非常）必要

   It is necessary to …

   ② **Subj.（没）有必要+do sth.**

   It is (not) necessary for subj. to …

   - 系统训练十分必要。
   - 教学经验不足的汉语教师有必要进行纠错技巧的系统培训。

第五课　纠错[1]反馈
Corrective Feedback

（文本形式：学术文章）

（选自靳洪刚发表[2]于《世界汉语教学》杂志 2011 Vol. 25:1, pp. 78–98的论文：《现代语言教学的十大原则》）

> ➢ 关键词：
>   直接纠错、间接纠错、计划性纠错、随机纠错、自发性纠错、重述性纠错
> ➢ 能力目标：
>   1. 学习者能理解诠释关于纠错反馈的学术文章。
>   2. 学习者能讨论纠错反馈研究的重点及方向。
>   3. 学习者能说明纠错反馈对学习第二语言的积极作用。
>   4. 学习者能举例说明纠错原则以及各类纠错技巧。
>   5. 学习者能举例说明每种纠错技巧的特点和功能。

---

[1] 纠错　jiūcuò　V.　to correct
[2] 发表　fābiǎo　V.　to publish

课文节选版 (Abridged Version)

《世界汉语教学》第25卷 2011年第1期　　　靳洪刚，《现代语言教学的十大原则》

"纠错反馈"(corrective feedback)原则[3]强调通过直接[4](direct/explicit)或间接[5](indirect/implicit)的纠错反馈方法，让学习者意识到自己的第二语言与目标语的差异，并提高自我纠错[6]意识，最终促进第二语言系统[7]的重新建立(Ellis, 2001)。

纠错原则可以通过两种形式在课堂中完成：一种为计划性纠错[8]，大多采取课堂讲解[9]、直接改错等方式；另一种为自然交际中随机纠错[10]，多采用直接或间接反馈、自我纠错、重述[11](recast)等方式。

计划性纠错技巧[12]最常用的有两种 (Ellis, 1994)：一是直接纠错。如就学生的错误在课上举例(problem illustration)纠正，目的是让学生意识到目标结构的语言规则[13]；二是导出错误法[14](garden path technique) (Tomasello and Herron, 1988, 1989)。这种方法是把学生带到容易出错的语言点[15]，导出学生可能出现的语言表达错误后，马上根据情况进行纠正[16]。比方说，在讲解中文形容词[17]和名词[18]搭配[19]时，教师可以从"单音节[20]形容词+名词"开始，如，"好人"、"大房子"、"小桌子"，然后到双音节[21]形容词，如，"好看"、"奇怪"。先让学生组词[22]，导出错误"好看人"，然后马上指出[23]，"好看+人"不符合[24]搭配规则，需要在"好看"和"人"之间加上"的"（"好看的人"），让学生明白这个语言规则。这种方法的好处是可以通过导出错误引起学习者对语言规则的注意。

[3]原则	yuánzé	N.	principle
[4]直接	zhíjiē	Adj.	explicit, direct
[5]间接	jiànjiē	Adj.	implicit, indirect
[6]自我纠错	zìwǒjiūcuò	NP.	self-correction
[7]系统	xìtǒng	N.	system
[8]计划性纠错	jìhuàxìngjiūcuò	NP.	planned error correction
[9]讲解	jiǎngjiě	V.	to explain, to lecture
[10]随机纠错	suíjīijiūcuò	NP.	spontaneous error correction
[11]重述	chóngshù	V.	to recast
[12]技巧	jìqiǎo	N.	technique, skill
[13]规则	guīzé	N.	rule
[14]导出错误法	dǎochūcuòwùfǎ	NP.	garden path technique
[15]语言点	yǔyándiǎn	N.	grammar point
[16]纠正	jiūzhèng	V.	to correct
[17]形容词	xíngróngcí	N.	adjective
[18]名词	míngcí	N.	noun
[19]搭配	dāpèi	V.	to collocate
[20]单音节	dānyīnjié	N.	monosyllable
[21]双音节	shuāngyīnjié	N.	disyllable
[22]组词	zǔcí	V.	to combine words, to form words into phrases
[23]指出	zhǐchū	V.	to point out
[24]符合	fúhé	V.	to accord with, be in keeping with sth.

自然交际中随机纠错可以分为三种：一是自发性纠错[25](self-initiated error correction)。这一方法是引导[26]学习者自己找错，如教师说"不对"，"再试试"，或"你说什么？"但不提供正确的答案，以便让学生自己完成纠错过程；二是交际中，在不打断[27]交流的前提下直接改正学习者的错误。如：

(1) 教师：今天怎么样？
　　学生：*我一点儿累。
　　教师：我<u>有</u>一点儿累。（强调"有"字）
　　学生：啊，对，我有一点儿累。

三是重述性纠错[28](recast)，可以有四种方式。第一是用升调[29]重复学生的错句；第二是用升调重复错句，紧接着[30]提供一个对句；第三是先回答错句的问题再进行纠错；第四是典型[31]的"重述"。方法是接着学生的错句，用疑问句[32]来提醒学生，暗示[33]前边所说的句子中有错误。如例(2)与例(1)几乎[34]一样，但是例(2)中重述部分的代词[35]是"你"而不是例(1)的"我"：

(2) 教师：今天怎么样？
　　学生：*我一点儿累。
　　教师：你<u>有</u>一点儿累吗？（强调"有"字）
　　学生：啊，对，我有一点儿累。

重述这种纠错方法采用间接的重复法，根据学习者所说的话一边交流，一边纠错。如例(3)：

(3) 学生：*这件衣服比我的不舒服。
　　老师：*比我的不舒服？（语调提高，语速放慢，句尾[36]加疑问声调）
　　学生：噢，这件衣服不……
　　老师：这件衣服<u>没有</u>你的舒服吗？（突出[37]"没有"）
　　学生：对，对，这件衣服没有我的舒服。
　　老师：那你买了吗？

---

[25]自发性纠错	zìfāxìngjiūcuò	NP.	self-initiated error correction
[26]引导	yǐndǎo	V.	to guide
[27]打断	dǎduàn	V.	to interrupt
[28]重述性纠错	chóngshùxìngjiūcuò	NP.	recasting
[29]升调	shēngdiào	N.	rising (vocal) tone
[30]紧接着	jǐnjiēzhe	Adv.	immediately, subsequently
[31]典型	diǎnxíng	Adj.	typical, representative
[32]疑问句	yíwènjù	N.	interrogative sentence
[33]暗示	ànshì	V./N.	to imply; implication
[34]几乎	jīhū	Adv.	almost, nearly, practically
[35]代词	dàicí	N.	pronoun
[36]句尾	jùwěi	N.	the end of a sentence
[37]突出	tūchū	V./Adj.	sticking out, outstanding

参考文献：

Ellis, N. (2001). Memory for language. In P. Robinson (Ed.), *Cognition and Second Language Instruction* (pp. 33–68). Cambridge, England: Cambridge University Press.

Ellis, R. (1994). A theory of instructed second language acquisition. In N. Ellis (Ed.), *Implicit and Explicit Language Learning*. London: Academic.

Jin, Hong Gang. (2011). 10 Methodological principles of modern language teaching. *Journal of Chinese Teaching in the World (SJHYJX)*, vol. 25:1, pp. 78–98.

Tomasello, M. and Herron, C. (1988). Down the garden path: inducing and correcting overgeneralization errors in the foreign language classroom. *Applied Psycholinguistics* vol. 9, pp. 237–46.

Tomasello, M. and Herron, C. (1989). Feedback for language transfer errors: the garden path technique. *Studies in Second Language Acquisition*, vol. 13, pp. 513–17.

语言重点：

1. **促进+NP（…的建立/…的发展）**

   to promote the establishment/development of …

   - "纠错反馈"原则强调通过直接或间接的纠错反馈方法，让学习者意识到自己的第二语言与母语的差异，并提高自我纠错意识，最终促进第二语言系统的重新建立。
   - 课堂中教师的计划性纠错可以促进学习者语法知识体系的发展以及语言输出准确度的提高。

2. **直接/间接+VP**

   to directly/indirectly …

   - 计划性纠错大多采取课堂讲解、直接改错等方式。
   - 相对于直接纠错，间接纠错技巧对教师的挑战较大，要求丰富的教学经验。

3. **引导sb.+do sth.**

   to guide sb. to …

   - 自发性纠错是一种引导学习者自己找错的纠错方法。
   - 除了讲解语言点以外，教师也应引导学生提高独立思考、分析归纳和灵活运用基础知识的能力。

4. **在…的前提下，subj.+do sth.**

   under the premise of … , subj. does …

   - 二是交际中，在不打断交流的前提下直接改正学习者的错误。
   - 重述纠错时，在给出正确的目标结构的前提下，教师也要利用各种暗示，如声调、停顿、手势、板书、眼神等清楚地指出交流中的错误。

5. …，紧接着，…

   … , immediately/subsequently, …

   - 第二是用升调重复错句，紧接着提供一个对句。
   - 使用导出错误法纠错时，教师把学生带到容易出错的语言点，导出学生可能出现的语言表达错误后，紧接着，马上根据情况进行纠正。

练习活动

 理解诠释1：预习单

先看课文，然后完成下面的作业：

一、根据课文进行填空。

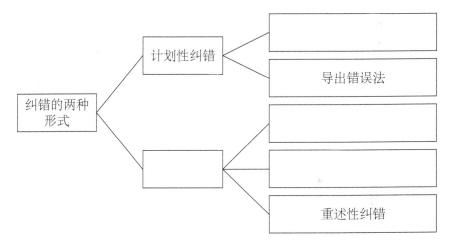

二、根据课文回答问题。
1. 纠错反馈对于学习第二语言是否具有积极的作用？请说明理由。

2. 重述性纠错包括几种方式？这几种方式分别是什么？请举例说明。

理解诠释2：扩展阅读

"纠错反馈"是近年来外语研究领域中备受关注的主题之一，与"引起注意"和"语言输出"并称为外语学习中的"三大件"。自20世纪80年代以来，课堂互动是第二语言习得研究领域相当重要的一个方面，而教师的纠错反馈是课堂互动中极其重要的一个环节，可以改善学生使用目标语的准确性。Lyster和Ranta (1997)通过对课堂互动的特点分析，将教师对学习者进行的纠错反馈方法分为明确纠错(explicit correction)、重述(recast)、诱导(elicitation)、元语言线索(metalinguistic clues)、要求澄清(clarification request)和重复(repetition)等六种形式，具体就是：（一）明确纠错。教师提供正确的形式，清楚表明学生说的什么话是不正确的。（二）重述。教师并不直接指出学生话语中的错误，而是间接地为学生提供正确的说法。（三）诱导。教师通过提问、停下来让学生接话、要求学生复述他们的话，以便诱导学生说出对的句子。（四）元语言线索。教师不直接提供正确的形式，而是对学生句子进行规则解释，让学生进行反思。（五）要求澄清。教师使用"你说什么？"和"我不明白。"以及"你说的是什么意思？"这类语意协商的词语。（六）重复。教师重复学生的错误，并利用上升语调引起学生的注意。

教师应该通过课堂观察，来了解纠错反馈在课堂中发挥的作用，以及不同种类的纠错反馈之间的区别，并进一步明确面对学生不同的错误时，教师采取哪种纠错反馈，以及哪些不同种类的纠错反馈对学生的纠错反应(uptake)有影响。这可以使教师检测自己纠错的效果，提高自己的教学技能。

没有一个纠错反馈形式是万能的。教师要不断尝试、丰富自己的纠错反馈技巧，以便在需要时能选择最适合的一种，针对学生的学习情况进行调整。不同的学习者对纠错反馈的形式有不同的反应，教师要根据具体情况灵活地加以运用，发挥其最佳的效能。

1. 教师对学习者的纠错反馈可以分为哪几种形式？

2. 请指出这位教师运用了哪种纠错形式？

   学生：我不太喜欢看亚洲(jiu1)电影。
   教师：亚洲(jiu1)？你的意思是？

   A. 元语言线索　　B. 要求澄清　　C. 重复　　D. 诱导

3. 请指出这位教师运用了哪种纠错形式？

   学生：我昨天见面了我的老师。
   教师：哦，是吗？你昨天跟你的老师见面了？
   学生：对，我跟我的老师见面了。

   A. 明确纠错　　B. 重述　　C. 重复　　D. 元语言线索

4. 判断下列哪个叙述是错误的？
   A. "纠错反馈"和"引起注意"、"语言输出"对第二语言学习来说都非常重要。
   B. "明确纠错"是六种纠错形式中最直接的纠错方法。
   C. "重述"和"重复"都需要重复学生的错误。
   D. 教师采用什么样的纠错方式要根据学习者的情况进行调整。

理解诠释3：听力理解

请看教学录像《学校附近的饭馆》http://v.youku.com/v_show/id_XOTAzMDUwMjY4.html，找出老师在课堂上使用的纠错指令，并判断老师使用的纠错技巧属于哪一类。

e.g.: 教师：今天怎么样？
　　　学生：我一点儿累。
　　　教师：不对。
　　　学生：哦，我有一点儿累。

教师纠错的指令	自发性纠错	不打断交流的直接纠错	重述性纠错
E.g. 不对	√		

教学录像文本

老师： 学校外边饭馆很多,哪家饭馆受欢迎?
学生： 有一家韩国风味的饭馆受我的欢迎。
老师： 受欢迎中间可以不可以说受我的欢迎?
学生： 不行,我喜欢一家韩国饭馆。
老师： 这家韩国饭馆的菜怎么样?
学生： 菜挺好吃。
老师： 除了菜好吃,还有别的特点吗?
学生： 它很公道(dao1)。
老师： 什么很公道(dao4)?
学生： 价钱很公道。
老师： 除了价钱很公道,菜很好吃以外,这家饭馆还有别的特点吗?
学生： 嗯,没有吧。
老师： 比方说它的环境怎么样?
学生： 哦,其实环境不太好(hao1)。
老师： 不太好(hao1)?
学生： 哦,不太好(hao3)。
老师： 对了,好。
学生： 环境不太好。
老师： 为什么你觉得这家饭馆的环境不太好?
学生： 桌子椅子都不太干净(jing1)。
老师： 哦,椅子不太干净(jing4)。
学生： 哦,椅子不太干净。(jing4)
老师： 好,还有别的方面吗?
学生： 因为受欢迎,太受欢迎,所以人太多,还有,有时候空调(tiao1)不行。
老师： 空调(tiao2)。
学生： 空调。有时候空调不行。
老师： 好极了,那这家饭馆的服务怎么样?
学生： 服务挺好的,他们都很客气。
老师： 他们是谁?
学生： 服务员都很客气,上菜得很快。
老师： 上菜得很快还是上菜上得很快?
学生： 上菜上得很快。
老师： 谁上菜上得很快?
学生： 服务员上菜上得很快。

人际交流1：面对面讨论

你和梁老师一起参加了今年夏天在北京的K-16暑期中文教师培训项目，在项目培训期间你们就"纠错反馈"的问题进行了讨论：

梁老师： 到今天我才意识到纠错反馈原来那么重要，不知道你有没有同感？

你的回答： 【建议词汇和结构：同感；避免；保证；促进NP（…的建立）；…（十分/非常）必要；相对于+NP, subj.…；A占B的百分之…；有助于；第二语言习得】

梁老师： 你在日常的课堂教学中使用纠错的频率高吗？什么情况下会纠错？主要用什么样的纠错办法？

你的回答： 【建议词汇和结构：在…（不打断交流）的前提下，subj. do sth.；直接/间接+VP；引导sb.+do sth.；促进NP（…的建立）；…（十分/非常）必要；相对于+NP, subj.…；A占B的百分之…】

梁老师： 其实我在日常的课堂教学中用得最多的就是课堂讲解的直接纠错法。可对于"导出错误法"了解得还不多，不知道你在课堂上有没有使用过这样的纠错技巧？

你的回答： 【建议词汇和结构：无法；语言点；引导sb.+do sth.；subj.（通过…的方法）检测…（学生是否掌握）；subj.（通过…）创造…的机会，（以便…）】

梁老师： 嗯，今后在课堂教学的过程中我也应该尝试这样的纠错方法。

人际交流2：微信(WeChat)交流

参加完夏天的K-16暑期中文教师培训项目以后，你和梁老师成为了很好的朋友，你们常常会在微信上就一些中文教学的问题进行讨论。今天，梁老师在微信上请教你一些关于纠错的问题，请给她回复。

【建议词汇和结构：打断；升调；典型；疑问句；暗示；停顿；手势；板书；眼神；subj.（一直）尝试+do sth.；do sth.对sb.（来说）是一种挑战；引导sb. do sth.；在…的前提下，subj. do sth.；…，紧接着，…】

96 Corrective Feedback

 表达演说：教学心得分享

经过一个学期的实践。你对"纠错反馈"有了一些自己的体会，明年的K-16暑期中文培训项目将邀请你给新一期的学员做一个关于"纠错反馈"的工作坊(workshop)。你的工作坊需要包括以下内容：

1. 纠错反馈的重要性。
2. 你的课堂使用了哪些纠错的方式，具体效果如何？
3. 在使用不同的纠错方式时，你遇到的挑战有哪些？你的解决办法是什么？

建议词汇和结构：大量；关键；反馈；subj.（十分/非常）必要；subj.采取…的方法/策略；subj.尽量+do sth.（尝试…/采取…）；A为B提供+NP；subj.不断+VP（调整/检测）；subj.（通过…的方式）检测…（学生的理解度/学生是否理解）；A和B是密切相关的；直接/间接+VP；相对于+NP，subj.

 反思任务

一、前期任务：
看完预习单中的教学视频，完成纠错反馈的检查单，并思考：

- 如果你是录像中的教师，对这个学生的语言错误进行纠错时，哪些部分你会采取相同的技巧？你认为哪些部分可以采取不同的（更好的）纠错技巧？为什么？

二、核心任务：
和另一位小组成员进行讨论：

- 比较并讨论你们观察的结果有何异同。
- 根据你的教学经验，应该如何掌握给学生纠错反馈的时机？在什么情况下，你会选择不马上纠错？为什么？
- 针对学生在发音、词汇、语法方面的错误，提供纠错反馈的技巧有何异同？

三、后期任务：
根据你和另一位小组成员在中期任务所完成的结果，为所有学员演示你们讨论出来的纠错方法。

 补充材料

[1] eLearnerEngaged. (2012, March 3). *How-to give feedback to students the right way*. [Video]. Retrieved from http://www.youtube.com/watch?v=TnLNI2fXt_M
[2] Wiggins, G. (2012, September). Seven keys to effective feedback. *Feedback for learning. Educational Leadership*, 70(1), 10–16. Retrieved from http://www.ascd.org/publications/educational-leadership/sept12/vol70/num01/Seven-Keys-to-Effective-Feedback.aspx
[3] 靳洪刚(2011)，《现代汉语教学的十大原则》，【《世界汉语教学》(2011年01期)】网络链接 http://www.docin.com/p-359969472.html

第六课　故事情景[1]教学法 (TPRS)
Teaching Proficiency through Reading and Storytelling

（文本形式：专业讨论）

> ➢ 关键词：
> TPRS、故事情景、语言、动作、语言点、故事的框架、可理解输入、重复
>
> ➢ 能力目标：
> 1. 学习者能理解诠释TPRS教学法的专业讨论。
> 2. 学习者能使用专业术语总结TPRS教学法的理论。
> 3. 学习者能举例说明TPRS教学法的三个步骤。
> 4. 学习者能说明在TPRS教学中如何提供可理解输入。
> 5. 学习者能讨论如何在教学中运用TPRS。

---

[1] 情景　qíngjǐng　N.　scene

课文全版 (Complete Version)

李老师是一位K-12的新老师，在观摩了经验丰富的白老师的中文课以后，两人开始了讨论。

白老师：我今年试用了一种新的教学法，叫"故事情景教学法"，英文是 "Teaching Proficiency through Reading and Storytelling"，简称TPRS。

李老师：是吗？什么是故事情景教学法？它的教学理论[2]是什么？

白老师：故事情景教学法，也就是TPRS，是一种把语言、动作[3]和故事结合在一起的教学方法。推广[4]TPRS的老师认为学生要想真正"学会"一门外语，只有通过接触[5]大量、丰富的可理解输入才能够习得[6]。传统的操练[7]是以输出[8]为主，而TPRS强调的是输入。

李老师：那也就是说，我们在教学时，不但要注意语言的输出，而且要重视语言输入。那故事情景教学法是如何组织课堂，为学生提供输入的呢？

白老师：备课时老师要先确定[9]语言点，选好三个生词、词组或句型，并用这三个语言点来创造一个故事的框架[10]。

李老师：什么叫"故事的框架"？

白老师：我给你举一个例子。比如说，我想教"要"、"给"和"不高兴"。我可以用这三个词建立一个这样的故事框架：

_____很喜欢_____，可是他没有_____。他不高兴。_____说："为什么你不高兴？"_____说："因为我没有_____。我要_____！"_____说："哦，我有_____，可是我不要。你要吗？"_____说："我要！"_____给_____ _____。_____很高兴。他说："谢谢！谢谢！"

这就是一个框架。你注意到没有？里面有很多空格[11]，这可以让学生填空[12]。比方说，故事里有两个人物，学生可以选择蝙蝠侠[13](Batman)和蜘蛛侠[14](Spiderman)，周杰伦和成龙，或者泰

---

[2]理论	lǐlùn	N.	theory
[3]动作	dòngzuò	N.	action, motion, movement
[4]推广	tuīguǎng	V.	to promote, to popularize
[5]接触	jiēchù	V.	to come into contact with
[6]习得	xídé	V.	to acquire
[7]操练	cāoliàn	V.	to drill
[8]输出	shūchū	V./N.	to output; output
[9]确定	quèdìng	V.	to ascertain, to confirm
[10]框架	kuàngjià	N.	frame, framework
[11]空格	kònggé	N.	blank space (on a form)
[12]填空	tiánkòng	V.	to fill in the blank
[13]蝙蝠侠	biānfúxiá	N.	Batman
[14]蜘蛛侠	zhīzhūxiá	N.	Spiderman

勒·斯威夫特(Taylor Swift)和肯伊·威斯特(Kanye West)。而且故事里的第一个人物想要的东西也可以让学生决定，比方说，一只狗或一块糖等。这样一来，虽然是老师主导[15]课堂，但是还是可以让学生参与[16]决策[17]。

用故事情景教学法来进行教学时，有三个步骤要遵循[18]。第一个步骤是明确重点[19]。老师一般会在黑板上把重要的语言点写下来，加上英文翻译。并且一个一个地介绍给学生，同时介绍一个相应[20]的手势或者动作来代表该语言点，让同学们和老师一块儿做。然后老师可以用语言点问学生一些简单的问题，比方说"你高兴不高兴？""你要什么？"等，让学生一边回答，一边做动作。第二个步骤是问故事。

李老师：问故事？怎么问呢？
白老师：老师没有故事，只有一个框架。需要通过问题让学生决定故事中的人物[21]、要什么东西等，这样，有意思的细节[22]就建立起来了。比方说，学生决定孔子要苹果以后，老师就可以问：

孔子要苹果吗？
孔子要不要苹果？
孔子要苹果还是香蕉？
孔子要苹果还是白老师要苹果？
孔子要苹果还是孔子吃苹果？
谁要苹果？
孔子要什么？
孔子为什么要苹果？

这样的问法叫做"问题循环[23]法"。在提问中，老师应使用新的语言点从各个角度问问题，这样可以让学生重复听，而且还可以根据学生的回答和动作判断[24]学生是否听懂。

李老师：哇，没想到可以问出那么多问题！那第三个步骤是什么？
白老师：第三个步骤是读故事。老师会为学生写一个故事，在故事中会重复使用相同的语言点，可是人物和情节[25]会发生变化。这种方法的好处是：一方面让学生觉得很新鲜[26]，可是另一方面，还在不

[15]主导	zhǔdǎo	Adj./V.	leading, dominant, guiding; to lead, to guide
[16]参与	cānyù	V.	to participate
[17]决策	juécè	V.	to make crucial/strategic decisions
[18]遵循	zūnxún	V.	to follow, to abide by
[19]明确重点	míngquèzhòngdiǎn	VP.	to establish the meaning of focal points
[20]相应	xiāngyìng	Adj.	corresponding
[21]人物	rénwù	N.	character, role
[22]细节	xìjié	N.	detail
[23]循环	xúnhuán	V.	to circulate, cycle
[24]判断	pànduàn	V.	to judge, to determine
[25]情节	qíngjié	N.	plot
[26]新鲜	xīnxiān	Adj.	fresh, new

断重复教学的重点。这样一来，学生就可以在重复中理解语言。一般上课的时候，老师会先念故事，然后问问题，给学生提供回答问题和参与的机会，以便检查学生理解的情况。比方说，老师念故事，学生提供手势；老师在一些地方停顿，让学生进行填空；老师故意出错，让学生来纠错。最后围绕[27]着故事里的新内容再提问，让学生翻译等。

李老师：那，您已经试用故事情景教学法差不多六个星期了，感觉如何？

白老师：感觉不错。用以前传统的教学法，教完六个星期，学生只会说自己叫什么名字、是哪国人、家里有几口人，很有限[28]。现在他们能够讲各种故事，上课也觉得有趣多了。而且，今年一些典型的错误也减少[29]了，比如"不有"和"二个"，因为"没有"和"两个"他们已经听到了无数[30]次了。还有，因为完成故事需要学生的参与，所以今年我更加了解我的学生，我们的关系也更加亲密[31]了。

李老师：听起来很不错。在使用故事情景教学法时，您遇到过什么困难吗？

白老师：当然有。为了让语言输入成为可理解输入，老师的速度[32]必须慢下来。可是我发现有时我会下意识[33]地加快速度，或者怕学生觉得重复太多，结果重复得还不够，所以我在这个方面还要继续努力。

李老师：白老师，谢谢您今天让我来听课，还给我举例说明故事情景教学法的教学过程。太谢谢了。

 语言重点：

1. …把A和B结合在一起/起来

to put A and B together; to combine A with B

- 故事情景教学法，也就是TPRS，是一种把语言、动作和故事结合在一起的教学方法。
- 在问题循环法这一步骤中，教师需要把学生的故事内容与重点语言知识结合在一起进行提问。

---

[27]围绕　wéirào　V.　to encircle, go round
[28]有限　yǒuxiàn　Adj.　limited
[29]减少　jiǎnshǎo　V.　to decrease, to reduce
[30]无数　wúshù　Adj.　countless
[31]亲密　qīnmì　Adj.　close, intimate
[32]速度　sùdù　N.　speed; pace
[33]下意识　xiàyìshí　Adv.　subconsciously

2. ① **Subj.重视…**

   Subj. values …

   ② **…受到sb.的重视**

   … is valued by sb.
   - 我们在教学时，不但要注意语言的输出，而且要重视语言输入。
   - 在故事情景教学的三个步骤中，由于重点语言知识多次反复出现，形成了大量的语言输入，因此可以受到学习者的重视。

3. **Subj.参与do sth.（决策/设计（…）/教学/备课）**

   Subj. participates in (decision making/design (…)/teaching/class preparation)
   - 这样虽然是老师主导，但是还是可以让学生参与决策。
   - 学生除了可以参与决策以外，也可以尝试参与设计课堂活动，这样一来，他们可以从教学者的角度来看所学的重点词汇与结构。

4. **Subj.用A来代表B**

   Subj. uses A to represent B
   - 老师用一个相应的手势或者动作来代表该语言点，让同学们和老师一块儿做。
   - 所谓的故事情景教学法是指"Teaching Proficiency through Reading and Storytelling"，所以现在语言教师常用TPRS来代表故事情境教学法。

5. **Subj.（不断）重复+V/N（听/问/使用/重点/问题）**

   Subj. (continuously) repeats (listening/asking/using/the main point/questions)
   - 在提问中，老师应使用新的语言点从各个角度问问题，这样可以让学生重复听。
   - 读故事时，教师可以不断重复教学的重点，这样一来，学生就可以在重复听中理解语言。

6. **典型的N（错误/例子/方法）**

   the typical (mistake/example/method)
   - 今年一些典型的错误也减少了。
   - 教师写故事时最好有意识地加入典型的例子使学生了解重点词汇或结构的用法。

第六课　故事情景[1]教学法 (TPRS)
Teaching Proficiency through Reading and Storytelling

（文本形式：专业讨论）

> ➢ 关键词：
>   TPRS、故事情景、语言、动作、语言点、故事的框架、可理解输入、重复
> ➢ 能力目标：
>   1. 学习者能理解诠释TPRS教学法的专业讨论。
>   2. 学习者能使用专业术语总结TPRS教学法的理论。
>   3. 学习者能举例说明TPRS教学法的三个步骤。
>   4. 学习者能说明在TPRS教学中如何提供可理解输入。
>   5. 学习者能讨论如何在教学中运用TPRS。

---

[1] 情景　qíngjǐng　N.　scene

课文节选版 (Abridged Version)

　　李老师是一位K-12的新老师，在观摩了经验丰富的白老师的中文课以后，两人开始了讨论。

白老师：我今年试用了一种新的教学法，叫"故事情景教学法"，英文是"Teaching Proficiency through Reading and Storytelling"，简称[2] TPRS。

李老师：是吗？什么是故事情景教学法？它的教学理论[3]是什么？

白老师：故事情景教学法，也就是TPRS，是一种把语言、动作[4]和故事结合在一起的教学方法。介绍TPRS的老师认为学生要想真正"学会"一门外语，只有通过接触[5]大量、丰富的可理解输入才能够习得[6]。传统操练[7]是以输出[8]为主，而TPRS强调的是输入。

李老师：那也就是说，我们在教学时，不但要注意语言的输出，而且要重视语言输入。那故事情景教学法是如何组织课堂，为学生提供输入的呢？

白老师：首先，备课时老师要先确定[9]语言点，选好三个生词、词组或句型，并用这三个语言点来创造一个故事的框架[10]。

李老师：什么叫"故事的框架"？

白老师：我给你一个例子。比如说，我想教"要"、"给"和"不高兴"。我可以用这三个词建立一个这样的故事框架：

　　　　＿＿＿＿很喜欢＿＿＿＿，可是他没有＿＿＿＿。他不高兴。
　　　　＿＿＿＿说："为什么你不高兴？"＿＿＿＿说："因为我没有
　　　　＿＿＿＿。我要＿＿＿＿！"＿＿＿＿说："哦，我有
　　　　＿＿＿＿，可是我不要。你要吗？"＿＿＿＿说：
　　　　"我要！"＿＿＿＿给＿＿＿＿。＿＿＿＿很高兴。
　　　　他说："谢谢！谢谢！"

　　这就是一个框架。你注意到没有？里面有很多空格[11]，这可以让学生填空[12]。比方说，故事里有两个人物，学生可以选择蝙蝠侠[13] (Batman)和蜘蛛侠[14] (Spiderman)，周杰伦和成龙，或者泰勒·斯威

[2]简称	jiǎnchēng	N./V.	abbreviation; to be called ... for short
[3]理论	lǐlùn	N.	theory
[4]动作	dòngzuò	N.	action, motion, movement
[5]接触	jiēchù	V.	to come into contact with
[6]习得	xídé	V.	to acquire
[7]操练	cāoliàn	V.	to drill
[8]输出	shūchū	V./N.	to output; output
[9]确定	quèdìng	V.	to ascertain, to confirm
[10]框架	kuàngjià	N.	frame, framework
[11]空格	kònggé	N.	blank space (on a form)
[12]填空	tiánkòng	V.	to fill in the blank
[13]蝙蝠侠	biānfúxiá	N.	Batman
[14]蜘蛛侠	zhīzhūxiá	N.	Spiderman

夫特(Taylor Swift)和肯伊·威斯特(Kanye West)。而且故事里的第一个人物想要的东西也可以让学生决定，比方说，一只狗或一块糖等。这样一来，虽然是老师主导[15]课堂，但是还是可以让学生参与[16]决策[17]。

用故事情景教学法来进行教学时，有三个步骤。第一个步骤是明确重点[18]。老师一般会在黑板上把重要的语言点写下来，加上英文翻译。而且一个一个地介绍给学生，同时介绍一个相应[19]的手势[20]或者动作来代表该语言点，让同学们和老师一块儿做。然后老师可以用语言点问学生一些简单的问题，比方说"你高兴不高兴？""你要什么？"等，让学生一边回答，一边做动作。第二个步骤是问故事。

李老师：问故事？怎么问呢？

白老师：老师没有故事，只有一个框架。需要通过问题让学生决定故事中的人物[21]、要什么东西等，这样，有意思的细节[22]就建立起来了。比方说，学生决定孔子要苹果以后，老师就可以问：

孔子要苹果吗？
孔子要不要苹果？
孔子要苹果还是香蕉？
孔子要苹果还是白老师要苹果？
孔子要苹果还是孔子吃苹果？
谁要苹果？
孔子要什么？
孔子为什么要苹果？

这样的问法叫做"问题循环[23]法"。

李老师：哇，真没想到可以问出这么多问题！那第三个步骤是什么？

白老师：第三个步骤是看故事。老师会为学生写一个故事，在故事中会重复使用相同的语言点，可是人物和情节[24]会发生变化。这种方法的好处是：一方面让学生觉得很新鲜[25]，可是另一方面，还在不断重复教学的重点。这样一来，学生就可以在重复中理解语言。一般上课的时候，老师会先念故事，然后问问题，给学生提供回答问题和参与的机会，以便检查学生理解的情况。比方说，老师

[15]主导	zhǔdǎo	Adj./V.	leading, dominant, guiding; to lead, to guide
[16]参与	cānyù	V.	to participate
[17]决策	juécè	V.	to make crucial/strategic decisions
[18]明确重点	míngquèzhòngdiǎn	VP.	to establish the meaning of focal points
[19]相应	xiāngyìng	Adj.	corresponding
[20]手势	shǒushì	N.	gesture
[21]人物	rénwù	N.	character, role
[22]细节	xìjié	N.	detail
[23]循环	xúnhuán	V.	to circulate, cycle
[24]情节	qíngjié	N.	plot
[25]新鲜	xīnxiān	Adj.	fresh, new

念故事，学生提供手势；老师在一些地方停顿[26]，让学生进行填空；老师故意出错，让学生来纠错。最后围绕[27]着故事里的新内容再提问题，让学生翻译等。

李老师：听起来很不错。在使用故事情景教学法时，您遇到过什么困难吗？

白老师：当然有。为了让语言输入成为可理解输入，老师的速度[28]必须慢下来。可是我发现有时我会下意识[29]地加快速度，或者怕学生觉得重复太多，结果重复得还不够，所以我在这方面要继续努力。

李老师：白老师，谢谢您今天让我来听课，还给我举例说明故事情景教学法的教学过程。太谢谢了。

 语言重点：

1. …把A和B结合在一起/起来

   to put A and B together; to combine A with B

   - 故事情景教学法，也就是TPRS，是一种把语言、动作和故事结合在一起的教学方法。
   - 在问题循环法这一步骤中，教师需要把学生的故事内容与重点语言知识结合在一起进行提问。

2. ① **Subj.重视…**

   Subj. values …

   ② …**受到sb.的重视**

   … is valued by sb.

   - 我们在教学时，不但要注意语言的输出，而且要重视语言输入。
   - 在故事情景教学的三个步骤中，由于重点语言知识多次反复出现，形成了大量的语言输入，因此可以受到学习者的重视。

3. **Subj.参与do sth.（决策/设计（…）/教学/备课）**

   Subj. participates in (decision making/design (…)/teaching/class preparation)

   - 这样虽然是老师主导，但是还是可以让学生参与决策。
   - 学生除了可以参与决策以外，也可以尝试参与设计课堂活动，这样一来，他们可以从教学者的角度来看所学的重点词汇与结构。

---

[26]停顿　tíngdùn　V.　to pause
[27]围绕　wéirào　V.　to encircle, go round
[28]速度　sùdù　N.　speed; pace
[29]下意识　xiàyìshí　Adv.　subconsciously

4. Subj.用A来代表B

Subj. uses A to represent B

- 老师用一个相应的手势或者动作来代表该语言点，让同学们和老师一块儿做。
- 所谓的故事情景教学法是指 "Teaching Proficiency through Reading and Storytelling"，所以现在语言教师常用TPRS来代表故事情境教学法。

5. Subj.（不断）重复+V/N（听/问/使用/重点/问题）

Subj. (continuously) repeats (listening/asking/using/the main point/questions)

- 在提问中，老师应使用新的语言点从各个角度问问题，这样可以让学生重复听。
- 读故事时，教师可以不断重复教学的重点，这样一来，学生就可以在重复听中理解语言。

练习活动

理解诠释1：预习单

先看课文，然后完成下面的作业：

一、根据课文进行填空。

所谓TPRS就是_____，是一种把_____、动作和_____结合在一起的教学方法。老师进行教学时，通过不断地问问题给学生提供大量、丰富的_____。老师利用选定的语言点和词组创造故事的_____，然后由学生来决定故事的_____和_____。这样一来，虽然由老师主导课堂，但是提供了学生_____决策的机会，不但有助于促进学生的理解度，同时也让他们觉得很新鲜。

二、下面是故事情景教学法的教学步骤，请按正常顺序进行排序。

a. 用手势代表语言点　　　　　　b. 用问题循环法问故事
c. 明确要教授的语言点　　　　　d. 用新的故事检查学生理解度
e. 确定故事框架　　　　　　　　f. 决定故事的情节和人物

_____→_____→_____→_____→_____

三、传统的句型操练与故事情景教学法有哪些不同？请你就两种方法强调的要点、教学进行方式和好处等三个方面进行比较。

理解诠释2：课程案例记录

今天，张教授给我们讲了关于TPRS教学法的理论以及其在课堂教学实践中的运用。首先，我们阅读了根据TPRS教学法编写的对外汉语教材《跟我学汉语》的前言，了解到所谓TPRS教学法是指一种把语言、动作和故事结合起来的教学方法。这种教学法让学生参与决策，成为教学的主人，老师则扮演启发和引导的角色。

接着，我们分组实践TPRS教学法。这种教学法表面上看起来容易，其实操作起来非常复杂。我和另一个同学一组。在确定了语言点以后，我们创造了故事框架，设计了上课的步骤和具体的教学形式。我们的教学步骤分为：教师口述，演示，学生模仿；学生相互口述，演示，相互模仿；教师口述情境，学生表演。而在教学形式上，我们一方面用手势代表相应的语言点，使重点明确；另一方面强调学生的参与，因此也加入了游戏的环节。我们选取的游戏为：孔子说(Simon says)。我们今天的授课内容和课堂教学目标为通过肢体演示和表演，让学生1)能够听到指示以后完成"坐下""站起来""跑""停""走""蹲下"等对应动作；2)能够根据年龄的不同将人群分组，并给以恰当的名称，如"男孩""女孩""老人"等；3)运用故事框架，进行表达演说。

最后，我们进行了教学演示。我所在的小组作为老师，另一个小组作为学生，将我们设计的课程演示出来。在演示的过程中，我们也发现了设计中的很多问题。比方说：故事情节太简单，学生操作太机械。

总之，这堂课的学习让我开始重视TPRS这种教学方法。我非常希望将这种教学法合理运用到自己的教学中。

1. TPRS教学法结合的内容不包含下列哪一项：
   A. 故事情节   B. 语言点   C. 打分标准   D. 手势、动作

2. 关于TPRS教学法，以下哪一个叙述是对的？
   A. 以教师为中心   B. 学生参与的机会不多
   C. 教师是课堂的引导者   D. 重视机械式操练

3. 造成TPRS教学法不成功的可能因素有：（多选）
   A. 故事情节太简单   B. 学生是教学的主人
   C. 用动作代表语言点   D. 可理解输入不够丰富

4. 你玩过"孔子说(Simon says)"这个游戏吗？你认为该游戏运用了哪些TPRS教学法的技巧？另外，这个游戏能不能算是一种TPRS教学法，为什么？

108 *Reading and Storytelling*

人际交流1：论坛

你和另一位同事代表你们学校参加了一场关于TPRS教学法的工作坊(workshop)，回来后组织了一个小型论坛，和其他同事分享心得：

主持人： 由于学校经费有限，上个星期由林老师和常老师代表参加了TPRS教学工作坊，两位老师学习了不少新东西。现在就请林老师先跟我们分享一下TPRS的教学理论。

你的回答： 【建议词汇和结构：⋯把A和B结合起来；subj.重视⋯；通过⋯（接触/大量的可理解输入/问题）检测/创造⋯；习得】

主持人： 谢谢林老师。故事情景教学法和传统的课堂有哪些差异？能不能给我们提出最少三个不同？

你的回答： 【建议词汇和结构：以⋯（教师/学生）为中心；⋯受到重视；输出；输入；主导；互动；新鲜；亲密；促进+NP；有限；典型的N（错误/例子/方法）；避免+NP】

主持人： 听起来好处不少。那，接下来，请给大家就TPRS教学法的具体实施步骤进行说明，好吗？

你的回答： 好的。【建议词汇和结构：首先⋯，其次⋯，最后⋯；确定；框架；相应的N；通过⋯（提问/大量的输入/动作）检测/重复⋯；用A来代表B；subj.（不断）重复+V/N（听/问/使用/重点）；循环；围绕；subj.参与do sth.（决策/设计/讨论/教学）】

主持人： 故事情景教学法表面上看起来容易，其实操作起来并不简单。由于时间的关系，我们不得不在此打住。如果还有问题，可以给两位老师写信。今天谢谢两位老师的分享，也谢谢大家的参与。

 人际交流2：电子邮件

在听完论坛的分享后，一位老师给你写信。请你读了之后给他回信。

林老师：

您好。上个星期听了您的分享后，我决定尝试TPRS教学法。不过，我发现设计一堂课真不简单，除了您提到的重点和步骤外，我还有几个问题想请教您：

第一、使用故事情景教学法时，老师应该用自然语速还是应该放慢语速？

第二、老师在说故事时怎么检查学生理解的情况？

第三、为何TPRS能有助于减少学生的典型错误？

期待您的回复，谢谢您的指导。

祝　教安！

杨雨生　上

【建议词汇和结构：…有必要+do sth.；速度；接触；大量；可理解输入；subj.（不断）重复+V/N（听/问/使用/重点）；技巧；用A来代表B；相应的N；语言点；词组；动作；情节；人物；纠错；通过…（提问/大量的输入/动作）判断/检测…；无数；引导sb.+do sth.；subj.参与do sth.（决策/设计/讨论/教学）】

表达演说：分享教学/学习经验

请你准备一个5分钟的演讲，跟同学分享一下自己使用TPRS教学法的经验（若没有教学经验，请分享学习外语时，老师使用TPRS教学的情况），并且举例说明。分享教学/学习经验时，请包括以下内容：

1. 你/你的老师曾经在课堂上使用过故事情景教学法吗？如果用过，学生的反应如何？如果没用过，原因可能是什么？
2. 你认为故事情景教学法有哪些好处？它结合了三种沟通模式中的哪几种？（请举例，并且就每一种沟通模式进行说明。）
3. 根据你的经验（或者你将来尝试），使用TPRS教学法时可能会遇到哪些困难？请你至少提出两点，提供大家在你发表后进行讨论。

建议词汇和结构：A为B提供+NP；丰富；新鲜感；参与；Do sth.对sb.（来说）是一种挑战；subj.采取（提问/说故事/句型操练）的方法；…（没）有必要+do sth.；促进+NP；有意义；调整；框架；人物；情节；停顿；词汇量；有限；subj.（不断）重复+V/N（听/问/使用/操练/重点）；纠错；速度；下意识

反思任务

一、前期任务
用下列语言形式设计一个故事框架

- V得+adj.（e.g. 跑得很快，吃得很多，写得很好）
- 时间词（e.g. 上午/中午/下午 or …点…分）
- 别+do sth.

二、核心任务
与小组成员讨论各自设计的框架，最后每组决定一个"框架"，并讨论教学步骤。

三、后期任务
根据讨论结果，为别的小组展示一堂用故事情景教学法进行的课。

补充材料

[1] Perceptions about Storytelling in Teaching Chinese as a Second/Foreign Language: Opportunities and Challenges. Proceedings of the 7th International Conference on Educational Reform (ICER 2014), Innovations and Good Practices in Education: Global Perspectives, retrieved from http://www.icer.msu.ac.th/index/paper/fullpaper/50.Kate%20Nguyen.pdf

[2] Decher, Beth. (2008). Body Language: The Effectiveness of Total Physical Response Storytelling in Secondary Foreign Language Instruction. Retrieved from http://www.macalester.edu/educationreform/actionresearch/action%20research%20-%20beth.pdf

[3] Kariuki, Patrick N. K. and Bush, Elizabeth Danielle. (2008). The Effects of Total Physical Response by Storytelling and the Traditional Teaching Styles of a Foreign Language in a Selected High School. Presented at the Annual Conference of the Mid-South Educational Research Association, Knoxville, Tennessee, November 5–7. Retrieved from http://files.eric.ed.gov/fulltext/ED503364.pdf

[4] TPRS teaching demo [PowerPoint slide]. Retrieved from http://www.youtube.com/watch?v=xhPYezd_yVI

第七课　任务教学设计
Task-based Instructional Design

（文本形式：面试）

> ➢ 关键词：
> 信息断层、预期结果、前期任务、核心任务、后期任务、角色、分组
>
> ➢ 能力目标：
> 1. 学习者能理解诠释关于任务教学的专业讨论。
> 2. 学习者能使用专业术语讨论任务教学的特点及教学目的。
> 3. 学习者能列出任务的五个基本组成部分并用实例说明。
> 4. 学习者能叙述、说明任务设计的三个阶段，并能介绍、分析自己做过的任务。

课文全版 (Complete Version)

何老师、麦老师和孔老师是三位年轻的外语教师。他们刚获得本科[1]学位[2]，正在找工作。今天他们去费城[3]国际联合[4]私立高中面试[5]。

史老师： 谢谢各位到我们的学校来参加面试。今天下午面试的主要内容是讨论外语教学法。我们采取的形式是集体讨论[6]。大家知道，任务教学法是外语教学领域[7]一种十分重要的教学模式[8]。就这个主题，请大家各自分享一些自己的看法和经验。请大家千万别紧张。首先，请各位简单地谈谈你们对使用任务进行教学的看法。

何老师： 我认为课上使用任务绝对[9]不是为了让学生觉得好玩而已，当然这一点也很重要。但是更重要的是利用任务让学生进行"有效互动[10]"与"语言使用"，也就是说，让学生通过完成一系列真实任务，来学习如何使用第二语言跟别人互动交流。因此，在设计任务之前，老师应先考虑任务的五个基本组成部分，首先，从任务出发制定教学目标，如任务所需要的词汇及语法结构、任务的功能等；其次，为学生提供完成任务的语言输入，可以是听力、阅读、也可以是视频材料[11]；第三是任务条件，也就是说，任务的语言信息是个别人知道，还是大家都知道。好的任务往往有信息断层[12]，这样可以让学生主动[13]互动提问；第四是任务完成的程序[14]；最后是任务的预期结果[15]，也就是说，学生完成任务后，可以获得一个具体的结果，比如，得出一个结论[16]，找出了凶手[17]等。不能随便讨论讨论就结束了。

孔老师： 何老师说的对。我想就任务的程序，再补充[18]一点，任务设计又可分为三个阶段：前期任务[19]、核心任务[20]、后期任务[21]。在前期

---

[1]本科	běnkē	N.	undergraduate, undergraduate course
[2]学位	xuéwèi	N.	academic degree
[3]费城	fèichéng	N.	Philadelphia
[4]联合	liánhé	V.	to unite
[5]面试	miànshì	V./N.	to interview; interview
[6]集体讨论	jítǐtǎolùn	VP./NP.	group discussion
[7]领域	lǐngyù	N.	domain, field
[8]教学模式	jiàoxuémóshì	NP.	pedagogical model
[9]绝对	juéduì	Adj./Adv.	absolute; absolutely
[10]有效互动	yǒuxiàohùdòng	NP.	effective interaction
[11]视频材料	shìpíncáiliào	NP.	video material
[12]信息断层	xìnxīduàncéng	NP.	information gap
[13]主动	zhǔdòng	Adj.	to be on the initiative, active
[14]程序	chéngxù	N.	procedure
[15]预期结果	yùqījiéguǒ	NP.	expected outcome
[16]结论	jiélùn	N.	conclusion
[17]凶手	xiōngshǒu	N.	assassin, murderer
[18]补充	bǔchōng	V.	to supplement
[19]前期任务	qiánqīrènwù	NP.	pre-task
[20]核心任务	héxīnrènwù	NP.	core-task
[21]后期任务	hòuqīrènwù	NP.	post-task

任务阶段，老师要说明任务内容，提供具体的指导，包括角色[22]、情况、需要讨论的问题、使用的定式与词汇等等，如此一来，可以避免许多进行中的问题与困难。还有一点，在实施任务[23]的时候，老师要给学生充分[24]的准备时间。研究证实，准备时间与学生输出的流利度[25]、复杂度[26]有很大的相关性。DeKeyser (2001) 指出，系统、有意义、语境清晰[27]的任务对语言准确度以及语言使用自动化过程[28]都有很大的帮助。

麦老师：两位老师说的很对。那我接着谈核心任务与后期任务吧。核心任务是指课上进行的有意义、真实的活动。通过讨论、角色扮演[29]等形式，让学生完成任务。在学生完成任务时，老师会观察到学生的语言使用和交际互动情况。我认为此时主要的角色应由学生担任[30]，老师要把注意力[31]集中[32]在调整互动上。核心任务完成之后就进入了后期任务，同样需要给学生一段时间来准备，让学生把核心任务的内容用另一种形式再做一次，比如小组报告或个人报告，各有优势[33]。学生报告之后，我会鼓励同学们提问，再一起分析[34]活动的过程与结果。此时，我不但会再次[35]强调重点词汇与语言定式，也会借此机会[36]帮助学生解决在完成任务的过程中所碰到的问题。

史老师：真不错。你们对任务设计都非常了解。不过，不知道哪位老师可以给我们介绍一下自己做过的任务？

孔老师：我来说一个吧！我做过的任务设计不少，其中最喜欢侦探[37]故事。在前期任务阶段，我会把学生分成几组，然后给组内每个学生一段文章。学生得回家准备，理解负责的故事内容，查出生词的意思，然后隔天[38]向同学叙述[39]他所负责的故事。于是在核心任务阶段，小组同学必须一起决定故事的先后顺序[40]，讨论其中

[22]角色	juésè	N.	role
[23]实施任务	shíshīrènwù	VP.	to carry out a task/assignment
[24]充分	chōngfèn	Adj.	sufficient, adequate
[25]流利度	liúlìdù	N.	fluency
[26]复杂度	fùzádù	N.	complexity
[27]清晰	qīngxī	Adj.	clear
[28]过程	guòchéng	N.	process
[29]角色扮演	juésèbànyǎn	VP./NP.	role play
[30]担任	dānrèn	V.	to undertake
[31]注意力	zhùyìlì	N.	attention
[32]集中	jízhōng	V./Adj.	to centralize, concentrate, focus; centralized
[33]优势	yōushì	N.	advantage, superiority
[34]分析	fēnxī	V.	to analyze
[35]再次	zàicì	Adv.	once again, once more
[36]借此机会	jiècǐjīhuì	Idiom	to take advantage of this opportunity
[37]侦探	zhēntàn	N.	detective
[38]隔天	gétiān	Adv.	on the next day
[39]叙述	xùshù	V.	to narrate
[40]先后顺序	xiānhòushùnxù	NP.	sequence

的细节，最后找出凶手。在这个过程中，学生会针对不明白的字词或细节提问。

何老师：对，我也用过这个方法，学生都非常喜欢。我还想补充一点：任务的设计有三个原则，即断层原则、决策原则、信息双向[41]原则。首先，在设计课文时，不要让每个学生看一样的课文。每个学生都只掌握部分信息，这样，学生的信息之间存在断层(gap)，便于让学生主动交流；其次，通过小组讨论、分享、合作，最后完成决策或得出结论，这样任务自然就有了预期结果。最后，由于任务过程中必须进行有问有答[42]、不断协商，所以信息的交流是双向的。

史老师：嗯，你们三位的讨论都很有创意[43]。那么，你们认为任务教学有什么优点[44]？

麦老师：通过任务，我不但能掌握学生的注意力，而且能给学生提供运用不同语言技能的机会，还可以让学生在课上主动说话表达。课堂活动不再是机械[45]地练习定式和词汇，而是一个有意义的学习环境。

史老师：任务设计的确有优势。不过，设计任务时是否也面临一些困难呢？

孔老师：对，我认为即使任务设计是十分有效的教学法，但仍然有一些困难难以[46]克服[47]。比方说老师必须详细地规划[48]任务的内容，否则学生不一定能充分发挥[49]语言能力。

史老师：今天的讨论很有意义。由于时间的关系，我们的面试到此结束。各位都是非常优秀[50]的老师，可惜我们只能录用[51]一位外语老师。不过，无论你们到哪儿去教书，肯定都能成为优秀的外语老师。谢谢大家。

语言重点：

1. **Subj.** 获得（了）⋯学位/证书

    Subj. to earn ... (academic degree, certificate, etc.)

    - 他们刚获得本科学位，正在找工作。
    - 为了获得教师资格证书，他特意参加了一个以提高教学水平为目标的培训项目。

---

[41]双向	shuāngxiàng	Adj.	two-way
[42]有问有答	yǒuwènyǒudá	VP.	sb. asks a question, sb. answers
[43]创意	chuàngyì	N.	creativity
[44]优点	yōudiǎn	N.	merit, advantage, strength
[45]机械	jīxiè	Adj./Adv.	mechanical; mechanically
[46]难以	nányǐ	Adv.	difficult to
[47]克服	kèfú	V.	to overcome
[48]规划	guīhuà	V.	to plan
[49]发挥	fāhuī	V.	to bring (skill, talent) into full play
[50]优秀	yōuxiù	Adj.	outstanding
[51]录用	lùyòng	V.	to recruit

2. **Subj.**把…（注意力/精力）集中在…上

   Subj. focuses (attention/energy) on …

   - 我认为此时主要的角色应由学生担任，老师要把注意力集中在调整互动上。
   - 在设计任务时，教师必须把主要精力集中在规划任务的内容与操作步骤上，否则学生不一定能充分发挥语言能力。

3. ① …，**Subj.**（应该/可以/会）借此机会 **do sth.**

   … , Subj. (should/can/will) take advantage of this opportunity to do sth.

   ② **Subj.**（应该/可以/会）借…的机会 **do sth.**

   Subj. (should/can/will) take advantage of the opportunity of … to do sth.

   - 此时，我不但会再次强调重点词汇与语言定式，也会借此机会帮助学生解决在完成任务的过程中所碰到的问题。
   - 在前期任务阶段，老师要说明任务内容，提供具体的指导，包括角色、情况、需要讨论的问题，老师也可以借介绍任务的机会介绍任务过程中需要使用的定式与词汇等等。

4. **Subj.**克服+NP（困难/紧张心理/心理障碍）

   Subj. overcomes (hardships/nervousness/psychological obstacles)

   - 没错，我认为即使任务设计是十分有效的教学法，但仍然有一些困难难以克服。
   - 在实施任务的时候，老师要给学生充分的准备时间。这样一来，不仅可以提高学生输出的流利度与复杂度，而且可以使其克服紧张心理。

5. ① **Obj.**难以+V

   Obj. is difficult to V.

   ② **Subj.** 难以+VP

   It is difficult for subj. to VP.

   - 没错，我认为即使任务设计是十分有效的教学法，但仍然有一些困难难以克服。
   - 如果学生的信息之间不存在断层，学生便难以主动交流，完成决策或得出结论。

第七课　任务教学设计
Task-based Instructional Design

（文本形式：面试）

> ➢ 关键词：
> 信息断层、预期结果、前期任务、核心任务、后期任务、角色、分组
> ➢ 能力目标：
>   1. 学习者能理解诠释关于任务教学的专业讨论。
>   2. 学习者能使用专业术语讨论任务教学的特点及教学目的。
>   3. 学习者能列出任务的五个基本组成部分并用实例说明。
>   4. 学习者能叙述、说明任务设计的三个阶段，并能介绍、分析自己做过的任务。

课文节选版 (Abridged Version)

何老师、麦老师和孔老师是三位年轻的外语教师。他们刚获得本科[1]学位[2]，正在找工作。今天他们去费城[3]国际联合[4]私立高中面试[5]。

史老师： 谢谢各位到我们的学校来参加面试。今天下午面试的主要内容是讨论外语教学法。我们采取的形式是集体讨论[6]。大家知道，任务教学法是外语教学领域[7]一种十分重要的教学模式[8]。我们就这个主题，请大家各自分享一些自己的看法和经验。请大家千万别紧张。首先，请各位简单地谈谈你们对使用任务进行教学的看法。

何老师： 我认为课上使用任务绝对[9]不是为了让学生觉得好玩而已，当然这一点也很重要。但是更重要的是利用任务让学生进行"有效互动[10]"与"语言使用"，也就是说，让学生通过完成一系列真实任务，来学习如何使用第二语言跟别人互动交流。因此，在设计任务之前，老师应先考虑任务的五个基本组成部分，首先，从任务出发制定教学目标，如任务所需要的词汇及语法结构、任务的功能等；其次，为学生提供完成任务的语言输入，可以是听力、阅读、也可以是视频材料[11]；第三是任务条件，也就是说，任务的语言信息是个别人知道，还是大家都知道。好的任务往往有信息断层[12]，这样可以让学生主动[13]互动提问；第四是任务完成的程序[14]；最后是任务的预期结果[15]，也就是说，学生完成任务后，可以获得一个具体的结果，比如，得出一个结论[16]，找出了凶手[17]等。不能随便讨论讨论就结束了。

[1]本科	běnkē	N.	undergraduate, undergraduate course
[2]学位	xuéwèi	N.	academic degree
[3]费城	fèichéng	N.	Philadelphia
[4]联合	liánhé	V.	to unite
[5]面试	miànshì	V./N.	to interview; interview
[6]集体讨论	jítǐtǎolùn	VP./NP.	group discussion
[7]领域	lǐngyù	N.	domain, field
[8]教学模式	jiàoxuémóshì	NP.	pedagogical model
[9]绝对	juéduì	Adj./Adv.	absolute; absolutely
[10]有效互动	yǒuxiàohùdòng	NP.	effective interaction
[11]视频材料	shìpíncáiliào	NP.	video material
[12]信息断层	xìnxīduàncéng	NP.	information gap
[13]主动	zhǔdòng	Adj.	to be on the initiative, active
[14]程序	chéngxù	N.	procedure
[15]预期结果	yùqījiéguǒ	NP.	expected outcome
[16]结论	jiélùn	N.	conclusion
[17]凶手	xiōngshǒu	N.	assassin, murderer

孔老师： 何老师说的对。我想就任务的程序，再补充[18]一点，任务设计又可分为三个阶段[19]：前期任务[20]、核心任务[21]、后期任务[22]。在前期任务阶段，老师要说明任务内容，提供具体的指导[23]，包括角色[24]、情况、需要讨论的问题、使用的定式与词汇等等，如此一来，可以避免许多进行中的问题与困难。还有一点，在实施任务[25]的时候，老师要给学生充分[26]的准备时间。研究证实[27]，准备时间与学生输出的流利度[28]、复杂度[29]有很大的相关性。DeKeyser (2001)指出，系统、有意义、语境清晰[30]的任务对语言准确度以及语言使用自动化过程[31]都有很大的帮助。

麦老师： 两位老师说的很对。那我接着谈核心任务与后期任务吧。核心任务是指课上进行的有意义、真实的活动。通过讨论，角色扮演[32]等形式，让学生完成任务。在学生完成任务时，老师会观察到学生的语言使用和交际互动情况。我认为此时主要的角色应由学生担任[33]，老师要把注意力[34]集中[35]在调整互动上。核心任务完成之后就进入了后期任务，同样需要给学生一段时间来准备，让学生把核心任务的内容用另一种形式再做一次，比如小组报告或个人报告，各有优势[36]。学生报告之后，我会鼓励同学们提问，再一起分析[37]活动的过程与结果。此时，我不但会再次[38]强调重点词汇与语言定式，也会借此机会[39]帮助学生解决在完成任务的过程中所碰到的问题。

史老师： 真不错。你们对任务设计都非常了解。不过，不知道哪位老师可以给我们介绍一下自己做过的任务？

[18]补充	bǔchōng	V.		to supplement
[19]阶段	jiēduàn	N.		phase, stage
[20]前期任务	qiánqīrènwù	NP.		pre-task
[21]核心任务	héxīnrènwù	NP.		core-task
[22]后期任务	hòuqīrènwù	NP.		post-task
[23]指导	zhǐdǎo	V.		to guide, to direct
[24]角色	juésè	N.		role
[25]实施任务	shíshīrènwù	VP.		to carry out a task/assignment
[26]充分	chōngfèn	Adj.		sufficient, adequate
[27]证实	zhèngshí	V.		to prove, to validate
[28]流利度	liúlìdù	N.		fluency
[29]复杂度	fùzádù	N.		complexity
[30]清晰	qīngxī	Adj.		clear
[31]过程	guòchéng	N.		process
[32]角色扮演	juésèbànyǎn	VP./NP.		role play
[33]担任	dānrèn	V.		to undertake
[34]注意力	zhùyìlì	N.		attention
[35]集中	jízhōng	V./Adj.		to centralize, concentrate, focus; centralized
[36]优势	yōushì	N.		advantage, superiority
[37]分析	fēnxī	V.		to analyze
[38]再次	zàicì	Adv.		once again, once more
[39]借此机会	jiècǐjīhuì	Idiom		to take advantage of this opportunity

孔老师： 我来说一个吧！我做过的任务设计不少，其中最喜欢侦探[40]故事。在前期任务阶段，我会把学生分成几组，然后给组内每个学生一段文章。学生得回家准备，理解负责的故事内容，查出生词的意思，然后隔天[41]向同学叙述[42]他所负责的故事。于是在核心任务阶段，小组同学必须一起决定故事的先后顺序[43]，讨论其中的细节，最后找出凶手。在这个过程中，学生会针对不明白的字词或细节提问。

何老师： 对，我也用过这个方法，学生都非常喜欢。我还想补充一点：任务的设计有三个原则，即断层原则、决策原则、信息双向[44]原则。首先，在设计课文时，不要让每个学生看一样的课文。每个学生都只掌握[45]部分信息，这样，学生的信息之间存在断层(gap)，便于让学生主动交流；其次，通过小组讨论、分享、合作，最后完成决策或得出结论，这样任务自然就有了预期结果。最后，由于任务过程中必须进行有问有答、不断协商，所以信息的交流是双向的。

史老师： 嗯，你们三位的讨论都很有创意[46]。由于时间的关系，我们的面试到此结束。谢谢大家。

语言重点：

1. **Subj.**获得（了）…学位/证书

    Subj. to earn … (academic degree, certificate, etc.)

    ● 他们刚获得本科学位，正在找工作。
    ● 为了获得教师资格证书，他特意参加了一个以提高教学水平为目标的培训项目。

2. **Subj.**把…（注意力/精力）集中在…上

    Subj. focuses (attention/energy) on …

    ● 我认为此时主要的角色应由学生担任，老师要把注意力集中在调整互动上。
    ● 在设计任务时，教师必须把主要精力集中在规划任务的内容与操作步骤上，否则学生不一定能充分发挥语言能力。

---

[40]侦探	zhēntàn	N.	detective
[41]隔天	gétiān	Adv.	on the next day
[42]叙述	xùshù	V.	to narrate
[43]先后顺序	xiānhòushùnxù	NP.	sequence
[44]双向	shuāngxiàng	Adj.	two-way
[45]掌握	zhǎngwò	V.	to master
[46]创意	chuàngyì	N.	creativity

3. ① …, **Subj.**（应该/可以/会）借此机会 **do sth.**

   … , Subj. (should/can/will) take advantage of this opportunity to do sth.

   ② **Subj.**（应该/可以/会）借…的机会 **do sth.**

   Subj. (should/can/will) take advantage of the opportunity of … to do sth.

- 此时，我不但会再次强调重点词汇与语言定式，也会借此机会帮助学生解决在完成任务的过程中所碰到的问题。
- 在前期任务阶段，老师要说明任务内容，提供具体的指导，包括角色、情况、需要讨论的问题，老师也可以借介绍任务的机会介绍任务过程中需要使用的定式与词汇等等。

练习活动

 理解诠释1：预习单

先看课文，然后完成下面的作业：

一、根据课文进行填空。

　　教师采用任务教学的目的是利用任务让学生进行＿＿＿＿＿＿与＿＿＿＿＿＿。在设计任务以前，教师应该考虑五个基本组成部分。首先，从任务出发，制定＿＿＿＿＿＿，如，语言结构和语言功能，所谓的语言结构又包括＿＿＿＿＿和＿＿＿＿＿＿结构；其次，为学生提供完成任务的＿＿＿＿＿＿，可以是＿＿＿＿＿＿＿材料，＿＿＿＿＿材料和＿＿＿＿＿＿材料；第三是任务条件，好的任务常常包括＿＿＿＿，在设计任务时有三个原则，即，＿＿＿＿＿原则，＿＿＿＿＿原则，＿＿＿＿＿原则；第四个是任务完成的程序，包括＿＿＿＿、＿＿＿＿、＿＿＿＿三个阶段；最后是＿＿＿＿＿＿比方说，通过讨论得出一个结论，通过侦探故事＿＿＿＿＿＿。

二、以侦探故事的语言任务设计为例，说明在进行任务的程序中，帮助学生建立了哪些方面的意识？（可多选）

A. 语言输入　B. 语言意识　C. 差异意识　D. 语言输出　E. 语义协商

1. 教师把学生分成几组，然后给组内每个学生一段内容不同的文章。＿＿＿＿
2. 学生回家准备，理解负责的故事内容，查出生词的意思。＿＿＿＿
3. 学生向同学叙述他所负责的故事。＿＿＿＿
4. 小组同学一起决定故事的先后顺序，讨论细节，最后找出凶手。＿＿＿＿

理解诠释2：扩展阅读

> **任务设计程序说明单**
> ——谁偷了照相机
>
> **任务说明：**
>   这是一个侦探故事。星期四上课以前，你应该读完分配给你的故事，并且回答作业中的问题。在课堂中，你会向同学叙述你所知道的故事内容，也会听别的同学叙述故事的其他部分。这样一来，你们就可以知道完整的故事。接下来，通过和同学一块儿沟通、讨论，请你们找出到底是谁偷了照相机。
>
> **任务进行的程序：**
> 一、每个学生会分配到一段故事，每段故事的内容都不一样。
> 二、请你详细阅读你的故事，充分了解故事的经过和细节，然后回答星期二作业中和故事有关的问题。请不要把你的故事告诉其他同学。
> 三、在星期四的课堂中，你要告诉小组成员你所知道的故事内容。你能叙述越多细节越好，因此，上课以前请熟记你的故事。
> 四、听其他同学叙述故事时，如果你对故事的情节、相关细节或者字句有问题，可以随时向他提问。
> 五、在听完并了解完整的故事以后，你们的小组必须合作找出究竟谁是小偷，并且说明他是怎么偷照相机的。
> 六、最后，请你们选一位小组代表报告你们的调查结果，并说明你们基于什么理由做出这样的结论。其他小组成员可以协助小组代表做进一步的解释。
> 七、周末写作任务：请你撰写一份书面调查报告。在这份报告中，除了犯罪事实以外，你也可以发表个人对这个犯罪事件的看法。

1. 用自己的话总结这个任务设计的三个阶段分别是什么？
   ①前期任务：
   ②核心任务：
   ③后期任务：

2. 这张任务设计程序说明单上的哪些程序具体体现了任务设计的三个原则？（可多选）
   ①断层原则：
   ②信息双向原则：
   ③决策原则：

人际交流1：观摩课以后的讨论

李老师是一位K-12的新老师。在观摩了你的中文课以后，向你请教：

李老师： 许老师，刚才您的课真是太精彩了！在课上，您使用了任务教学法。我发现学生都很有兴趣，觉得很好玩儿，最重要的是他们通过完成任务进行了有效互动和语言使用。我还有几个问题想请教一下您。首先，在前期任务阶段，教师应该做什么？为什么？

你的回答： 【建议词汇和结构：A给B提供（具体的指导/任务内容的说明）；⋯包括⋯（角色/情况/定式/词汇）；subj.重视⋯；⋯如此一来，⋯（避免⋯）】

李老师： 其次，您认为上课的时候给学生任务是不是最好的办法？为什么？

你的回答： 【建议词汇和结构：实施任务；⋯的时候，给sb.充分的准备时间；A和B有很大的相关性；流利度；复杂度；避免+NP；subj.（研究/调查）证实⋯】

李老师： 最后，根据您的经验，任务本身应该有什么特点？实施这样的前期任务的好处是什么呢？

你的回答： 【建议词汇和结构：系统；有意义；语境清晰；⋯有助于+NP/VP（语言准确度）；避免+NP；subj.参与do sth.】

人际交流2：回复电子邮件

课后请教过你之后，李老师还有一些困惑，所以又给你写了一封电子邮件。请你给她回信。【建议词汇和结构：所谓的N是指⋯；有意义；真实；⋯包括⋯；讨论；辩论；角色扮演；信息交换；⋯有助于+NP/VP（引起互动/生生互动）；主角；subj.把+注意力/精力+集中/放在+VP（调整⋯/纠错/观察⋯/引导⋯）上；语言使用；准确度；复杂度】

许老师：

　　您好！今天上午观摩了您的课以后，我也想尝试使用任务进行教学。但是关于核心任务和后期任务，我还有一些困惑，想请教一下您：

第一，所谓的核心任务是指什么样的活动？其形式包括什么？
第二，在任务实施的过程中，教师和学生分别是什么角色？
第三，后期任务可以采用什么形式？这些形式各有什么优势？
第四，教师在后期任务阶段的角色是什么？
期待您的回复！

　　　　　　　　　　　　　　　　　　　　　　　李小东

表达演说：面试演讲

纽约国际私立高中要招聘一位中文教师。为了参加这次面试，请你准备一个5分钟的演讲，分享一个你所设计/实施过的任务，请包括以下内容：

1. 详细介绍这个任务设计的三个阶段。在每一个阶段，老师和学生的角色分别是什么？
2. 任务教学的优势是什么？请举例说明。
3. 在设计任务时，教师会面临什么困难？你认为应该如何克服这些困难？

建议词汇和结构：A给B提供NP；具体的指导；任务内容的说明；…包括…；角色；情况；定式；词汇；subj.重视…；…的时候，给sb.充分的准备时间； …如此一来，…（有助于/避免…）；A和B有很大的相关性；实施任务；subj.不断+VP（引起互动/调整…/引导…）；主角；生生互动；关键；subj.把+注意力/精力+集中/放在+VP（调整…/纠错/观察…/引导…）上；语言使用；准确度；复杂度；流利度

反思任务

一、前期任务：
根据任务教学设计的原则设计一个你要在教学示范实施的任务活动，你可以按照下面的框架来考虑自己的示范。

任务的五个基本组成部分	内容
教学目标	任务所需的词汇和语法结构：
	任务的功能：
用什么材料提供语言输入	
任务条件	
任务的程序	前期任务：
	核心任务：
	后期任务：
任务的预期结果	

二、核心任务：
和小组成员一起讨论各自设计的任务活动。讨论时，你也需要给小组成员提供意见和建议。

三、后期任务：
根据中期任务的讨论结果，修改你的任务设计。并在教学示范时体现并实施。

补充材料

[1] David Nunan. 2004. *Task-based Language Teaching*. Cambridge, England: Cambridge University Press. Retrieved from http://www.educ.ualberta.ca/staff/olenka.bilash/best%20of%20bilash/Task-based%20Language%20Teaching.pdf

[2] 我们的旅行计划（视频文件）网络链接 http://edu.chinese.cn/Edu/zh-CN/demonstration_lessons/article/2012-4/582.html

[3] Robert Martinez. 2013, June 17. Methodology Pills for Induced Reflection – No.10 Task-based Learning. (Video file). Retrieved from http://www.youtube.com/watch?v=ordimhxa_Bs

第八课　汉语语音与声调教学
On Instruction of Chinese Pronunciation and Tones

（文本形式：电子邮件）

> ➢ 关键词：
>   发音、声调、声母、韵母、舌位、卷舌、送气、圆唇
> ➢ 能力目标：
>   1. 学习者能理解诠释关于汉语发音及声调教学的专业讨论及论文。
>   2. 学习者能使用专业术语列举语音与声调教学的重要性。
>   3. 学习者能具体描述常见的发音难点。
>   4. 学习者能使用发音教学的相关专业词汇说明学生发音、声调困难的原因。
>   5. 学习者能针对发音难点说明教学策略。

课文全版 (Complete Version)

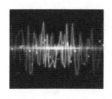

王丽和陈伟都是在美国中学任教[1]的汉语教师，新学期即将开始，两人在电子邮件里讨论对语音教学的看法。

陈老师：

新学期就要开始了，开学的准备工作都差不多了吧？前阵子[2]我看了一些关于语音[3]教学的文章[4]，想与您分享[5]，希望我们可以多多交流。

很多学者[6]认为，汉语的语音教学最重要的是教学生掌握发音部位[7]和方法。开始教声母[8]发音时，与其给学生讲解发音理论[9]，不如先给学生提供正确的发音示范[10]，让学生一边模仿[11]一边练习，同时，也可以配合[12]手势（如升调或降调[13]）或图示[14]。这些都有助于学生了解发音部位。

学生在学习第二语言时，容易受到母语的影响，出现母语负迁移[15]的现象，以母语为英语的学生为例，有两个较易出错的情况：

1. 无法卷舌[16]：

因英语没有相同的卷舌音，学生在面对zh、ch、sh、r等声母时，舌位[17]容易太靠前，舌头卷得不到位[18]，学者们建议利用图像[19]给学生看舌头的位置以及卷舌的动作过程图，让学生逐步[20]模仿。

[1]任教	rènjiào	V.	to be a teacher (formal)
[2]前阵子	qiánzhènzi	NP.	a short time ago
[3]语音	yǔyīn	N.	speech sound
[4]文章	wénzhāng	N.	article
[5]分享	fēnxiǎng	V.	to share
[6]学者	xuézhě	N.	scholar
[7]发音部位	fāyīnbùwèi	NP.	place of articulation
[8]声母	shēngmǔ	N.	initial consonant
[9]发音理论	fāyīnlǐlùn	NP.	theory of pronunciation
[10]示范	shìfàn	V./N.	to demonstrate; demonstration
[11]模仿	mófǎng	V.	to imitate, copy, model oneself
[12]配合	pèihé	V.	to act in concert with, to coordinate with
[13]降调	jiàngdiào	N.	falling tone
[14]图示	túshì	N.	instructional illustration
[15]负迁移	fùqiānyí	NP.	negative transfer
[16]卷舌	juǎnshé	V.	to retroflex
[17]舌位	shéwèi	N.	tongue position
[18]到位	dàowèi	V.	to reach the designated position
[19]图像	túxiàng	N.	image, picture
[20]逐步	zhúbù	Adv.	progressively, step-by-step

2. 辨别[21]送气[22]与否：
 汉语的p，t，k，q，ch，c和b，d，g，j，zh，z以送不送气为辨别的关键，学生可能将"吃菜"说成"吃再"。因此很多有经验的教师会请学生将一张纸放在嘴前，发送气音时纸会震动[23]，而发不送气音时纸则不会震动。用这种方法，可以让学生感觉发音时的气流[24]。除此之外，也可举一些对比性的例子，如"饱"和"跑"，"肚"和"兔"，使学生了解两个语音之间的不同。

 以上只是我的一点心得[25]，若[26]有不足[27]之处还请您多多指正[28]！
　敬祝
教安

王丽敬上
2014年12月28日

王老师：
 谢谢分享您的读书心得和宝贵[29]经验。上封信中，您讨论了关于汉语声母的教学，下面我想针对[30]汉语的韵母[31]，特别是i、u、ü，分享一些个人的教学心得。
 英语为母语的学生，对i和u并不陌生，但英语并没有ü的发音，学生不清楚圆唇[32]程度，容易造成发音不到位的问题。因此我个人建议，可以先发i和u，然后由i或u过渡[33]到ü。若由i开始，保持舌位不变，同时将嘴唇变圆并同时向前，就可发ü，但若由u开始，u是最高圆唇元音[34]，舌头一定要向后隆起[35]，发音时嘴的圆唇程度[36]不变，将舌头隆起，舌位向前发ü。让学生练习时，先发u再发ü，不断交替[37]练习，让学生在练习中体会唇形[38]与舌位移动[39]的关系。

---

[21]辨别	biànbié	V.	to differentiate, to distinguish, to discriminate
[22]送气	sòngqì	V.	to aspirate
[23]震动	zhèndòng	V.	to vibrate
[24]气流	qìliú	N.	airflow
[25]心得	xīndé	N.	experience, what one has learned from work, study, etc.
[26]若	ruò	Prep.	if
[27]不足	bùzú	Adj.	insufficient
[28]指正	zhǐzhèng	V.	to point out mistakes so that they can be corrected
[29]宝贵	bǎoguì	Adj.	precious
[30]针对	zhēnduì	V.	to aim/direct at
[31]韵母	yùnmǔ	N.	vowel (of a Chinese syllable)
[32]圆唇	yuánchún	V.	to round one's lips
[33]过渡	guòdù	V.	to cross over, to transition (to)
[34]元音	yuányīn	N.	vowel
[35]隆起	lóngqǐ	V.	to bulge, to rise
[36]程度	chéngdù	N.	degree, extent
[37]交替	jiāotì	V.	to alternate
[38]唇形	chúnxíng	N.	shape of the lips
[39]移动	yídòng	V.	to move, to shift

另外，我也想谈一点声调教学的体会。汉语的声调对区辨[40]意义有很大的影响，是语音教学的重点。

汉语的四个声调可分为五等分，一声为55，二声为35，三声为214，四声为51。

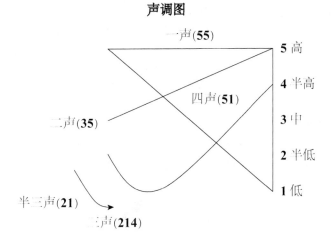

声调图

总的来说，以英语为母语的学生常有声调错误，分别是在缺乏[41]声调和读错声调这两个方面。造成缺乏声调的主要原因是英语是无声调语言，学生会把汉语的音节都发成一个调即中平调[42]。读错声调则是因学生经常把不同的声调相混淆[43]，如二声变三声，一声变四声，或用英语的语调[44]变化，代替[45]汉语的声调。

关于声调教学，我有两个建议：

1. 声调教学顺序：

   声调教学应从易到难，首先教最高调第一声，为其他三个声调定下基础调位[46]；接着教第四声，一声的高度可以当作四声的起点[47]；然后教第二声，以第四声的终点[48]为二声的起点，避免二声上升幅度[49]不够的情况；最后，学习第三声。

[40]区辨	qūbiàn	V.	to differentiate, to distinguish
[41]缺乏	quēfá	V.	to lack, to be short of
[42]中平调	zhōngpíngdiào	N.	mid-level tone
[43]混淆	hùnxiáo	V.	to confuse, to mix up
[44]语调	yǔdiào	N.	intonation, tone
[45]代替	dàitì	V.	to replace
[46]调位	diàowèi	N.	toneme
[47]起点	qǐdiǎn	N.	starting point
[48]终点	zhōngdiǎn	N.	ending point
[49]幅度	fúdù	N.	range, breadth

2. 由半三声[50]进入全三声

三声在汉语的四个声调中难度最高，学生容易在一开始起调不是太高就是太低，与二声混淆。但在实际语言交流中，半三声出现的频率[51]非常高，达到百分之八十。因此，半三声应该做为主要声调，和一声同时介绍，让学生先了解、掌握半三声，再进入全三声。

以上只是我个人的一点浅见[52]，与您的教学经验相比，我还需要多磨练[53]，请您不吝赐教[54]！

祝您身体健康！

陈伟敬上
2014年12月31日

语言重点：

1. …，(Subj.)与其A，不如B

…，(Subj.) rather B, than A

- 开始教声母发音时，与其给学生讲解发音理论，不如先给学生提供正确的发音示范，让学生一边模仿一边练习，同时，也可以配合手势（如升调或降调）或图示。
- 英语为母语的学生，对i和u并不陌生，但英语并没有ü的发音，学生不清楚圆唇程度，容易造成发音不到位的问题。因此我个人建议，与其直接教ü，不如先教i和u，然后由i或u过渡到ü。

2. …有助于+VP

to be contributive to/helpful with regard to

- 配合手势或图示有助于学生了解发音部位或气流方向等等。
- 声调教学应从易到难，首先教最高调第一声，为其他三个声调定下基础调位，这样有助于其他声调的学习。

3. …出现…的现象/问题/情况

there occurs a phenomenon/problem/situation of …

- 学生在学习第二语言时，容易受到母语的影响出现母语负迁移的现象。
- 三声在汉语的四个声调中难度最高，学生容易出现起调太高或太低的问题，有时也会出现与二声混淆的情况。

---

[50]半三声	bànsānshēng	NP.	half third tone (in a Mandarin syllable)
[51]频率	pínlǜ	N.	frequency
[52]浅见	qiǎnjiàn	N.	a humble opinion, a superficial view
[53]磨练	móliàn	V./N.	to temper oneself; discipline
[54]不吝赐教	búlìncìjiào	Idiom	to be generous in granting instruction

4. **Subj.受到sth./sb.的影响/限制**

    Subj. is influenced/restricted by sth./sb.

    - 学生在学习第二语言时，容易受到母语的影响出现母语负迁移的现象。
    - 由于受到发音习惯的限制，学生在面对zh、ch、sh、r等声母时，舌位容易太靠前，舌头卷得不到位。

5. **针对N，subj.…**

    aiming at/with regard to N, subj. …

    - 下面我想针对汉语的韵母，特别是 i、u、ü，分享一些简单的教学心得。
    - 针对三声难以习得的问题，现今多数汉语教师均采取由半三声进入全三声的策略。

6. **…造成/导致…的问题/情况/困难**

    … to lead to/result in problems/situations/difficulties

    - 学生不清楚圆唇程度，容易造成发音发不到位的问题。
    - 由于英语是无声调语言，这容易造成学生把汉语的音节都发成一个调的情况，即中平调。而导致读错声调的原因则是因学生经常把不同的声调相混淆，如二声变三声，一声变四声，或用英语的语调变化，代替汉语的声调。

7. **Subj.掌握+N（发音要领/规则/方法/知识/语法点）**

    Subj. grasps/masters N (the main points of pronunciation/rules/methods/knowledge/grammar)

    - 汉语的语音教学最重要的是教学生掌握发音部位和方法。
    - 学生只掌握语音规则远远不够，他们需要反复多次模仿练习，在实际交流中形成语音的发音习惯。

第八课　汉语语音与声调教学
On Instruction of Chinese Pronunciation and Tones

（文本形式：电子邮件）

> ➢ 关键词：
>   发音、声调、声母、韵母、舌位、卷舌、送气、圆唇
> ➢ 能力目标：
>   1. 学习者能理解诠释关于汉语发音及声调教学的专业讨论及论文。
>   2. 学习者能使用专业术语列举语音与声调教学的重要性。
>   3. 学习者能具体描述常见的发音难点。
>   4. 学习者能使用发音教学的相关专业词汇说明学生发音、声调困难的原因。
>   5. 学习者能针对发音难点说明教学策略。

课文节选版 (Abridged Version)

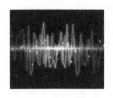

王丽和陈伟都是在美国中学任教[1]的汉语教师，新学期即将开始，两人在电子邮件里讨论对语音教学的看法。

陈老师：

新学期就要开始了，开学的准备工作都差不多了吧？前阵子[2]我看了一些关于语音[3]教学的文章[4]，想与您分享[5]，希望我们可以多多交流。

很多学者[6]认为，汉语的语音教学最重要的是教学生掌握发音部位[7]和方法。开始教声母[8]发音时，与其给学生讲解发音理论[9]，不如先给学生提供正确的发音示范[10]，让学生一边模仿[11]一边练习，同时，也可以配合[12]手势（如升调或降调[13]）或图示[14]。这些都有助于学生了解发音部位或气流[15]方向等等。

英语为母语的学生有两个较易出错的情况：

1. 无法卷舌：

因英语没有相同的卷舌[16]音，学生在面对zh、ch、sh、r等声母时，舌位[17]容易太靠前，舌头卷得不到位[18]，学者们建议利用图像给学生看舌头的位置以及卷舌的动作过程图，让学生逐步模仿。

---

[1]任教	rènjiào	V.	to be a teacher (formal)
[2]前阵子	qiánzhènzi	NP.	a short time ago
[3]语音	yǔyīn	N.	speech sound
[4]文章	wénzhāng	N.	article
[5]分享	fēnxiǎng	V.	to share
[6]学者	xuézhě	N.	scholar
[7]发音部位	fāyīnbùwèi	NP.	place of articulation
[8]声母	shēngmǔ	N.	initial consonant
[9]发音理论	fāyīnlǐlùn	NP.	theory of pronunciation
[10]示范	shìfàn	V./N.	to demonstrate; demonstration
[11]模仿	mófǎng	V.	to imitate, copy, model oneself
[12]配合	pèihé	V.	to act in concert with, to coordinate with
[13]降调	jiàngdiào	N.	falling tone
[14]图示	túshì	N.	instructional illustration
[15]气流	qìliú	N.	airflow
[16]卷舌	juǎnshé	V.	to retroflex
[17]舌位	shéwèi	N.	tongue position
[18]到位	dàowèi	V.	to reach the designated position

2. 辨别[19]送气[20]与否：
　　汉语的p、t、k、q、ch、c和b、d、g、j、zh、z以送不送气为辨别的关键，学生可能将"吃菜"说成"吃再"。因此很多有经验的教师会请学生将一张纸放在嘴前，发送气音时纸会震动[21]，而发不送气音时纸则不会震动。除此之外，也可举一些对比性的例子，如"饱"和"跑"，"肚"和"兔"，使学生了解两个语音之间的不同。

　　以上只是我的一点心得[22]，若有不足[23]之处还请您多多指正[24]！
　　　敬祝
　　教安

　　　　　　　　　　　　　　　　　　　　　　　　王丽敬上
　　　　　　　　　　　　　　　　　　　　　　　　2014年12月28日

王老师：
　　谢谢分享您的读书心得和宝贵[25]经验。上封信中，您讨论了关于汉语声母的教学，下面我想针对[26]汉语的韵母[27]，特别是i、u、ü，分享一些个人的教学心得。
　　英语为母语的学生，对i和u并不陌生，但英语并没有ü的发音，学生不清楚圆唇[28]程度，容易造成发音不到位的问题。因此我个人建议，可以先教i和u，然后由i或u过渡[29]到ü。若由i开始，保持舌位不变，同时将嘴唇变圆并同时向前，就可发ü，但若由u开始，u是最高圆唇元音[30]，舌头一定要向后隆起[31]，发音时嘴的圆唇程度[32]不变，将舌头隆起，舌位向前发ü。让学生练习时，先发u再发ü，不断交替[33]练习，让学生在练习中体会唇形[34]与舌位移动[35]的关系。
　　另外，我也想谈一点声调教学的体会。汉语的声调对区辨[36]意义有很大的影响，是语音教学的重点。

[19]辨别	biànbié	V.	to differentiate, to distinguish, to discriminate
[20]送气	sòngqì	V.	to aspirate
[21]震动	zhèndòng	V.	to vibrate
[22]心得	xīndé	N.	experience, what one has learned from work, study, etc.
[23]不足	bùzú	Adj.	insufficient
[24]指正	zhǐzhèng	V.	to point out mistakes so that they can be corrected
[25]宝贵	bǎoguì	Adj.	precious
[26]针对	zhēnduì	V.	to aim/direct at
[27]韵母	yùnmǔ	N.	vowel (of a Chinese syllable)
[28]圆唇	yuánchún	V.	to round one's lips
[29]过渡	guòdù	V.	to cross over, to transition (to)
[30]元音	yuányīn	N.	vowel
[31]隆起	lóngqǐ	V.	to bulge, to rise
[32]程度	chéngdù	N.	degree, extent
[33]交替	jiāotì	V.	to alternate
[34]唇形	chúnxíng	N.	shape of the lips
[35]移动	yídòng	V.	to move, to shift
[36]区辨	qūbiàn	V.	to differentiate, to distinguish

汉语的四个声调可分为五等分，一声为55，二声为35，三声为214，四声为51（见下图）。

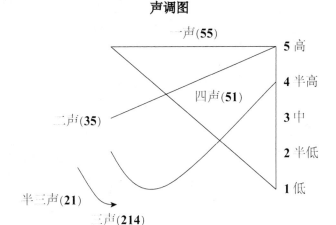

关于声调教我有两个建议：

1. 声调教学顺序：

   声调教学应从易到难，首先教最高调第一声，为其他三个声调定下基础调位[37]；接着教第四声，一声的高度可以当作四声的起点[38]；然后教第二声，以第四声的终点[39]为二声的起点，避免二声上升幅度[40]不够的情况；最后，学习第三声。

2. 由半三声[41]进入全三声

   三声在汉语的四个声调中难度最高，学生容易在一开始起调不是太高就是太低，与二声混淆。但在实际语言交流中，半三声出现的频率[42]非常高，达到百分之八十。因此，半三声应该做为主要声调，和一声同时介绍，让学生先了解、掌握半三声，再进入全三声。

   以上只是我个人的一点浅见[43]，与您的教学经验相比，我还需要多磨练[44]，请您不吝赐教[45]！

   祝您身体健康！

陈伟敬上
2014年12月31日

---

[37]调位	diàowèi	N.	toneme
[38]起点	qǐdiǎn	N.	starting point
[39]终点	zhōngdiǎn	N.	ending point
[40]幅度	fúdù	N.	range, breadth
[41]半三声	bànsānshēng	NP.	half third tone (in a Mandarin syllable)
[42]频率	pínlǜ	N.	frequency
[43]浅见	qiǎnjiàn	N.	a humble opinion, a superficial view
[44]磨练	móliàn	V./N.	to temper oneself; discipline
[45]不吝赐教	búlìncìjiào	Idiom	to be generous in granting instruction

语言重点：

1. **…，(Subj.)与其A，不如B**

   … , (Subj.) rather B, than A

   - 开始教声母发音时，与其给学生讲解发音理论，不如先给学生提供正确的发音示范，让学生一边模仿一边练习，同时，也可以配合手势（如升调或降调）或图示。
   - 英语为母语的学生，对i和u并不陌生，但英语并没有ü的发音，学生不清楚圆唇程度，容易造成发音不到位的问题。因此我个人建议，与其直接教ü，不如先教i和u，然后由i或u过渡到ü。

2. **…有助于+VP**

   to be contributive to/helpful with regard to

   - 配合手势或图示有助于学生了解发音部位或气流方向等等。
   - 声调教学应从易到难，首先教最高调第一声，为其他三个声调定下基础调位，这样有助于其他声调的学习。

3. **针对N，subj.…**

   aiming at/with regard to N, subj. …

   - 下面我想针对汉语的韵母，特别是 i、u、ü，分享一些简单的教学心得。
   - 针对三声难以习得的问题，现今多数汉语教师均采取由半三声进入全三声的策略。

4. **…造成/导致…的问题/情况/困难**

   … to lead to/result in problems/situations/difficulties

   - 学生不清楚圆唇程度，容易造成发音发不到位的问题。
   - 由于英语是无声调语言，这容易造成学生把汉语的音节都发成一个调的情况，即中平调。而导致读错声调的原因则是因学生经常把不同的声调相混淆，如二声变三声，一声变四声，或用英语的语调变化，代替汉语的声调。

5. **A对B有(很大/深刻的)影响**

   A has a (great) effect upon B

   - 汉语的声调对区辨意义有很大的影响。
   - 手势（如升调或降调）或图示对学生了解发音部位或气流方向等等有很大影响。

6. **Subj.掌握+N（发音要领/规则/方法/知识/语法点）**

   Subj. grasps/masters N (the main points of pronunciation/rules/methods/knowledge/grammar)

   - 汉语的语音教学最重要的是教学生掌握发音部位和方法。
   - 学生只掌握语音规则远远不够，他们需要反复多次模仿练习，在实际交流中形成语音的发音习惯。

练习活动

理解诠释1：预习单

先看课文，然后完成下面的作业：

一、根据课文进行填空。
  学生把"吃饱了"说成"吃跑了"是因为学生无法＿＿＿＿＿＿，而学生总是发不好"zh、ch、sh"是因为＿＿＿＿＿＿，所以汉语语音教学最重要的是让学生掌握＿＿＿＿＿＿和＿＿＿＿＿＿。

二、根据五度标记法，请分别标记"偏、误、模、仿"这四个汉字的声调，并在方框内分别画出这四个字的声调图。

例： 谈：二声（阳平），35
一声（阴平）＿＿＿＿＿
二声（阳平）＿＿＿＿＿
三声（上声）＿＿＿＿＿
四声（去声）＿＿＿＿＿

三、根据课文，判断下面的叙述是否正确？要是不正确请改正。

- 借助一张纸的方法可以教学生区别i, u和ü这组发音。
- 发u和ü这两个音时，唇形不变。
- 一个学了5年中文的学生总是把"我"说成"wó"，属于化石化现象。
- 汉语中，韵母的发音不存在送气与否的问题。
- 声调教学从易到难的顺序是：一声，四声，二声，三声。
- 在汉语中，半三声出现的频率高达80%。
- 双音节教学中应放慢速度，增加前后音节的停顿。

理解诠释2：扩展阅读

参考资料：http://www.goingker.com/kshy/study.html

z，c，s与zh，ch，sh的发音方法及舌位对比图

字母	发音特征		舌位图	发音方法	练习
z	舌尖音塞擦音清音	不送气音 / 舌尖前音		舌尖平伸，抵住上齿背	总则自在
zh		不送气音 / 舌尖后音		舌尖上翘，抵住硬腭前部	软腭上升，堵塞鼻腔通路，声带不颤动，较弱的气流把阻碍冲开一条窄缝，从窄缝中挤出，摩擦成声。	庄重主张
c		送气音 / 舌尖前音		舌尖平伸，抵住上齿背	粗糙参差
ch		送气音 / 舌尖后音		舌尖上翘，抵住硬腭前部	车床长城
s	舌尖音塞擦音清音	舌尖前音		舌尖接近上齿背	气流从窄缝中挤出，摩擦成声，声带不颤动。	思索松散
sh		舌尖后音		舌尖上翘，接近硬腭前部，留出窄缝	世说山水

1. 根据舌位对比图，下面哪个声母属于舌尖前音？
   A. z　　　　B. r　　　　C. zh　　　　D. ch

2. 根据上图，"z"和"c"在发音方法上存在什么差异？
   A. 塞擦音和擦音的不同　B. 不送气和送气的不同　C. 舌位的不同

3. 请从发音方法和舌位的变化两个方面来说明"中"和"充"两个字的声母在发音上的不同。

人际交流1：面对面讨论

今年夏天K-16暑期中文教师培训项目邀请北京语言大学的金教授来为学员们做了一个关于"语音教学"的讲座。在讲座开始以前，金老师围绕"语音教学"这个主题问了学员几个问题。

金教授：　各位学员大家好，很荣幸能有这个机会和大家分享我在语音教学方面的一些体会。听说今天参加讲座的学员都是在美国任教的中文老师，所以在开始讲座以前，我想先了解一下你们在语音教学方面的情况。首先，在课堂教学的过程中，你们有没有注意过语音方面出现的母语负迁移的现象？如果有，请给我一个例子。

你的回答：【建议词汇和结构：舌位；声母；韵母；Subj.受到…的影响/限制；subj.掌握+N（发音要领/规则/方法）；以…为例；Obj.难以+V（掌握/控制）】

金教授：　刚才很多学员都谈到了"zh""ch""sh"的问题。有没有学员有好的教学方法可以分享给大家？

你的回答：【建议词汇和结构：舌位；图像；模仿；避免+NP；V得到位/不到位；逐步+do sth.；…有助于…；针对N, subj.…；造成/导致…的问题/情况】

金教授：　谢谢各位学员的分享，其实声母和韵母教学还有很多值得探讨的方面，但是今天我主要将向你们分享声调教学的体会。在座的各位觉得声调教学重要吗？为什么？

你的回答：【建议词汇和结构：区辨；缺乏；误解；混淆；语调；代替；造成/导致…的问题/情况】

金教授：　正如大家所说，声调教学非常重要，但是很多老师尤其是非母语中文老师在进行声调教学时都遇到了很大的挑战，在此，我将分享一些我的浅见，希望对大家未来的教学有所帮助。……

人际交流2：电子邮件交流

　　金教授的"语音教学"讲座让K-16的学员收获颇丰。不久以后K-16暑期中文项目的其中一位学员给金教授发来了电子邮件，想向他请教一些关于声调教学的问题。下面是邮件的具体内容，请你看完以后代金教授给这位学员回信。【建议词汇和结构：调位；起点；重点；幅度；频率；区辨；尝试；针对+N, subj.…；subj.掌握+N（调位/发音部位/要领）；尽量+VP；Subj.把…重点放在…上/方面（，如此一来…）；Subj.不断+VP】

金教授：
　　您好！
　　我叫郝怡佳，是ACCK-16暑期中文培训项目的学员。前不久您为我们做的关于"语音教学"的讲座真是让我受益匪浅。回国以后，我采用了很多您在讲座上提到的语音教学的方法，这些方法都非常有效。真心感谢您的分享。
　　最近我在教学过程中还遇到了一个问题：一些学生在发三声的时候总是发不对，有的学生三声的问题好像已经化石化了。针对这样的问题，不知您有没有好的办法？请您不吝赐教！期待您的回复。
　　祝您工作顺利！

　　　　　　　　　　　　　　　　　　　　　　　　郝怡佳

 表达演说：教学报告

　　在学完本课以后，请你完成一篇500字的以发音教学为主题的报告，报告请包括以下内容：

1. 非母语教师在进行发音教学时常常遇到哪些困难？
2. 学生在学习发音时会出现哪些偏误？这些偏误产生的原因是什么？
3. 如何针对学生出现的发音问题进行教学？

建议词汇和结构：发音；声调；声母；韵母；舌位；卷舌；送气；圆唇；图像；针对+N, subj.…；subj.掌握+N（调位/发音部位/要领）；尽量+VP；尝试；subj.把…重点放在…上/方面（，如此一来…）；subj.不断+VP；V得到位/不到位；逐步+do sth.；模仿；…有助于…；针对N, subj.…；造成/导致…的问题/情况

反思任务

一、前期任务:
你将会收到一封学生的电子邮件,其中包括一段录音http://v.youku.com/v_show/id_XMjEwNDk1NDA4.html。请阅读电子邮件,并尝试依据录音中出现的语音问题制作一份语音检测单。

> 尊敬的老师:
> 　　您好!
> 　　我是加州圣马力诺市高中的一名学生。我学3年中文了。我很喜欢中文,可是我在发音方面有一些问题,您可以帮助我吗?谢谢您!
> 　　祝您工作顺利!
> 　　　　　　　　　　　　　　　　　　　　　　　　　　　小宝

二、核心任务:
就录音中出现的语音问题进行小组讨论,进一步完善语音问题检测单,并针对其中的问题找出有效的解决方法。

三、后期任务:
每位小组成员分别针对小宝录音中出现的一项问题,用语音的方式向小宝提出改善发音的建议。

 ## 补充材料

[1] Qian-jie Fu, Xin Luo. (2004). Enhancing Chinese tone recognition by manipulating amplitude envelope: Implications for cochlear implants. Retrieved from http://web.ics.purdue.edu/~luo5/JASA3659.pdf
[2] 王理嘉(2005),《汉语拼音方案与世界汉语语音教学》,【《世界汉语教学》(2005)】网络链接 http://jwc.tsu.edu.cn/sdqcg/lunwen/09/2005/2005_02_05.PDF
[3] 叶军(2003),《对外汉语教学语音大纲》,【云南师范大学学报(2003年01期)】网络链接 http://www.docin.com/p-436144481.html
[4] 拼音学习(音频文件)网络链接 http://kid.chinese.cn/pinyin/index.html

第九课　汉字教学
On Instruction of Chinese Literacy

（文本形式：专业演讲）

> ➢ 关键词：
>   汉字、阅读、语音意识、笔画、部首、部件、笔顺、组词、拆字
> ➢ 能力目标：
>   1. 学习者能理解诠释关于汉字教学的专业讨论及学术文章。
>   2. 学习者能使用专业术语叙述、说明汉字教学的重要性。
>   3. 学习者能够比较、分析不同的汉字教学策略。
>   4. 学习者能列举有效汉字学习策略的步骤。
>   5. 学习者能使用正式套语对汉字教学进行演讲。

课文全版 (Complete Version)

美国西北大学张教授应K-12项目之邀,到语言大学演讲"汉字教学"。以下是她的演讲:

大家好,很荣幸[1]今天和大家一起讨论关于汉字教学的课题。我的演讲将分为五个部分,首先是汉字教学的重要性,第二是汉字书写意识的培养,第三是汉字的教学方法探讨[2],第四是汉字的复习方法,最后是现场[3]老师们的交流分享。

一、汉字教学的重要性

阅读与汉字息息相关[4],认读[5]汉字是阅读与写作的基础[6]。阅读受到背景知识、语言信息以及文字书写知识三个因素影响。现在的研究发现(Just and Carpenter, 1987; Juel et al., 1986; Koda, 2007),识字不够就无法阅读。从学生第一年的识字能力就可以预测[7]今后的阅读能力。此外,没有阅读背景知识就无法进行深度[8]阅读。有些学生对汉字学习抱一种抗拒[9]的心态[10],不愿意把时间花在汉字练习上,认为只要能听会说就行了,不会读写又有什么关系?他们不知道其实一个人的字词识别[11]能力直接影响他的交际能力。因此,培养学生的汉字书写意识格外[12]重要。

二、培养汉字的书写意识

汉字的书写意识包括语音意识、笔画[13]意识和部首[14]、部件[15]意识,这是因为汉字是由字形[16]、字音、字义[17]组成的。以"天"为例,字形是"天",发音是"tiān",意思是sky,形、音、义三者密不可分[18]。研究发现汉语初学者对汉语字词的读音正确与否直接影响汉字的意义识别(Everson, 1998),我们从中得到的教学启示[19]是:学习汉字要先学读音再学写字,也就是先会说,再会写。

谈完语音意识,我接着要谈笔画意识。笔画是字形的基础,规律[20]的笔画顺序能帮助学生有效地记忆[21]汉字,减少记忆负担,有利于汉字很快

[1]荣幸	róngxìng	Adj.	honored
[2]探讨	tàntǎo	V.	to inquire into; probe into
[3]现场	xiànchǎng	N.	on-site
[4]息息相关	xīxīxiāngguān	VP.	be closely related to, be closely linked
[5]认读	rèndú	V.	to read and recognize (characters)
[6]基础	jīchǔ	N.	foundation, base
[7]预测	yùcè	V.	to predict
[8]深度	shēndù	Adj./N.	deep, thorough; depth, deepness
[9]抗拒	kàngjù	V.	to resist, defy
[10]心态	xīntài	N.	mentality, mindset
[11]识别	shíbié	V.	to discriminate, to identify
[12]格外	géwài	Adv.	especially, particularly
[13]笔画	bǐhuà	N.	stroke (of a character)
[14]部首	bùshǒu	N.	radical of a Chinese character
[15]部件	bùjiàn	N.	part(s) of a character
[16]字形	zìxíng	N.	form of a character
[17]字义	zìyì	N.	meaning (of words)
[18]密不可分	mìbùkěfēn	VP.	inextricably linked; inseparable
[19]教学启示	jiàoxuéqǐshì	NP.	enlightenment/inspiration (for teaching)
[20]规律	guīlǜ	N.	regularity
[21]记忆	jìyì	V./N.	to memorize; memory

从大脑中提取[22]。笔顺[23]为什么重要？打个比方[24]，我们的大脑[25]好比[26]电脑，记忆存储[27]和提取是有规律的，在大脑中建立的神经通路[28]是固定[29]的。如果记忆的信息每一次都不同，存储的地方就不同，提取方式也不同。例如，你这次写"口"字是画一个圈，下一次是从右写到左，再下一次又是另一种方式，光一个"口"就有三个记忆存储通路[30]，不但浪费[31]记忆容量[32]，而且当你要从大脑中提取"口"的时候，也会花掉更多时间去寻找确定。这就像一个人不把东西放在固定的地方，于是要找那个东西的时候，就想不起来到底放在哪里了。因此，教师怎么能不强调笔顺的重要性呢？

最后，我们要谈到部首、部件意识。汉字大致[33]可分为独体字[34]和合体字[35]。汉字并不完全是图画，而是由一个或几个部分组成的，而这些组成部分就是部首和部件，对掌握汉字起着很大的作用。学生知道了部首、部件和组合[36]方式后，学习汉字也就不那么难了。

三、汉字的教学方法探讨

过去，很多人之所以认为学汉字很困难是因为缺乏方法，这就是为什么有些学生投入[37]了大量的时间和精力[38]，学习效果[39]却不理想[40]的主要原因。最近中国的一位学者报告了一项实验[41]：她把学生分成两组，给一组学生先看汉字，帮他们拆解[42]汉字中的组成部件，要求他们抄写[43]，然后和原字比较有何不同，最后再试着用故事帮助他们记忆；而另一组学生，老师单单只让他们反复[44]地抄写汉字。研究结果显示[45]，第一组学生平均[46]抄

[22]提取	tíqǔ	V.	to retrieve
[23]笔顺	bǐshùn	N.	stroke order
[24]打个比方	dǎgebǐfāng	VP.	for example
[25]大脑	dànǎo	N.	brain
[26]好比	hǎobǐ	V.	to be just like
[27]存储	cúnchǔ	V.	to store
[28]神经通路	shénjīngtōnglù	NP.	[neurology] neural pathway
[29]固定	gùdìng	Adj.	fixed
[30]存储通路	cúnchǔtōnglù	NP.	[neurology] storage pathway
[31]浪费	làngfèi	V.	to waste
[32]记忆容量	jìyìróngliàng	NP.	memory capacity
[33]大致	dàzhì	Adv.	roughly, approximately
[34]独体字	dútǐzì	N.	a character that cannot be further deconstructed, e.g. 山，日，女
[35]合体字	hétǐzì	N.	a character that can be further deconstructed to parts, e.g. 江，男，妹
[36]组合	zǔhé	N./V.	combination; to combine
[37]投入	tóurù	V.	to throw (oneself) into, to invest in
[38]精力	jīnglì	N.	energy
[39]效果	xiàoguǒ	N.	effect
[40]不理想	bùlǐxiǎng	Adj.	imperfect, unsuitable
[41]一项实验	yíxiàngshíyàn	NP.	(an) experiment
[42]拆解	chāijiě	V.	to deconstruct
[43]抄写	chāoxiě	V.	to copy (by writing)
[44]反复	fǎnfù	Adv.	repeatedly
[45]显示	xiǎnshì	V.	to show, to reveal
[46]平均	píngjūn	Adj.	average; equally

写4.93次，正确率[47]就达到75%，而另一组平均抄写10.74次，正确率却只有57%。这个差异表明[48]：学习策略有利于正确地记忆汉字。

那么，学习汉字时有什么好方法呢？除了动手写以外，组词练习和拆字[49]练习也很有帮助。前者如"天明"，"天"是"天气"的"天"，"明"是"明天"的"明"；后者如"奇"，上面是"大"，下面是"可"。经过这样的提示[50]，学生很快就能记住一个新字了。

四、汉字的复习方法

老师应该怎么帮助学生复习汉字？首先，要把认读与书写结合起来，有计划地让学生复习，例如每天读一小段文章，在有意义、有目的的情况下，让汉字重复出现，加强[51]学生的印象。字单[52]的设计也很重要，这是一张我给一年级学生的字单，上面特别标明[53]拼音、意义、笔画数、部首、相关字词等，让学生在练习新字时，有意识地产生语音意识、字形意识和部首、部件意识，并且培养学生按笔顺书写的好习惯，如此一来，学习汉字就再也不是件难事了。

五、经验交流与分享：

以上是综合[54]我个人经验与学者研究的报告。在座的[55]都是经验丰富的老师，在您的教学中一定用过许多有效的方法或游戏。今天大家难得[56]有机会聚在一起[57]，能不能请大家分享一下汉字教学的经验或有效的方法呢？

下面是一些暑期中文教师培训班教师的经验分享记录：

1. 分析字词：把字写在白板后，让学生分析字的部件。
2. 使用工具：让学生使用不同的工具，如颜料[58]、毛笔、粉笔等，在纸上、地板上或黑板上写字，或手写在砂纸(sand paper)上。
3. 查字典：例如，让学生一起查字典，把有同样的部首的字或词联系起来。
4. 用花朵写字：在花蕊[59]上写部首，在花瓣[60]上写部件，让学生写完后再贴在教室里。

[47]正确率	zhèngquèlǜ	N.	ratio of accuracy
[48]表明	biǎomíng	V.	to make known, make clear, state clearly
[49]拆字	chāizì	V.	to deconstruct (a character)
[50]提示	tíshì	V./N.	to point out, to prompt; hint
[51]加强	jiāqiáng	V.	to reinforce, to enhance, to strengthen
[52]字单	zìdān	N.	character sheet
[53]标明	biāomíng	V.	to mark clearly
[54]综合	zōnghé	V.	to synthesize
[55]在座的	zàizuòde	N.	somebody present (at a meeting, banquet, etc.)
[56]难得	nándé	Adj.	hard to come by, rare
[57]聚在一起	jùzàiyìqǐ	VP.	to get together, to reunite
[58]颜料	yánliào	N.	paint, dye, pigment
[59]花蕊	huāruǐ	N.	stamen, pistil
[60]花瓣	huābàn	N.	petal

5. 想象汉字：例如，"片"，像是一个空手道[61]的人；"长"，是字母K中间加一横[62]。
6. 意义联想："茶"，有人在草（艹）木中间采茶。
7. 笔顺接力[63]：全班上台接力写字，大家检查笔顺是否正确。

语言重点：

1. **Subj.（对…）抱（着）…（抗拒/积极/试试看）的心态**

   Subj. has a (resistant/positive/trying) attitude toward sth.

   - 有些学生对汉字学习抱一种抗拒的心态，不愿意把时间花在汉字练习上。
   - 该学者的实验表明学习策略有利于正确地记忆汉字，因此我们应该对汉字学习抱着积极的心态，寻找有效的学习策略。

2. **只要…就行了，…（又）有什么关系？**

   as long as … is fine, what does … have to do with it?

   - 有些学生认为只要能听会说就行了，不会读写又有什么关系？
   - 对于笔顺学习这一问题，很多学习者有一个普遍的错误认识：只要写完以后别人看得懂就行了，我们用什么笔顺又有什么关系？

3. **Subj.由…组成**

   Subj. is composed of …

   - 汉字是由字形、语音、语义组成的。
   - 这张一年级学生的字单由拼音、意义、笔画数、部首、相关字词等几部分组成。

4. **A（就）好比B，…**

   can be compared to; A is just like B

   - 打个比方，我们的大脑好比电脑，记忆存储和提取是有规律的，在大脑中建立的神经通路是固定的。
   - 笔顺就好比找到汉字的地图，记得正确的笔顺就能快速准确地提取输出汉字的字形。

5. **Subj.之所以……是因为…**

   the reason subj. … is (because) …

   - 过去，很多学习者之所以认为学汉字很困难是因为缺乏方法。
   - 非母语教师之所以会受到很多学生的欢迎，是因为他们往往能从学习者的角度预期学生的困难。

---

[61]空手道　　kōngshǒudào　　N.　　Karate
[62]横　　　　héng　　　　　　N.　　horizontal character stroke
[63]接力　　　jiēlì　　　　　　V.　　to relay, work by relays

第九课　汉字教学
On Instruction of Chinese Literacy

（文本形式：专业演讲）

> 关键词：
> 汉字、阅读、语音意识、笔画、部首、部件、笔顺、组词、拆字
> 能力目标：
> 1. 学习者能理解诠释关于汉字教学的专业讨论及学术文章。
> 2. 学习者能使用专业术语叙述、说明汉字教学的重要性。
> 3. 学习者能够比较、分析不同的汉字教学策略。
> 4. 学习者能列举有效汉字学习策略的步骤。
> 5. 学习者能使用正式套语对汉字教学进行演讲。

课文节选版 (Abridged Version)

美国西北大学张教授应K-12项目之邀[1]到语言大学演讲"汉字教学"。以下是她的演讲:

大家好,很荣幸[2]今天和大家一起讨论关于汉字教学的课题[3]。我的演讲[4]将分为五个部分,首先是汉字教学的重要性,第二是汉字书写意识的培养,第三是汉字的教学方法探讨[5],第四是汉字的复习方法,最后是现场[6]老师们的交流分享。

一、汉字教学的重要性

阅读与汉字有关,认读[7]汉字是阅读与写作的基础[8]。阅读受到背景知识、语言信息,以及文字书写知识三个因素[9]影响。现在的研究发现(Just and Carpenter, 1987; Juel et al., 1986; Koda, 2007),没有阅读背景知识就无法进行深度[10]阅读,而且从学生第一年的识字能力[11]可以预测[12]今后的阅读能力。有些学生对汉字学习抱一种抗拒[13]的心态[14],不愿意把时间花在汉字练习上,认为只要能听会说就行了,不会读写又有什么关系?他们不知道其实一个人的字词识别[15]能力直接影响他的交际能力。因此,培养学生的汉字书写意识格外[16]重要。

二、培养汉字的书写意识

汉字的书写意识包括语音意识、笔画[17]意识和部首[18]、部件[19]意识,这是因为汉字是由字形[20]、字音、字义[21]组成的。以"天"为例,字形是"天",发音是"tiān",意思是sky,形、音、义三者密不可分[22]。研究发现汉语初学者对汉语字词的读音正确与否直接影响汉字的意义识别

---

[1]应邀	yìngyāo	VP.	to accept the invitation
[2]荣幸	róngxìng	Adj.	honored
[3]课题	kètí	N.	topic
[4]演讲	yǎnjiǎng	V./ N.	to speak; speech
[5]探讨	tàntǎo	V.	to inquire into; probe into
[6]现场	xiànchǎng	N.	on-site
[7]认读	rèndú	V.	to read and recognize (characters)
[8]基础	jīchǔ	N.	foundation, base
[9]因素	yīnsù	N.	factor
[10]深度	shēndù	Adj./N.	deep, thorough; depth, deepness
[11]能力	nénglì	N.	ability, capability, competence
[12]预测	yùcè	V.	to predict
[13]抗拒	kàngjù	V.	to resist, defy
[14]心态	xīntài	N.	mentality, mindset
[15]识别	shíbié	V.	to discriminate, to identify
[16]格外	géwài	Adv.	especially, particularly
[17]笔画	bǐhuà	N.	stroke (of a character)
[18]部首	bùshǒu	N.	radical of a Chinese character
[19]部件	bùjiàn	N.	part(s) of a character
[20]字形	zìxíng	N.	form of a character
[21]字义	zìyì	N.	meaning (of words)
[22]密不可分	mìbùkěfēn	VP.	inextricably linked; inseparable

(Everson, 1998)，我们从中得到的教学启示[23]是：学习汉字要先学读音再学写字，也就是先会说，再会写。

接下来谈笔画意识。笔画是字形的基础，规律[24]的笔画顺序能帮助学生有效地记忆[25]汉字，减少记忆负担，有利于汉字很快从大脑中提取[26]。

最后，我们要谈到部首、部件意识。汉字大致[27]可分为独体字[28]和合体字[29]。汉字并不完全是图画，而是由一个或几个部分组成的，而这些组成部分就是部首和部件。学生知道了部首、部件和组合[30]方式后，学习汉字也就不那么难了。

三、汉字的教学方法探讨

过去，很多人之所以认为学汉字很困难是因为缺乏[31]方法，这就是为什么有些学生投入[32]了大量的时间和精力[33]，学习效果[34]却不理想[35]的主要原因。近期中国的一位学者报告了一项实验[36]：她把学生分成两组，给一组学生先看汉字，帮他们拆解[37]汉字中的组成部件，要求他们抄写[38]，然后和原字比较有何不同，最后再试着用故事帮助他们记忆；而另一组学生，老师单单只让他们反复[39]地抄写汉字。研究结果显示[40]，第一组学生平均[41]抄写4.93次，正确率[42]就达到75%，而另一组平均抄写10.74次，正确率却只有57%。这个差异表明[43]：学习策略有利于正确地记忆汉字。

那么，学习汉字时有什么好方法呢？除了动手写以外，组词练习和拆字[44]练习也很有帮助。前者如"天明"，"天"是"天气"的"天"，

[23]教学启示	jiàoxuéqǐshì	NP.	enlightenment/inspiration (for teaching)
[24]规律	guīlǜ	N.	regularity
[25]记忆	jìyì	V./N.	to memorize; memory
[26]提取	tíqǔ	V.	to retrieve
[27]大致	dàzhì	Adv.	roughly, approximately
[28]独体字	dútǐzì	N.	a character that cannot be further deconstructed, e.g. 山，日，女
[29]合体字	hétǐzì	N.	a character that can be further deconstructed to parts, e.g. 江，男，妹
[30]组合	zǔhé	N./V.	combination; to combine
[31]缺乏	quēfá	V.	to lack
[32]投入	tóurù	V.	to throw (oneself) into, to invest in
[33]精力	jīnglì	N.	energy
[34]效果	xiàoguǒ	N.	effect
[35]不理想	bùlǐxiǎng	Adj.	imperfect, unsuitable
[36]一项实验	yíxiàngshíyàn	NP.	(an) experiment
[37]拆解	chāijiě	V.	to deconstruct
[38]抄写	chāoxiě	V.	to copy (by writing)
[39]反复	fǎnfù	Adv.	repeatedly
[40]显示	xiǎnshì	V.	to show, to reveal
[41]平均	píngjūn	Adj.	average; equally
[42]正确率	zhèngquèlǜ	N.	ratio of accuracy
[43]表明	biǎomíng	V.	to make known, make clear, state clearly
[44]拆字	chāizì	V.	to deconstruct (a character)

"明"是"明天"的"明";后者如"奇",上面是"大",下面是"可"。经过这样的提示[45],学生很快就能记住一个新字了。

四、汉字的复习方法

老师应该怎么帮助学生复习汉字?首先,要把认读与书写结合起来,有计划地让学生复习,例如每天读一小段文章,在有意义、有目的的情况下,让汉字重复出现,加强[46]学生的印象。字单的设计也很重要,这是一张我给一年级学生的字单,上面特别标明[47]拼音、意义、笔画数、部首、相关字词等,让学生在练习新字时,有意识地产生语音意识、字形意识和部首、部件意识,并且培养学生按笔顺[48]书写的好习惯,如此一来,学习汉字就再也不是件难事了。

五、经验交流与分享:

以上是综合[49]我个人经验与学者研究的报告。在座[50]都是经验丰富的老师,在您的教学中一定用过许多有效的方法或游戏。今天大家难得[51]有机会聚在一起[52],能不能请大家分享一下汉字教学的经验或有效的方法呢?

下面是一些暑期中文教师培训项目教师的经验分享记录:

1. 分析字词:把字写在白板后,让学生分析字的部件。
2. 使用工具:让学生使用不同的工具,如颜料[53]、毛笔、粉笔等,在纸上、地板上或黑板上写字。
3. 查字典:例如:让学生一起查字典,把有同样的部首的字或词联系起来。
4. 用花朵写字:在花蕊[54]上写部首,在花瓣[55]上写部件,让学生写完后再贴在教室里。
5. 想象汉字:例如:"片",像是一个空手道[56]的人;"长",是字母K中间加一横[57]。
6. 意义联想:"茶",有人在草(艹)木中间采茶。
7. 笔顺接力[58]:全班上台接力写字,大家检查笔顺是否正确。

[45]提示	tíshì	V./N.	to point out, to prompt; hint
[46]加强	jiāqiáng	V.	to reinforce, to enhance, to strengthen
[47]标明	biāomíng	V.	to mark clearly
[48]笔顺	bǐshùn	N.	stroke order
[49]综合	zōnghé	V.	to synthesize
[50]在座的	zàizuòde	N.	somebody present (at a meeting, banquet, etc.)
[51]难得	nándé	Adj.	hard to come by, rare
[52]聚在一起	jùzàiyìqǐ	VP.	to get together, to reunite
[53]颜料	yánliào	N.	paint, dye, pigment
[54]花蕊	huāruǐ	N.	stamen, pistil
[55]花瓣	huābàn	N.	petal
[56]空手道	kōngshǒudào	N.	Karate
[57]横	héng	N.	horizontal character stroke
[58]接力	jiēlì	V.	to relay, work by relays

语言重点：

1. **Subj.**（对…）抱（着）…（抗拒/积极/试试看）的心态

   Subj. has a (resistant/positive/trying) attitude toward sth.

   - 有些学生对汉字学习抱一种抗拒的心态，不愿意把时间花在汉字练习上。
   - 该学者的实验表明学习策略有利于正确地记忆汉字，因此我们应该对汉字学习抱着积极的心态，寻找有效的学习策略。

2. 只要…就行了，…（又）有什么关系？

   as long as … is fine, what does … have to do with it?

   - 有些学生认为只要能听会说就行了，不会读写又有什么关系？
   - 对于笔顺学习这一问题，很多学习者有一个普遍的错误认识：只要写完以后别人看得懂就行了，我们用什么笔顺又有什么关系？

3. **Subj.**由…组成

   Subj. is composed of …

   - 汉字是由字形、语音、语义组成的。
   - 这张一年级学生的字单由拼音、意义、笔画数、部首、相关字词等几部分组成。

4. **Subj.**之所以……是因为…

   the reason subj. … is (because) …

   - 过去，很多学习者之所以认为学汉字很困难是因为缺乏方法。
   - 非母语教师之所以会受到很多学生的欢迎，是因为他们往往能从学习者的角度预期学生的困难。

练习活动

 理解诠释1：预习单

先看课文，然后完成下面的作业：

一、下面的描述分别对应哪种汉字书写意识？请连线。

应该按照汉字的笔画顺序记忆　　　　　　　　　汉字部件意识
学习汉字时，应该先学读音再学写汉字　　　　　笔画意识
学习汉字时不能只是简单地反复抄写汉字　　　　语音意识

二、把下面十个汉字根据独体字和合体字的分类进行填空。
白、拆、因、出、耳、目、五、边、记、密

独体字	合体字

三、在上面的十个汉字中选择三个合体字，写出这些合体字的字形、语音、语义、笔顺和部首。

汉字			
字形			
语音			
语义			
笔顺			
部首			

四、根据课文，归纳总结汉字的复习方法。如果你在汉字教学的过程中有好的经验，请和大家分享。

理解诠释2：偏旁和部首

　　偏旁是合体字中常见的组成部分。人们习惯把汉字的上、下、左、右各部分统称偏旁。

　　偏旁是合体字的构字部件。古代人把左右结构的合体字的左方称为"偏"，右方称为"旁"，现在合体字各部位的部件统称为偏旁。如"语"字，由"言字旁"和"吾"两个偏旁组成；"盆"字由"分"和"皿字底"两个偏旁组成；"问"字由"门字框"和"口"两个偏旁组成。

　　部首是表义的偏旁。偏旁与部首是整体与部分的关系。把表义的偏旁叫做"部首"，起源于以《说文解字》为代表的古代字典。古代字典把具有共同形旁的字归为一部，称为"部首"。如"妈"、"妹"、"妙"、"姑"等字，具有共同的形旁"女"，"女"就是这部分字的部首。《新华字典》和《现代汉语词典》都有"部首检字表"。

　　部首是汉字中很有特色的构字部件，它构字能力强、利用率高，一个"三点水"（氵）与其他部件组合，可以构成500多个字。部首一般都有名称和明显的意义,可以帮助学生了解字义、记忆字形。部首有"旁"、"头"、"底"、"框"、"心"五种类型,一般说来,在上称"头",如花字中的"艹",称草字头;在下称"底",如盆字中的"皿",称皿字底;在左称"旁",如铁字中的"钅",称金字旁;在右称"边",如料字中的"斗",称斗字边;在外称"框",如冈字中的"冂",称同字框。利用部首纠正错别字也能收到很好的效果,例如,学生常把"爬"字的左边写成"瓜",把"恭"的下边写成"水"字的样子,如果他们明白了"爬"要用"爪"、"恭"是内心的一种感情,就不会把"爪"写成"瓜"、把""(心字底)写成"水"了。

常见偏旁部首:

部首	名称	意义	部首	名称	意义
冫	两点水	多与冰或寒冷有关	冖	秃宝盖	多与覆盖有关
卩	单耳刀	多与人或屈体有关	刂	立刀旁	多与金属有关
夂	建字底	多与脚的动作、行动有关	人	人字头	多与人有关
辶	走之旁	多与行走、行动有关	纟	绞丝旁	多与丝、线、织有关
贝	贝字旁	多与钱财有关	日	日字旁	多与太阳、时间有关
灬	四点底	多与火有关	月	月字旁	多与时间、身体有关
心	心字底	多与内心活动有关	礻	示字旁	多与祭祀、祝愿有关
钅	金字旁	多与金属有关	目	目字旁	多与眼睛有关
疒	病字旁	多与疾病有关	衤	衣字旁	多与衣服有关
竹	竹字头	多与竹类植物有关	王	王字旁	多与玉有关
亻	单立人	多与人有关	讠	言字旁	多与说话有关
阝	左耳旁	多与土石或升降等有关	阝	右耳旁	多与城镇、地名等有关
艹	草字头	多与花草植物有关	扌	提手旁	多与手或手的动作有关
口	口字旁	多与口或表语气有关	囗	方框儿	多指围起来
彳	双立人	多与行走或道路有关	犭	反犬旁	多与兽类动物有关
饣	食字旁	多与食物或吃有关	氵	三点水	多与水有关
忄	竖心旁	多与内心活动有关	宀	宝盖头	多与房屋有关

1. 关于"偏旁",下列哪个叙述是错的:
   A. 偏旁是构字部件
   B. 偏旁可以在字的上、下、左、右边,或者字的中间
   C. 部首是表明意义的偏旁
   D. 每个汉字都有偏旁

2. 在汉字教学中,为何需要强调部首?(四选二)
   A. 部首有助于学生了解字义   B. 可以利用部首构成很多字
   C. 部首的笔画很少,很简单   D. 可以避免母语的负迁移

3. 部首一般都有名称。由于几个汉字的读音一样,一般人为了区辨字形,在告诉别人哪个字的时候,会加以描述。比如认识的"识",是"言字旁",右边一个"只";"笔"是竹字头,下面一个"毛"。请你利用这个方法描述一下"忙"、"实"、"闷"和"淇"这四个字。

4. 如果有人告诉你 "精""清""请""睛"的部首是一样的,这个说法有问题吗?如果有,请你指出错误并加以解释。

人际交流1:心得交流

张教授应K-12项目之邀,到语言大学演讲"汉字教学"。你听了以后觉得很有收获,和另一位来参加的老师讨论了起来。

王老师: 我以前虽然知道阅读很重要,上课时也会花一些时间教写字,但是没想到学生的交际能力会直接受到字词识别能力的影响。

你的回答: 是啊。【建议词汇和结构:A和B息息相关;只要…就行了,…(又)有什么关系;基础;Subj.受到sth.的限制/影响;预测;培养;格外+(重要/紧张)】

王老师: 你说的一点都不错。刚才张教授提到汉字的书写意识包括三个部分,分别是语音、笔画和什么,你记下来了吗?为什么他特别强调笔顺的重要性呢?

你的回答: 另外一个是部首、部件意识。【建议词汇和结构:之所以…是因为…;规律;减轻/加重(工作/学习/记忆)的负担;提取;神经通路;储存通路;固定;A(就)好比B,…;浪费】

王老师: 我以后上课得好好强调笔顺的重要性了。对了,你一般是怎么帮助学生克服学习汉字的心理障碍的,能不能跟我分享一下?

你的回答: 好啊。【建议词汇和结构:subj.(对…)抱(着)…(抗拒/积极/试试看)的心态;通过…(提问/大量的输入/认读)检测/重复…;subj.(不断)重复+V/N(读/写/出现);拆解;字形;字义;部件;部首;提示;加强】

王老师: 太好了,谢谢,谢谢。我们今后应该多找机会交流,互相学习。

人际交流2：电子邮件

一个在家教的朋友给你写信，提到他最近遇到的困难。请你读了之后给她回信。

志荣：

　　好久不见，你最近好吗？我前一阵子接了一个家教，是个高中生。他很聪明，学得很快，但就是不愿意花时间和精力学汉字，对汉字学习抱着很强的抗拒心态。

　　你我都知道汉字是阅读的基础，而阅读又和交际能力密不可分。你自己学过中文，现在又是中文老师，能不能跟我分享分享你的学习经验或教学经验？这将对我和我的学生有很大的帮助。谢谢。

　　祝　顺心

　　　　　　　　　　　　　　　　　　　　　　　美幸

【建议词汇和结构：A和B息息相关；只要…就行了，…（又）有什么关系；subj.受到sth.的限制/影响；…有必要+do sth.；识别；独体字；合体字；subj.由…组成；拆解；字形；字义；规律；记忆；提取；反复；抄写；加强；A（就）好比B，…】

 表达演说：心得报告

请你写一份400–500字的心得报告，谈谈你对张教授"汉字教学"演讲的心得。由于这份报告写完后要交给语言大学的教授批阅，因此请你在报告的最后客气地请他指正。

这份心得报告请至少分三段书写，内容包括：

1. 汉字教学的重要性（学者的研究有什么教学启示？）
2. 汉字教学方法（实验结果表明了什么？）
3. 这个演讲对你的启发（比如反思自己的学习/教学过程、你以后将如何规划课程…等）

建议词汇和结构：之所以…是因为…；subj.（对…）抱（着）…【抗拒/积极/试试看】的心态；…造成/导致…的问题/情况/困难；预测；A和B密不可分；探讨；能力；基础；语音意识；笔画意识；部首部件意识；subj.由…组成；规律；记忆；提取；…，(subj.)与其A…，不如B；反复；缺乏+N；格外+（重要/紧张）；减轻/加重（工作/学习/记忆）的负担；…有助于…；不吝赐教

反思任务

一、前期任务

选择5个汉字，并准备一节汉字课介绍这五个汉字，介绍内容包括以下几个部分：

1. 如何给学生介绍这个汉字的部件、部首、笔顺以及笔画。
2. 如何给学生介绍这个字的来历、造字方法、发展的过程。
3. 将采用什么有意思的课堂活动来让学生学习这个汉字。

二、核心任务

三位成员一组，彼此介绍自己的汉字课。每位小组成员除了介绍自己的汉字课以外，还要给别的小组成员反馈意见，分享自己的教学经验。

三、后期任务

每位小组成员根据中期任务的讨论结果，选择一个汉字介绍一个有效的教授方法，形成书面报告。

补充材料

[1] Shen, Helen H. and Ke, Chuanren. (2007). *Radical Awareness and Word Acquisition Among Nonnative Learners of Chinese*. Retrieved from http://onlinelibrary.wiley.com/doi/10.1111/j.1540-4781.2007.00511.x/abstract
[2] Shen, Helen H. (2010). Imagery and verbal coding approaches in Chinese vocabulary instruction. *Language Teaching Research*, vol. 14:4, pp. 485–499. Retrieved from http://ltr.sagepub.com/content/14/4/485.short
[3] Michael E. Everson (2011). Word Recognition among Learners of Chinese as a Foreign Language: Investigating the Relationship between Naming and Knowing. *The Modern Language Journal*, vol. 82:2, pp. 194–204. Retrieved from http://onlinelibrary.wiley.com/doi/10.1111/j.1540-4781.1998.tb01192.x/abstract
[4] 汉字五千年（视频文件）网络链接 http://edu.chinese.cn/zh-CN/onlinelearning/node_22118.htm
[5] 写字帖

Part II
文化篇 (Culture)

第一课　《隐形[1]的翅膀[2]》歌词赏析[3]
　　　　　—网络文章改写
A Popular Chinese Song and its Social Impact

（文本形式：博客）

> ➢ 关键词：
>   励志歌曲、坚定、信念、成长、目标、追求、梦想
> ➢ 能力目标：
>   1. 学习者能理解诠释歌词的内涵和思想感情。
>   2. 学习者能介绍、描述歌曲中的人物形象。
>   3. 学习者能赏析中文励志歌曲。
>   4. 学习者能比较、分析中美励志歌曲的异同。

---

[1] 隐形　yǐnxíng　Adj.　invisible
[2] 翅膀　chìbǎng　N.　wing
[3] 赏析　shǎngxī　V.　to appreciate and analyze

课文全版 (Complete Version)

《隐形的翅膀》歌词：http://www.9ku.com/geci/74858.htm

词曲：王雅君

歌手：张韶涵

《隐形的翅膀》是一首流行歌曲，与此同时[4]，也是一首励志[5]歌曲，非常适合现在的年轻人，因此受到广泛[6]的关注和好评[7]。

所谓的"隐形的翅膀"是指什么呢？毫无疑问[8]，指的是坚定[9]的信念[10]。

每一次 都在徘徊孤单中坚强
每一次 就算很受伤也不闪泪光

在成长的道路上，绝大部分人都不是一帆风顺[11]的，都在徘徊[12]中前行，有时候也会感到孤单[13]。每一次失败，都会让人的心越来越成熟。这种成熟是被迫[14]的，因为成长的道路不能依赖[15]于前人的经验，必须自己走过去，才能明白。所以，只有坚强[16]才能让自己慢慢地成长。在这条道路上，很多人，渐渐地学会了就算受伤[17]也不会流泪[18]。因为，泪水[19]代表懦弱[20]和幼稚[21]。

我知道 我一直有双隐形的翅膀
带我飞 飞过绝望

这双隐形的翅膀，其实就是一种坚定的信念。坚信[22]自己能成功，坚信自己不比别人差。每个人，都相信自己有一双翅膀，这双翅膀会带我们飞过绝望[23]。其实在成长的道路上，有时候绝望只是现实离自己的目标很

[4]与此同时	yǔcǐtóngshí	Adv.	meanwhile, at the same time
[5]励志	lìzhì	Adj.	inspirational; be determined to fulfill one's aspirations
[6]广泛	guǎngfàn	Adj.	broad, extensive, wide-ranging
[7]好评	hǎopíng	N.	favorable criticism/comment
[8]毫无疑问	háowúyíwèn	Idiom.	without a doubt
[9]坚定	jiāndìng	Adj.	firm; steadfast
[10]信念	xìnniàn	N.	belief; conviction; faith
[11]一帆风顺	yìfānfēngshùn	Idiom.	plain sailing, all smooth sailing (successful)
[12]徘徊	páihuái	V.	to hang about; to pace back and forth, to hesitate, to linger
[13]孤单	gūdān	Adj.	alone, lonely
[14]被迫	bèipò	V.	to be forced, to be compelled
[15]依赖	yīlài	V.	to rely on, to depend on
[16]坚强	jiānqiáng	Adj.	strong, firm, staunch
[17]受伤	shòushāng	V.	to be injured; to get hurt
[18]流泪	liúlèi	V.	to shed tears
[19]泪水	lèishuǐ	N.	tears
[20]懦弱	nuòruò	Adj.	cowardly; weak
[21]幼稚	yòuzhì	Adj.	childish
[22]坚信	jiānxìn	V.	to firmly believe
[23]绝望	juéwàng	N./Adj.	desperation/despair; hopeless

远而已，远远没有到绝望的程度。只要自己不放弃，就有机会飞得高，飞得远。

不去想 他们拥有美丽的太阳

身边有许多一帆风顺的人，有的事业成功，有的有好运气，看到别人轻松地生活，也许你会不禁[24]产生一种不平的心理，但是这种心理不平衡[25]对我们没有任何好处。所以，虽然他们的太阳是美丽的，但是，我们不会羡慕他们的世界。对我们而言，最重要的就是做好自己。

我看见 每天的夕阳[26]也会有变化

每天的夕阳都在变化，也许是色彩[27]的变化，也许是夕阳下的风景[28]在改变，也许是夕阳下的人在改变。这个部分表达的意思是只要不断努力，追求梦想，自己的世界也会渐渐地发生变化。这种变化也会进一步坚定自己的信念。

我知道 我一直有双隐形的翅膀
带我飞 给我希望

有时候，带给我们希望的是家人和朋友，但是，很多时候是我们自己。没想到自己会发生这样的变化，没想到自己会在失败中慢慢地成长。

我终于 看到 所有梦想都开花
追逐[29]的年轻 歌声多嘹亮[30]
我终于翱翔[31] 用心凝望[32]不害怕
哪里会有风 就飞多远吧

最好的几句歌词就在这里。通过坚持，我们成功了。我们看到所有的梦想都在开花[33]，所以我们开始享受成功的快乐，大声的歌唱。

在自己的天空翱翔的时候不再害怕，因为我们已经做好了准备。我们用心凝望着这个曾经让我们困惑[34]的世界。这种不知道自己能做什么的困惑，同样存在于中国的高等学府[35]里，大学生们用几年的时间问自己，到底我能做什么。他们用自己的努力去回答这个问题。一次次的实习申请，一次次的面试，一份又一份的简历。在这个过程中，他们用心凝望，渐渐地找到了答案，他们明白自己能做很多事情。对于他们而言，哪里有风，

[24]不禁	bùjīn	Adv.	can't help (doing sth.); can't refrain from
[25]平衡	pínghéng	Adj.	balanced, in a state of equilibrium
[26]夕阳	xīyáng	N.	the setting sun
[27]色彩	sècǎi	N.	hue, tinge
[28]风景	fēngjǐng	N.	scenery, landscape
[29]追逐	zhuīzhú	V.	to pursue, to chase
[30]嘹亮	liáoliàng	Adj.	loud and clear
[31]翱翔	áoxiáng	V.	to soar, to flutter
[32]凝望	níngwàng	V.	to gaze or stare at
[33]开花	kāihuā	V.	to blossom, to flower
[34]困惑	kùnhuò	N./Adj.	perplexity; confused
[35]高等学府	gāoděngxuéfǔ	NP.	institution of higher learning

他们就能飞多远。尽管这种情况会因为个人的具体情况而产生不同，但是，歌词要表示的，就是人们所追求的梦想。

隐形的翅膀 让梦恒久[36]比天长
留一个愿望 让自己想象

我们都希望我们的梦能够比天长。与此同时，每个人的心中都会留一个很美的愿望，为了那个梦想，不断努力。因为有梦想，就会永远充满希望。

综上所述[37]，通过《隐形的翅膀》我们看到了一位有着坚定信念，在成长的道路上，虽然经历了一次又一次的失败，但仍然不放弃，坚持追求自己的梦想，最终获得成功的青年形象[38]。正是因为这个健康向上的青年形象，才使这首歌曲成为近年来众多励志歌曲中的经典之作[39]。

 语言重点：

1. …，与此同时，…

   at the same time/meanwhile …

   - 《隐形的翅膀》是一首流行歌曲，与此同时，也是一首励志歌曲。
   - 北京是一座拥有众多跨国公司的国际化大都市，与此同时，它也是中国的政治和文化中心。

2. A受到（B的）广泛+V（关注/好评/重视/欢迎）

   A receives B's extensive attention/favorable criticism/value/welcome

   - 这首励志歌曲非常适合现在的年轻人，因此受到广泛的关注和好评。
   - 随着星谈项目有效教学策略的推广，利用各种科技及媒体教材组织教学的方式受到广泛的欢迎。

3. 毫无+N（疑问/信念/目标/变化/准备）

   Without the least amount of/without a trace of (a) doubt/conviction/goal/change/preparation

   - 毫无疑问，"隐形的翅膀"指的是坚定的信念。
   - 在成长的道路上一定会有很多毫无目标的人在徘徊。

---

[36]恒久	héngjiǔ	Adj.	permanent, enduring
[37]综上所述	zōngshàngsuǒshù	Idiom.	in conclusion, in summary, to sum up
[38]形象	xíngxiàng	N.	image; form; figure
[39]经典之作	jīngdiǎnzhīzuò	NP.	classic

4. **A依赖于B（sb./sb.的帮助/前人的经验/…关系/…条件）**

   A depends on B (sb./sb.'s help/the experience of predecessors/ … relationship/ … conditions)

   - 成长的道路不能依赖于前人的经验，必须自己走过去，才能明白。
   - 过去发展中国家的经济增长依赖于发达国家，现在这种状况正在开始改变，中国是这一变化最主要的例子。

5. **Subj.渐渐地+VP（学会/明白/发生变化/产生）**

   Subj. gradually + VP (learns/understands/undergoes changes/gives rise to)

   - 在这条道路上，很多人，渐渐地学会了就算受伤也不会流泪。
   - 这个部分表达的意思是只要不断努力，追求梦想，自己的世界也会渐渐地发生变化。

6. **Subj.（只是…而已，）远远没有到…（绝望/放弃/发达国家）的程度**

   Subj. (is merely … and that is all) far from reaching the level/degree of (desperation/giving up/developed countries)

   - 其实在成长的道路上，我们有时候绝望只是现实离自己的目标很远而已，远远没有到绝望的程度。
   - 近几年中国只是经济发展迅速而已，但是远远没有到发达国家的程度。

7. **Subj.不禁+VP（产生…心理/怀疑/流泪/感到）**

   Subj. can't help (generating … mentality/doubt/weeping/feeling)

   - 看到别人轻松的生活，也许你会不禁产生一种不平的心理。
   - 目前多数年轻人会利用外国影视作品来学习外语，让人不禁怀疑他们会更多注意影视作品的内容还是语言。

8. **对（于）sb.而言，…**

   Regarding sb., … ; as far as sb. is concerned …

   - 我们不会羡慕他们的世界。对我们而言，最重要的就是做好自己。
   - 对于母语为英语的学生而言，汉语语音中的卷舌音常常是发音的难点。

9. **Subj.因（为）…而+do sth.**

   Subj. because/on account of/owing to … and so + do sth.

   - 这种情况会因为个人的具体情况而产生不同。
   - 许多来到华人地区生活的人，常常因不理解特殊的禁忌文化而感到不可思议。

10. ① **sb.充满+abstract N**（希望/信心/自信）

   Sb. is full of/brimming with + abstract N. (hope/faith/confidence)

   ② **sb.对+NP/VP**（未来/实现梦想）充满+希望/信心/自信

   Sb. is full of/brimming with + hope/faith/confidence for (the future/realizing their dreams)

   - 因为有梦想，就会永远充满希望。
   - 坚定的信念让我们对未来充满信心。

11. 综上所述，…

   in conclusion, in summary, to sum up

   - 综上所述，通过《隐形的翅膀》我们看到了一位有着坚定信念，在成长的道路上，虽然经历了一次又一次的失败，但仍然不放弃，坚持追求自己的梦想，最终获得成功的青年形象。
   - 综上所述，流行歌曲不仅是语言流行趋势与变化的表现，也展现了社会价值观念与主流文化的改变。

第一课　《隐形[1]的翅膀[2]》歌词赏析[3]
—网络文章改写
A Popular Chinese Song and its Social Impact

（文本形式：博客）

> ➢ 关键词：
> 励志歌曲、坚定、信念、成长、目标、追求、梦想
> ➢ 能力目标：
> 1. 学习者能理解诠释歌词的内涵和思想感情。
> 2. 学习者能介绍、描述歌曲中的人物形象。
> 3. 学习者能赏析中文励志歌曲。
> 4. 学习者能比较、分析中美励志歌曲的异同。

---

[1]隐形　yǐnxíng　Adj.　invisible
[2]翅膀　chìbǎng　N.　wing
[3]赏析　shǎngxī　V.　to appreciate and analyze

课文节选版 (Abridged Version)

《隐形的翅膀》歌词：http://www.9ku.com/geci/74858.htm
词曲：王雅君
歌手：张韶涵

《隐形的翅膀》是一首流行歌曲，与此同时[4]，也是一首励志[5]歌曲，非常适合现在的年轻人，因此受到广泛[6]的关注和好评[7]。

所谓的"隐形的翅膀"指的是坚定[8]的信念[9]。

每一次 都在徘徊孤单中坚强
每一次 就算很受伤也不闪泪光

在成长的道路上，大部分人都不是一帆风顺[10]的，都在徘徊[11]中前行，有时候也会感到孤单[12]。每一次失败，都会让人的心越来越成熟。只有坚强[13]才能让自己慢慢地成长。在这条道路上，很多人，渐渐[14]地学会了就算受伤[15]也不会流泪[16]。因为，泪水[17]代表懦弱[18]和幼稚[19]。

我知道 我一直有双隐形的翅膀
带我飞 飞过绝望

这双隐形的翅膀，其实就是一种坚定的信念。坚信[20]自己能成功，坚信自己不比别人差。每个人都相信自己有一双翅膀，这双翅膀会带我们飞过绝望[21]。只要自己不放弃，就有机会飞得高，飞得远。

不去想 他们拥有美丽的太阳

身边有许多一帆风顺的人，有的事业成功，有的有好运气。虽然他们的太阳是美丽的，但是，我们不会羡慕他们的世界。对我们而言，最重要的就是做好自己。

[4]与此同时	yǔcǐtóngshí	Adv.	meanwhile, at the same time
[5]励志	lìzhì	Adj.	inspirational; be determined to fulfill one's aspirations
[6]广泛	guǎngfàn	Adj.	broad, extensive, wide-ranging
[7]好评	hǎopíng	N.	favorable criticism/comment
[8]坚定	jiāndìng	Adj.	firm; steadfast
[9]信念	xìnniàn	N.	belief; conviction; faith
[10]一帆风顺	yìfānfēngshùn	Idiom.	plain sailing, all smooth sailing (successful)
[11]徘徊	páihuái	V.	to hang about; to pace back and forth, to hesitate, to linger
[12]孤单	gūdān	Adj.	alone, lonely
[13]坚强	jiānqiáng	Adj.	strong, firm, staunch
[14]渐渐	jiànjiàn	Adv.	gradually
[15]受伤	shòushāng	V.	to be injured; to get hurt
[16]流泪	liúlèi	V.	to shed tears
[17]泪水	lèishuǐ	N.	tears
[18]懦弱	nuòruò	Adj.	cowardly; weak
[19]幼稚	yòuzhì	Adj.	childish
[20]坚信	jiānxìn	V.	to firmly believe
[21]绝望	juéwàng	N./Adj.	desperation/despair; hopeless

我看见 每天的夕阳也会有变化

每天的夕阳[22]都在变化，也许是色彩[23]的变化，也许是夕阳下的风景[24]在改变，也许是夕阳下的人在改变。这个部分表达的意思是只要不断努力，追求梦想，自己的世界也会渐渐地发生变化。这种变化，也会进一步坚定自己的信念。

我知道 我一直有双隐形的翅膀
带我飞 给我希望

有时候，带给我们希望的是家人和朋友，但是，很多时候是我们自己。

我终于 看到 所有梦想都开花
追逐的年轻 歌声多嘹亮[25]
我终于 翱翔 用心凝望不害怕
哪里会有风 就飞多远吧

最好的几句歌词就在这里。通过坚持，我们成功了。我们看到所有的梦想都在开花[26]，所以我们开始享受成功的快乐，大声的歌唱。

在自己的天空翱翔[27]的时候不再害怕，因为我们已经做好了准备。我们用心凝望[28]着这个曾经让我们困惑[29]的世界。这种不知道自己能做什么的困惑，同样存在于中国的高等学府[30]里，大学生们用几年的时间问自己，到底我能做什么。他们用自己的努力去回答这个问题。一次次的实习申请，一次次的面试，一份又一份的简历[31]。在这个过程中，他们用心凝望，渐渐地找到了答案，他们明白自己能做很多事情。对于他们而言，哪里有风，他们就能飞多远。歌词要表示的，就是人们所追求的梦想。

隐形的翅膀 让梦恒久[32]比天长
留一个愿望 让自己想象

我们都希望我们的梦能够比天长。与此同时，每个人的心中都会留一个很美的愿望[33]，为了那个梦想，不断努力。因为有梦想，就会永远充满希望。

---

[22]夕阳	xīyáng	N.	the setting sun
[23]色彩	sècǎi	N.	hue, tinge
[24]风景	fēngjǐng	N.	scenery, landscape
[25]嘹亮	liáoliàng	Adj.	loud and clear
[26]开花	kāihuā	V.	to blossom, to flower
[27]翱翔	áoxiáng	V.	to soar, to flutter
[28]凝望	níngwàng	V.	to gaze or stare at
[29]困惑	kùnhuò	N./Adj.	perplexity; confused
[30]高等学府	gāoděngxuéfǔ	NP.	institution of higher learning
[31]简历	jiǎnlì	N.	resume
[32]恒久	héngjiǔ	Adj.	permanent, enduring
[33]愿望	yuànwàng	N.	wish

168   *A Popular Chinese Song*

综上所述[34]，通过《隐形的翅膀》我们看到了一位有着坚定信念，在成长的道路上，虽然经历了一次又一次的失败，但仍然不放弃，坚持追求自己的梦想，最终获得成功的青年形象[35]。正是因为这个健康向上的青年形象，才使这首歌曲成为励志歌曲中的经典之作[36]。

 语言重点：

1. …，与此同时，…

    at the same time/meanwhile …

    - 《隐形的翅膀》是一首流行歌曲，与此同时，也是一首励志歌曲。
    - 北京是一座拥有众多跨国公司的国际化大都市，与此同时，它也是中国的政治和文化中心。

2. **A受到（B的）广泛+V（关注/好评/重视/欢迎）**

    A receives B's extensive attention/favorable criticism/value/welcome

    - 这首励志歌曲非常适合现在的年轻人，因此受到广泛的关注和好评。
    - 随着星谈项目有效教学策略的推广，利用各种科技及媒体教材组织教学的方式受到广泛的欢迎。

3. **Subj.渐渐地+VP（学会/明白/发生变化/产生）**

    Subj. gradually + VP (learns/understands/undergoes changes/gives rise to)

    - 在这条道路上，很多人，渐渐地学会了就算受伤也不会流泪。
    - 这个部分表达的意思是只要不断努力，追求梦想，自己的世界也会渐渐地发生变化。

4. **对（于）sb.而言，…**

    Regarding sb., … ; as far as sb. is concerned …

    - 我们不会羡慕他们的世界。对我们而言，最重要的就是做好自己。
    - 对于母语为英语的学生而言，汉语语音中的卷舌音常常是发音的难点。

5. ① **sb.充满+abstract N（希望/信心/自信）**

    Sb. is full of/brimming with + abstract N. (hope/faith/confidence)

    ② **sb.对+NP/VP（未来/实现梦想）充满+希望/信心/自信**

    Sb. is full of/brimming with + hope/faith/confidence for (the future/realizing their dreams)

    - 因为有梦想，就会永远充满希望。
    - 坚定的信念让我们对未来充满信心。

---

[34]综上所述   zōngshàngsuǒshù   Idiom.   in conclusion, in summary, to sum up
[35]形象   xíngxiàng   N.   image; form; figure
[36]经典之作   jīngdiǎnzhīzuò   NP.   classic

6. 综上所述，…

in conclusion, in summary, to sum up

- 综上所述，通过《隐形的翅膀》我们看到了一位有着坚定信念，在成长的道路上，虽然经历了一次又一次的失败，但仍然不放弃，坚持追求自己的梦想，最终获得成功的青年形象。
- 综上所述，流行歌曲不仅是语言流行趋势与变化的表现，也展现了社会价值观念与主流文化的改变。

练习活动

理解诠释1：预习单

先看课文，然后完成下面的作业：

一、听歌曲http://www.youtube.com/watch?v=ShltcsGsZjA，填写歌词并标注拼音。

隐形的翅膀

词曲：王雅君　　歌手：张韶涵

每一次 都在徘徊（拼音：　　）孤单中坚强
每一次 就算很_____也不闪泪光
我知道 我一直有双隐形的翅膀（拼音：　　）
带我飞 飞过绝望（拼音：　　）
不去想 他们拥有_____
我看见 每天的夕阳（拼音：　　）也会有变化
我知道 我一直有双隐形的翅膀
带我飞 给我希望
我终于 看到 所有_____都开花
追逐的年轻 歌声多嘹亮（拼音：　　）
我终于 翱翔（拼音：　　）用心凝望（拼音：　　）不害怕
哪里会有风 就飞多远吧
不去想 他们拥有美丽的太阳
我看见 每天的夕阳也会有变化
我知道 我一直有双隐形的翅膀
带我飞 给我希望
我终于 看到 所有梦想都开花
追逐（拼音：　　）的年轻 歌声多嘹亮
我终与 翱翔 用心凝望不害怕
哪里会有风 就飞多远吧
隐形的翅膀 让梦恒久（拼音：　　）比天长
留一个_____让自己想象

二、根据课文对歌词的解释，用自己的话向大家讲述歌词中青年的故事。（200字以内）

📖 **理解诠释2：扩展阅读**

改编自http://wenku.baidu.com/view/41d208c1bb4cf7ec4afed0e2.html

　　当今社会，流行音乐受到年轻人的广泛欢迎。流行歌曲的内容虽然有很多以爱情为主题，但是不能把流行歌曲的内容全部归结到爱情主题上，因为当中也有许多歌曲是励志的。不管是初中生，高中生还是大学生，都非常喜欢听励志类的歌曲。这些歌曲内容健康向上，成为年轻人的精神动力。

　　调查显示，大部分中学生更喜欢听关于爱情和励志类的歌曲。针对中学生喜欢听关于爱情的流行歌曲这一现象，心理学家做出了解答：中学生正处在心理和生理发育的特殊时期。在这个时期，中学生的性知识开始萌动，常常表现为对异性从开始的有意疏远到对异性充满好奇和渴望，从而对朦胧的爱情生活十分向往。听跟爱情有关的流行歌曲比较能满足他们情感上的需求。

　　为什么中国中学生喜欢听励志类的歌曲呢？有人说，这是因为中国的孩子是最苦的。不管他们是自愿的还是被迫的，总是得完成大量的学习任务。父母把希望寄托在他们身上，与此同时，他们也承受着巨大的心理压力。中国的孩子如此劳累，不仅只是自身的问题，同时也和中国的教育体制、家长的教育方式有关。当孩子因为学习上遇到的困难而失去信心时，往往会选择听一些例如《阳光总在风雨后》、《水手》等励志类歌曲。这些歌曲教年轻人不要怕面对失败，不要放弃，要坚强，不要依赖于别人，要靠自己去克服困难。

　　成长的道路上，一定会有很多失败与困惑，让人不禁想放弃自己追求的梦想。经典的励志歌曲有一股力量，比方说《隐形的翅膀》、《最初的梦想》、《我的未来不是梦》、《真心英雄》、《蜗牛》、《飞得更高》、《我是一只小小鸟》等等。每次听这些歌曲都会使你全身充满力量，勇敢站起来，继续努力。励志歌曲既有时刻提醒你保持方向的意思，也有鼓励的作用，让人们坚定信念。

1. 用自己的话总结为什么中学生喜欢听关于爱情的流行歌曲？

2. 用自己的话总结为什么中国中学生喜欢听励志类的歌曲？

3. 根据文章，中国孩子如此劳累跟哪些方面有着密切的关系？（可多选）
　　A. 中国教育体制　　　B. 成长的困惑
　　C. 父母的希望　　　　D. 生理发育特殊时期

4. 励志歌曲有哪些作用？（可多选）
　　A. 鼓励　　B. 提醒　　C. 满足情感需求　　D. 帮助坚定信念

人际交流1：办公室答疑

你的学生听完《隐形的翅膀》这首歌以后有一些困惑，所以到办公室来请你答疑：

学生： 老师，歌词前两句"在徘徊孤单中坚强"，"就算很受伤也不闪泪光"的意思都和坚强有关系。为什么作者反复提到坚强呢？

你的回答： 【建议词汇和结构：一帆风顺；A依赖于B（sb./sb.的帮助/前人的经验）；subj.渐渐地+VP（学会/明白）；懦弱；幼稚】

学生： 隐形的翅膀带她飞过绝望，给她希望。所谓的"隐形的翅膀"指的是什么呢？

你的回答： 【建议词汇和结构：所谓的N是指…；毫无+N（疑问/信念/目标）；坚定；坚信；subj.因为…而+do sth.】

学生： 在"不去想他们拥有美丽的太阳"这句歌词中，"他们"指的是谁？"美丽的太阳"代表什么呢？整句歌词想要表达什么？

你的回答： 【建议词汇和结构：一帆风顺；羡慕；subj.不禁+VP（产生…心理/怀疑/感到）；对sb.而言，…；sb.对+NP/VP（未来/实现梦想）充满+希望/信心/自信】

人际交流2：在脸书(Facebook)上征求意见

下面是一位K-12的老师在脸书上发布的一条近况，请给他回复。【建议词汇和结构：A受到（B的）广泛+V（关注/好评）；…，与此同时，…；对sb.而言，…；subj.不禁+VP（产生…心理/怀疑/感到）；毫无+N（疑问/信念/目标）；sb.对+NP/VP（未来/实现梦想）充满+希望/信心/自信；sb.充满+abstract N（希望/信心/自信）；A依赖于B（sb./sb.的帮助/前人的经验）；subj.渐渐地+VP（学会/明白）】

> 📝 近况　📷 相片/影片　▶ 生活要事
>
> 各位朋友，我打算给学生推荐一些中文励志歌曲，大家有什么好建议吗？求歌曲名，你对这首歌曲的理解以及这首歌曲带给你的感受。谢谢！

表达演说：读后感

请你写一篇400–500字的读后感，谈谈你看完《"隐形的翅膀"赏析》这篇文章以后的感想。请包括以下内容：

1. 总结课文作者对这首歌曲的理解。
2. 你自己对这首歌曲的理解。
3. 歌曲的哪个部分给你最深的感受？结合自己的亲身经历进行说明。
4. 其他：你自己想讨论的角度。

建议词汇和结构：A受到（B的）广泛+V（关注/好评）；毫无+N（疑问/信念/目标）；对sb.而言，…；subj.不禁+VP（产生…心理/怀疑/感到）；sb.对+NP/VP（未来/实现梦想）充满+希望/信心/自信；sb.充满+abstract N（希望/信心/自信）；A依赖于B（sb./sb.的帮助/前人的经验）；subj.渐渐地+VP（学会/明白）；…，与此同时，…；综上所述，…

反思任务

一、前期任务：
当你的学生或朋友因为学习或者生活中的问题而失去信心开始困惑、徘徊的时候，为了鼓励他们，让他们面对失败，坚定信念，不要放弃，你会给他们推荐哪首中文的励志歌曲呢？请采访中国人，了解他们心目中经典的励志歌曲，并说明这首歌曲之所以经典的原因。

二、核心任务：

- 在采访到的结果中，选择一首你最喜欢的歌曲，在网上听歌，并写下歌词。
- 结合网上的评论，理解歌词的意思。
- 最少采访5位中国人，谈谈他们对这首歌曲的理解以及这首歌曲给他们带来的感受。

三、后期任务：
用PPT报告的形式赏析歌词：解释为什么要选择这首歌曲，说明歌曲代表的意义，介绍采访结果（别人对这首歌曲的理解以及这首歌曲给他们带来的感受），阐述自己对歌词的理解。

补充材料

[1] 听歌学汉语《北京欢迎你》
    网络链接 http://video.chinese.cn/article/2010-04/06/content_121551.htm
[2] 听歌学汉语《甜蜜蜜》
    网络链接 http://video.chinese.cn/article/2011-03/10/content_233999.htm
[3] 儿童歌谣（视频文件）
    网络链接 http://edu.chinese.cn/Edu/zh-CN/nursery_rhymes/index.html

第二课　中国教育现状
The Current State of China's Education

（文本形式：报刊文章）

> ➢ 关键词：
>   应试教育、素质教育、创新、教育体系、资源分配、体制改革
> ➢ 能力目标：
>   1. 学习者能理解诠释有关中国教育的专业讨论及论文。
>   2. 学习者能讨论并说明目前中国教育存在的问题。
>   3. 学习者能简单介绍美国的教育制度。
>   4. 学习者能比较、分析中美教育的异同。

课文全版 (Complete Version)

在中国，教育一直是被抨击[1]最多的问题，而在中国教育存在的诸多[2]问题当中，笔者[3]认为最严重的问题是以下两个。

第一个是学生的素质[4]问题。

中国学生在基础知识[5]的掌握上表现优秀，然而在创新[6]方面却少有建树[7]。为什么中国学生会具有这种基础好，创新差的特点呢？这恐怕就得归咎于[8]当前中国的应试教育制度[9]了。所谓的应试教育是指一种偏重于[10]通过考试的分数来衡量[11]学生水平，以把少数人从多数人中选拔[12]出来为目标的教学模式。由于中国当前的教育体系[13]一切服从[14]于应试，把考试分数等同于教育质量[15]，因此，中国的学校以及教师就不得不为了应付[16]考试，追求[17]升学率[18]而紧紧围绕着考试和升学的需要，只教与考试有关的内容。而对学生来说，学习的目标是升学，而不是培养个人的兴趣。这种带有明显[19]功利性[20]的教与学让学校教育一味[21]提高教学要求，加快教学进度，加大考试难度。随着学习负担[22]的日益[23]加重[24]，学生便逐渐丧失[25]了对新鲜事物的探索精神[26]，最后不可避免[27]地成为了只会读死书、死读书的学习机器。

[1] 抨击	pēngjī	V.	to attack, to assail, to lash out at
[2] 诸多	zhūduō	Adj.	a good deal, a lot of
[3] 笔者	bǐzhě	N.	author
[4] 素质	sùzhì	N.	quality/character (of a person)
[5] 基础知识	jīchǔzhīshi	NP.	basic knowledge
[6] 创新	chuàngxīn	N.	creativity, innovation
[7] 建树	jiànshù	N.	achievement, contribution
[8] 归咎于	guījiùyú	VP.	to attribute a fault to, to put the blame on
[9] 应试教育制度	yìngshìjiàoyù zhìdù	NP.	exam-oriented education system
[10] 偏重于	piānzhòngyú	VP.	to stress one aspect at the expense of another
[11] 衡量	héngliáng	V.	to weigh, to measure, to judge
[12] 选拔	xuǎnbá	V.	to select, to choose (worthy person)
[13] 教育体系	jiàoyùtǐxì	NP.	education system
[14] 服从	fúcóng	V.	to obey, to comply with, be subordinated to
[15] 教育质量	jiàoyùzhìliàng	NP.	quality of education
[16] 应付	yìngfù	V.	to deal with, to cope with
[17] 追求	zhuīqiú	V.	to pursue, to seek, to chase
[18] 升学率	shēngxuélǜ	N.	rate of advancement to next grade of school
[19] 明显	míngxiǎn	Adj.	obvious
[20] 功利性	gōnglìxing	Adj./N.	utilitarian, utility
[21] 一味	yíwèi	Adv.	blindly, invariably
[22] 负担	fùdān	N.	burden
[23] 日益	rìyì	Adv.	increasingly
[24] 加重	jiāzhòng	V.	to aggravate, to increase the weight of
[25] 丧失	sàngshī	V.	to lose, to forfeit, to be deprived of
[26] 探索精神	tànsuǒjīngshén	NP.	the spirit of exploration
[27] 不可避免	bùkěbìmiǎn	Adv.	unavoidably

教育资源[28]严重不均衡[29]是目前中国教育存在的第二个大问题。
　　中国的教育资源不均衡问题主要表现在三个方面：一是城乡之间的差距[30]：中国50％以上的人口在农村，而90％以上的重点学校[31]却在城市。由于在教育资源分配[32]上存在着较为严重的城乡分化[33]，导致了一些农村中小学学生存在辍学[34]、失学[35]等现象，甚至很多人产生了"读书无用论[36]"的思想，这进一步加大了城乡教育的差距。二是地区之间的差距：东西部之间巨大的经济差距导致教育差距也非常大。据笔者了解，2011年，青海全省用于教育的拨款[37]还不及[38]北京市朝阳区一个区的教育拨款的一半。最后是阶层差别[39]。最近，有研究指出：中国学生就读[40]学校的好坏与其家庭的社会经济地位之间存在着密切的关系，也就是说有钱人的孩子，不管是否聪明好学[41]，都能够得到优质[42]的教育资源，这种教育上的优势会转化[43]成为他们未来的优势。这样，所谓的精英阶层[44]将会不断集中，在社会上逐渐形成一个几乎无法攻破[45]的利益集团[46]。最后的结果便是社会的两极分化[47]越来越严重。

　　综上所述，笔者认为，如今要在中国实行教育体制改革[48]，恐怕已不只是从应试教育向素质教育[49]转变那么简单了，中国教育要想有出路[50]，需要的是人们价值观念[51]的转变[52]、国家经济的均衡发展以及社会资源的合理分配等各个层面的改变。唯有如此，中国教育制度的改革才可突破瓶

[28]教育资源	jiàoyùzīyuán	NP.	educational resources
[29]均衡	jūnhéng	Adj.	balanced
[30]差距	chājù	N.	disparity, difference
[31]重点学校	zhòngdiǎnxuéxiào	NP.	key school (government chosen)
[32]分配	fēnpèi	V.	to distribute, to allot
[33]城乡分化	chéngxiāngfēnhuà	NP.	the urban–rural divide
[34]辍学	chuòxué	V.	to withdraw from a school, to drop out
[35]失学	shīxué	V.	to be deprived of education
[36]读书无用论	dúshūwúyònglùn	NP.	the theory that study is useless
[37]拨款	bōkuǎn	V.	to allocate (funds), budget, fund
[38]不及	bùjí	V.	to be inferior
[39]阶层差别	jiēcéngchābié	NP.	difference in hierarchy
[40]就读	jiùdú	V.	to study
[41]聪明好学	cōngmínghàoxué	Adj.	intelligent and fond of study
[42]优质	yōuzhì	Adj.	excellent quality
[43]转化	zhuǎnhuà	V.	to transform
[44]精英阶层	jīngyīngjiēcéng	NP.	the elite class
[45]攻破	gōngpò	V.	to make a breakthrough
[46]利益集团	lìyìjítuán	NP.	interest group
[47]两极分化	liǎngjífēnhuà	VP.	to polarize
[48]教育体制改革	jiàoyùtǐzhìgǎigé	NP.	educational system reform
[49]素质教育	sùzhìjiàoyù	NP.	all-round education (contrasted with 应试教育, exam-oriented education)
[50]出路	chūlù	N.	way out, exit, outlet
[51]价值观念	jiàzhíguānniàn	NP.	values
[52]转变	zhuǎnbiàn	V./N.	to change, transformation

颈[53]，中国教育的现状才能发生根本性的改变，中国的教育事业才能真正蓬勃发展[54]。

参考文章：
《中国教育的反思》作者：刘祥龙
《探寻中国教育问题解决之道》作者：俞敏洪 中国东方教育新浪博客
《中国教育打几分》作者：黄祺
《现状之一：人虽多，而才少》转载自 http://www.177liuxue.cn
《批判与反思 教育界的共同课题》作者：王攀峰 中国教育报

 语言重点：

1. ① …得归咎于…

    … (problem/blame) must be attributed to …

    ② **Subj.把…归咎于…**

    Subj. attributes A's (fault/problem) to B …

    - 为什么中国学生会具有这种基础好，创新差的特点呢？这恐怕就得归咎于当前中国的应试教育制度了。
    - 追根溯源，我们可以把社会两极分化越来越严重的现象归咎于教育资源分配的严重不均。

2. **Subj.把A等同于B**

    Subj. equates A with B

    - 中国当前的教育体系一切服从于应试，把考试分数等同于教育质量。
    - 中国的大学排名，往往把"规模大、学生多"等同于"水平高、实力强"。

3. ① **Subj.加快…（教学/工作/建设/工程）进度**

    Subj. accelerates (education's/work's/building's/construction's) speed of advancement

    ② **Subj.加大…（考试/教材/改革/管理）难度/（改革/管理）力度**

    Subj. enlarges/expands (the test's/teaching material's/reform's/management's) degree of difficulty/(reform's/management's) degree of strength

    - 这种带有明显功利性的教与学让学校教育一味提高教学要求，加快教学进度，加大考试难度。
    - 为了改变中国目前的教育现状，政府需加大提高学生创新素质与平均教育资源分配这两方面的改革力度。

---

[53]瓶颈　　píngjǐng　　N.　　bottleneck
[54]蓬勃发展　péngbófāzhǎn　VP.　to develop and flourish

4. **Subj.导致…**

    Subj. results in/brings about …

    - 由于在教育资源分配上存在着较为严重的城乡分化,导致了一些农村中小学学生存在辍学、失学等现象。
    - 学习负担的日益加重导致学生逐渐丧失对新鲜事物的探索精神,最后不可避免地成为了只会读死书、死读书的学习机器。

5. **A不及B的…(百分之几/几分之几/一半)**

    A is inferior to B

    - 青海全省用于教育的拨款还不及北京市朝阳区一个区的教育拨款的一半。
    - 虽然中国已经成为世界第二的经济大国,但人均消费水平却还不及美国的六分之一。

6. **A跟B(之间)存在/有(着)(紧密的/密切的)关系**

    A and B are closely related

    - 中国学生在初中阶段就读的学校好坏与其家庭的社会经济地位之间存在着相当密切的关系。
    - 中国教育制度改革能否突破瓶颈跟人们价值观念的转变、国家经济的均衡发展以及社会资源的合理分配等各个层面的改变之间存在着紧密的关系。

第二课　中国教育现状
The Current State of China's Education

（文本形式：报刊文章）

> ➢ 关键词：
>   应试教育、素质教育、创新、教育体系、资源分配、体制改革
> ➢ 能力目标：
>   1. 学习者能理解诠释有关中国教育的专业讨论及论文。
>   2. 学习者能讨论并说明目前中国教育存在的问题。
>   3. 学习者能简单介绍美国的教育制度。
>   4. 学习者能比较、分析中美教育的异同。

课文节选版 (Abridged Version)

有学者认为在中国目前存在[1]的所有问题中，教育问题是最严重[2]的。中国教育存在的问题主要有以下两个。

第一个是学生的素质[3]问题。

中国学生往往对基础知识[4]掌握得很好可是在创新[5]方面的能力却很差。为什么中国学生会具有这种基础好，创新差的特点呢？这恐怕就得归咎于[6]当前中国的应试教育制度[7]了。由于中国当前的教育体系[8]一切服从[9]于应试，把考试分数等同于[10]教育质量[11]，因此中国的学校以及教师为了追求[12]升学率[13]，就不得不为了应付[14]考试而紧紧围绕着考试的内容来进行教学，只教与考试有关的内容。而对学生来说，学习的目标是升学，而不是培养个人的兴趣。这样的结果便是学生最后不可避免[15]地成为了只会读死书、死读书的学习机器。

第二个是教育资源[16]严重不均衡[17]的问题。

中国目前的教育资源不均衡主要表现在三个方面：一是城乡[18]之间的差距[19]；中国50%以上的人口在农村，而90%以上的重点学校[20]却在城市。由于在教育资源分配[21]上存在着较为严重的城乡分化[22]，导致[23]了一些农村中小学学生存在辍学[24]、失学[25]等现象[26]，这进一步加大[27]了农村教育与城市

[1]存在	cúnzài	V.	to exist
[2]严重	yánzhòng	Adj.	serious, severe
[3]素质	sùzhì	N.	quality/character (of a person)
[4]基础知识	jīchǔzhīshi	NP.	basic knowledge
[5]创新	chuàngxīn	N.	creativity, innovation
[6]归咎于	guījiùyú	VP.	to attribute a fault to, to put the blame on
[7]应试教育制度	yìngshìjiàoyùzhìdù	NP.	exam-oriented education system
[8]体系	tǐxì	N.	system
[9]服从	fúcóng	V.	to obey, to comply with, be subordinated to
[10]等同于	děngtóngyú	VP.	to equate with
[11]教育质量	jiàoyùzhìliàng	NP.	quality of education
[12]追求	zhuīqiú	V.	to pursue, to seek, to chase
[13]升学率	shēngxuélǜ	N.	rate of advancement to next grade of school
[14]应付	yìngfù	V.	to deal with, to cope with
[15]不可避免	bùkěbìmiǎn	Adv.	unavoidably
[16]教育资源	jiàoyùzīyuán	NP.	educational resources
[17]均衡	jūnhéng	Adj.	balanced
[18]城乡	chéngxiāng	N.	urban and rural
[19]差距	chājù	N.	disparity, difference
[20]重点学校	zhòngdiǎn xuéxiào	NP.	key school (government chosen)
[21]分配	fēnpèi	V.	to distribute, to allot
[22]分化	fēnhuà	V./N.	to divide, differentiation
[23]导致	dǎozhì	V.	to lead to, to result in (negative result)
[24]辍学	chuòxué	V.	to withdraw from a school, to drop out
[25]失学	shīxué	V.	to be deprived of education
[26]现象	xiànxiàng	N.	phenomenon
[27]加大	jiādà	V.	to expand, to increase

教育的差距。二是地区[28]之间的差距，主要为东西部之间的差距问题。东西部之间巨大的经济差距导致教育差距也非常大。据[29]笔者[30]了解，2011年，青海全省[31]的教育拨款[32]还不到北京市朝阳区[33]一个区的教育拨款的一半。最后是阶层差别[34]。有调查说：有钱人的孩子，不管是不是聪明好学[35]，都能够上好学校，得到优质[36]的教育资源，这种教育上的优势会转化[37]成为他们未来的优势。这样，所谓的精英阶层[38]将会不断集中，最后的结果便是社会的两级分化[39]越来越严重。

综上所述，笔者认为，如今，要在中国实行教育体制改革[40]，恐怕已不只是从应试教育向素质教育[41]转变[42]那么简单了，中国教育要想有出路[43]，需要的是人们价值观念[44]的转变、国家经济的均衡发展[45]以及社会资源的合理[46]分配等各个层面[47]的改变。

参考文章：
《中国教育的反思》作者：刘祥龙
《探寻中国教育问题解决之道》作者：俞敏洪 中国东方教育新浪博客
《中国教育打几分》 作者：黄祺
《现状之一：人虽多，而才少》转载自 http://www.177liuxue.cn
《批判与反思 教育界的共同课题》作者：王攀峰 中国教育报

[28]地区	dìqū	N.	area, district, region
[29]据	jù	Prep.	according to
[30]笔者	bǐzhě	N.	author
[31]全省	quánshěng	N.	the whole province
[32]拨款	bōkuǎn	V.	to allocate (funds), budget, fund
[33]区	qū	N.	district
[34]阶层差别	jiēcéngchābié	NP.	difference in hierarchy
[35]聪明好学	cōngmínghàoxué	Adj.	intelligent and fond of study
[36]优质	yōuzhì	Adj.	excellent quality
[37]转化	zhuǎnhuà	V.	to transform
[38]精英阶层	jīngyīngjiēcéng	NP.	the elite class
[39]两极分化	liǎngjífēnhuà	VP.	to polarize
[40]教育体制改革	jiàoyùtǐzhìgǎigé	NP.	educational system reform
[41]素质教育	sùzhìjiàoyù	NP.	all-round education (contrasted with 应试教育, exam-oriented education)
[42]转变	zhuǎnbiàn	V./N.	to change, transformation
[43]出路	chūlù	N.	way out, exit, outlet
[44]价值观念	jiàzhíguānniàn	NP.	values
[45]均衡发展	jūnhéngfāzhǎn	VP./NP.	balanced development
[46]合理	hélǐ	Adj.	rational, reasonable
[47]层面	céngmiàn	N.	aspect

语言重点：

1. **Subj.具有……的特点/优势**

   Subj. has the unique characteristic of … /superiority in …

   - 为什么中国学生具有这种基础好，创新差的特点呢？
   - 和非母语者教师比，母语教师在语言方面具有一定优势。

2. ① …得归咎于…

   … (problem/blame) must be attributed to …

   ② **Subj.把…归咎于…**

   Subj. attributes A's (fault/problem) to B …

   - 为什么中国学生会具有这种基础好，创新差的特点呢？这恐怕就得归咎于当前中国的应试教育制度了。
   - 追根溯源，我们可以把社会两极分化越来越严重的现象归咎于教育资源分配的严重不均。

3. **Subj.把A等同于B**

   Subj. equates A with B

   - 中国当前的教育体系一切服从于应试，把考试分数等同于教育质量。
   - 中国的大学排名，往往把"规模大、学生多"等同于"水平高、实力强"。

4. **…存在…的问题/现象/差距**

   … exists … the problem of … /the phenomenon of … /the difference in …

   - 在中国教育存在的问题主要有以下两个：第一个是学生的素质问题，第二个是教育资源严重不均衡的问题。
   - 中国东西部之间存在的巨大的经济差距导致教育差距也非常大。

5. **Subj.导致…**

   Subj. results in/brings about …

   - 由于在教育资源分配上存在着较为严重的城乡分化，导致了一些农村中小学学生存在辍学、失学等现象。
   - 中国当前的应试教育制度导致学生最后成为了只会读死书、死读书的学习机器。

6. ① …，**Subj.** 不可避免地+VP

　　… , Subj. is unable to avoid + VP

　② …，…是不可避免的

　　… is inevitable

- 这样的结果便是学生最后不可避免地成为了只会读死书、死读书的学习机器。
- 教育资源分配不均的现象若继续发展下去，所谓的精英阶层不断集中，社会的两级分化越来越严重是不可避免的。

练习活动

理解诠释1：预习单

先看课文，然后完成下面的作业：

一、根据课文，作者认为中国教育存在的最严重的两个问题分别是什么？

二、比较中国教育与美国教育的异同，完成以下表格。

	中国教育	美国教育
学生对基础知识的掌握情况		
学生在创新方面的能力		
考试分数在教育中的重要性		
教与学是否具有功利性		
教育的城乡差距		
教育的地区差距		
教育的阶级差别		

理解诠释2：扩展阅读

《中国教育现状》一文的作者认为中国教育存在的两大问题是学生的素质问题与教育资源不均衡的问题。事实上，美国教育也存在着诸多问题，而美国人民抨击最多的问题其实也和这篇文章作者所指出的问题差不多。

首先，美国学生也存在着素质问题。美国学生虽然在创新方面颇有建树，但对基础知识的掌握却远不如中国和其它亚洲学生。美国大学在学生入学的时候以多种方式来衡量学生水平,虽然可以让学生自由探索新鲜事物,但学生可能一味追求自己的兴趣,而忽略基础知识的重要性。

其次,美国政府对教育的投入明显不足,特别是高等教育方面。由于这几年美国财政困难,许多学校的开支与收入无法平衡,这间接将贫困家庭的学生排斥在外。如果来自贫困家庭的学生成绩不是最优秀的,要读好的大学简直比登天还难。

最后,美国教育的城乡差距、地区差距与阶级差别也非常大,教育资源分配不均、辍学、失学的现象也非常普遍。在美国前50大城市中,高中生能毕业的比例不足百分之七十。

美国的教育体质要如何实行改革,突破瓶颈,合理分配资源,也需要看未来美国经济如何发展,政府如何处理。

1. 根据阅读文章,请用自己的话概括美国教育存在的问题有哪些。

2. 根据阅读文章,判断下列哪项叙述是错误的。
   A. 本文作者认为,美国学生对基础知识的掌握不够。
   B. 美国存在的教育问题不比中国少。
   C. 美国有百分之三十的高中生会辍学。
   D. 美国的教育资源存在分配不均的问题。

3. 根据阅读文章,下列哪项不是造成贫困家庭学生上好大学难的原因。
   A. 政府对高等教育的投入不足。
   B. 城乡差距和阶层差距。
   C. 贫困学生不注重对基础知识的掌握。
   D. 贫困学生高中的辍学率和失学率比较高。

人际交流1:面对面交流

赵校长是北京市朝阳区一所公立小学的校长,今年春天到你的学校参观访问,在观摩完几堂课以后,赵校长与你谈起了一些与学校教育有关的问题。

赵校长: 周老师,这次来你们学校参观访问真是让我大开眼界,也让我意识到中美的小学教育真的存在很多不同。从今天观摩的几堂课的情况来看,美国的小学好像不太重视学生对基础知识的掌握,不知道这是不是我的一个误解?

你的回答: 【建议词汇和结构:严重;素质;追求;均衡;广泛;subj.重视…;subj.具有…的特点/优势;…得归咎于…;subj.把A等同于B;…存在…的问题/现象;subj.不可避免地+VP(出现/引起…)】

赵校长: 我觉得你说的对,其实中国和美国的小学教育应该互取所长。中国的小学教育太偏重于应试教育而忽视了对学生创新能力的培养。这一点上,我们应该多向你们学习。这所学校是一所公立学校,我想知道在美国公立学校和私立学校之间存在什么差异呢?

你的回答：【建议词汇和结构：教育资源；均衡；差距；分配；地区；阶层差别；精英阶层；两级分化；价值理念；…，与此同时，…；A受到（B的）广泛+V.(关注/重视/欢迎)；毫无+N.(疑问)；…存在…的问题/现象；subj.不可避免地+VP.】

人际交流2：回复电子邮件

距离上次参观访问一个月以后，赵校长给你发来了电子邮件，请看完邮件以后，给赵校长一个回复。【建议词汇和结构：…，与此同时，…；对于…（学生/老师）而言；毫无+N（疑问）；subj.渐渐地+V（学会/发生变化）；不可避免；A跟B（之间）存在着密切的关系；subj.加快…（教学）的进度；subj.加大…（教材/管理）的难度/（创新）的比重】

> 周老师：
> 　　你好，最近怎么样？一切都还顺利吗？距离上次见面已经有一个多月的时间了。上次对贵校为期三天的参观访问真是让我收获颇丰，尤其是和你深入的讨论了美国的教育情况以后，更加深了我对美国教育制度的了解。
> 　　有感于贵校在培养学生创新精神方面取得的成绩，从下个学期起，我打算开始带领老师们做一些培养学生创新精神的尝试。我在观摩您的中文课的时候发现你采用了很多有意思的教学策略来激发学生的想象力，所以我想请你多介绍一些培养学生创造能力的方法，希望我们的英文老师们也能把这些方法运用到今后的第二语言课堂学习当中。
> 　　期待您的回复！
> 　　祝你一切顺利！
> 　　　　　　　　　　　　　　　　　　　　　　　　　赵明良

表达演说：大会演讲稿

今年夏天你将去中国参加一个"海内外基础教育大会"，在大会上你将发表一个以介绍中美教育差异为主题的演讲。你需要先草拟一个大会演讲稿，演讲稿的内容可以从以下几个方面考虑：学生对基础知识的掌握情况、学生在创新方面的能力、考试分数的重要性、教育的城乡差距、教育的地区差距、教育的阶级差别……

参考套语：
尊敬的各位来宾、各位与会者：
　　大家下午好，很荣幸能有这次机会在这里为大家做这个演讲，今天我将主要和大家讨论中美教育之间的差异问题。
　　………………………………………………………
　　以上就是我的演讲内容，感谢大家的聆听。欢迎各位提问。谢谢！

文化体验任务

一、前期任务：
根据课文内容，设计五个与中国教育制度相关的问题。
四位成员一组，交换并讨论各自所设计出来的问题，制作调查问卷。

二、核心任务：
利用前期任务所准备的调查问卷，四人一组对当地中小学的校长与老师进行采访，进一步了解中国当前中小学的教育情况。

三、后期任务
整理采访结果，四人一组在课堂上向别的小组和老师报告所了解到的中国教育的现状与问题。

补充材料

[1] 钟经平. 教育资源不均衡加剧 穷孩子为何难"跳龙门"
    网络链接 http://learning.sohu.com/20110830/n317771554.shtml
[2] 中国中学生动手能力差原因探析
    网络链接 http://blog.sina.com.cn/s/blog_4b8935c9010006vn.html
[3] 中美教育的十个最大差异
    网络链接 http://news.xinhuanet.com/overseas/2011-04/02/c_121260817.htm
[4] 6分钟解析我国教育现状（视频文件）
    网络链接 http://v.qq.com/cover/t/t3jzkfmek0avznp.html?vid=x0115x5aa7z

第三课　华人禁忌[1]
Chinese Taboos

（文本形式：杂志文章）

> 关键词：
> 禁忌、文化现象、习俗、送礼、吉利、谐音、风水、占卜
> 能力目标：
> 1. 学习者能列出至少5项华人禁忌并解释原因。
> 2. 学习者能说明美国社会的禁忌习俗。
> 3. 学习者能分享自己在生活中受到哪些禁忌的影响。
> 4. 学习者能表达自己对禁忌习俗的意见和看法。

---

[1] 禁忌　jìnjì　N.　taboo

课文全版 (Complete Version)

　　禁忌是人类社会特有[2]的一种文化现象，世界上几乎所有的民族[3]都有自己的禁忌习俗[4]，华人社区也不例外。华人的禁忌习俗特别多，而且在日常生活的各个领域都看得到。许多来到华人地区生活过的外国人，常常因不理解这些特殊的禁忌文化而感到不可思议[5]，甚至于心里觉得不舒服，到底华人禁忌有哪些呢？

　　华人送礼有一些禁忌，这往往和华人的语言发音特点相关。例如伞和扇子[6]，跟"散"的发音很相似，就是和亲友"散掉"的意思，所以作为礼物，伞和扇子都不合适。除此之外，华人不喜欢送别人时钟，因为"送钟"与"送终[7]"同音，所以被当成禁忌；送人刀或剪刀也不合适，因为有句成语叫"一刀两断[8]"。据说[9]送人刀或剪刀会导致分离。但是若一定要送人刀或剪刀，可以向对方拿取一些零钱，变成买卖[10]就没关系了，否则还是应该改送别的东西。还有送菊花[11]也不吉利[12]，因为这些东西是华人办丧礼[13]时才会送的。如果朋友或情人分吃一个梨[14]，就代表"分离"。送水果可以考虑送苹果，象征[15] "平安[16]"，但是不能送四个，因为"四"与"死"发音相近，听起来不吉利。因此香港门牌[17]号码常常没有"四"号，车牌号[18]大多数也没有以"四"开头的；台湾医院里没有四楼或四号病房，公共汽车也没有四路线[19]。不过，华人也有喜欢的数字，那就是"八"，因为"八"和"发"谐音[20]。比方说，香港过年时要吃发菜[21]，因为发菜是发财[22]的谐音。

[2]特有	tèyǒu	Adj.	particular, characteristic
[3]民族	mínzú	N.	ethnic group
[4]习俗	xísú	N.	custom
[5]不可思议	bùkěsīyì	Idiom	inconceivable, unthinkable
[6]扇子	shànzi	N.	fan
[7]送终	sòngzhōng	V.	to attend to a dying parent or other senior member of one's family; to bury a parent
[8]一刀两断	yìdāoliǎngduàn	V.	to break with ... once and for all
[9]据说	jùshuō	Idiom	it is said
[10]买卖	mǎimài	N.	business
[11]菊花	júhuā	N.	chrysanthemum
[12]吉利	jílì	Adj.	lucky
[13](办)丧礼	(bàn)sānglǐ	V.	(to have) a funeral
[14]梨	lí	N.	pear
[15]象征	xiàngzhēng	V.	to symbolize
[16]平安	píng'ān	Adj.	safe and sound
[17]门牌	ménpái	N.	door plate
[18]车牌号	chēpáihào	N.	license plate
[19]路线	lùxiàn	N.	route
[20]谐音	xiéyīn	V./N.	similar sounding words
[21]发菜	fàcài	N.	hair weeds (*nostoc flagelliforme*)
[22]发财	fācái	V.	to make a fortune

188 *Chinese Taboos*

　　在居住环境和场所方面，华人非常相信住宅[23]室内的风水[24]。从住宅土地的选择到门、窗面对的方向，及客厅、卧室、厨房内各种物品的摆设[25]方法或方向，各方面都得考虑，禁忌数量之多，不胜枚举[26]。此外，华人习惯以自己的住家为中心，这种思想观念使得人们在出门远行[27]时非常小心。每次出远门，都要经过占卜[28]或风水师，预测出门是否平安、顺利。这是因为出门远行意味着[29]离开自己的安全居住范围[30]，难免[31]会让人产生一种离开家乡[32]的失落感[33]和不安全感[34]。虽然许多禁忌都是为了避开[35]不吉利的事情，但偶尔[36]也有例外[37]，比方说，华人认为黑、白两色是不吉利的颜色，因而像结婚等喜庆[38]场合[39]多不喜欢看到黑或白色；而丧事则要求戴黑色的纱[40]，或穿白色的孝服[41]、戴白色的纸花[42]等。

　　许多民族都有禁忌习俗。在现代社会有很多人认为禁忌习俗就是一种陈旧古板[43]的想法，或是不科学[44]的迷信[45]。但是从另一方面来看，禁忌习俗无论在西方还是东方社会，都普遍存在，而且常常和占卜或风水等信仰相结合，这是出于避开不吉利的事物和追求[46]平安的心理。因此，我们应该看到禁忌的深层意义[47]，而不只是禁忌本身所表现的行为。

[23]住宅	zhùzhái	N.	residence, dwelling
[24]风水	fēngshuǐ	N.	traditional Chinese practice of determining the location and orientation of a house, tomb, etc.
[25]摆设	bǎishè	V.	to furnish and decorate (a room)
[26]不胜枚举	búshèngméijǔ	Idiom	the examples too numerous to mention
[27]远行	yuǎnxíng	V.	to go on a long journey
[28]占卜	zhānbǔ	V.	fortune telling, divination
[29]意味着	yìwèizhe	V.	to signify; to mean; to imply
[30]安全居住范围	ānquánjūzhùfànwéi	NP.	safety zone
[31]难免	nánmiǎn	Adv.	unavoidably
[32]家乡	jiāxiāng	N.	hometown
[33]失落感	shīluògǎn	N.	sense of loss, sense of failure to meet expectations
[34]安全感	ānquángǎn	N.	sense of security
[35]避开	bìkāi	V.	to avoid, to evade, to keep away from
[36]偶尔	ǒu'ěr	Adv.	occasionally
[37]例外	lìwài	N./V.	exception; to be an exception
[38]喜庆	xǐqìng	Adj.	joyous
[39]场合	chǎnghé	N.	occasion
[40]纱	shā	N.	band worn on the arm during a funeral
[41]孝服	xiàofú	N.	mourning cloth
[42]纸花	zhǐhuā	N.	paper flower
[43]陈旧古板	chénjiùgǔbǎn	Adj.	old-fashioned and inflexible
[44]不科学	bùkēxué	Adj.	unscientific
[45]迷信	míxìn	N.	superstition
[46]追求	zhuīqiú	V.	to pursue
[47]深层意义	shēncéngyìyì	NP.	deeper meaning

Chinese Taboos

 语言重点：

1. **Subj.**（禁忌/教育/成长）是一种…的现象/是一个…的问题（，几乎…都…），…也不例外

   Subj. (taboo/education/growing up) is a … phenomenon/problem (almost …), and is no exception

   - 禁忌是人类社会特有的一种文化现象，世界上几乎所有的民族都有自己的禁忌习俗，华人社区也不例外。
   - 教育是一个一直被抨击的问题，几乎每个国家都存在一定程度的教育问题，美国也不例外。

2. **Subj.**到底/究竟+wh-word/A不A/A还是B

   Subj. after all/in the end is + wh-word/A or not A/A or B?

   - 到底华人禁忌有哪些呢？
   - 禁忌习俗究竟是不科学的迷信还是民族文化？

3. ① **A象征（着）B**（平安/和平/分离/不吉利），因此…（。除非…，否则…）

   A symbolizes B (being safe and sound/peace/separation/unlucky), therefore … (unless … , otherwise …)

   ② **A是B**（平安/和平/分离/不吉利）的象征，因此…（。除非…，否则…）

   A is a symbol of B (being safe and sound/peace/separation/unlucky), therefore … (unless … , otherwise …)

   - 苹果象征"平安"，因此送水果可以考虑送苹果。
   - 刀或剪刀是分离的象征，因此送人这样的礼物不合适。除非送人刀或剪刀的时候，向对方拿取一些零钱，变成买卖关系，否则还是应该改送别的东西。

4. （…难免）让sb.产生一种…（失落/不安全）感

   … (hard to avoid) giving sb. a feeling of … loss/unsafety

   - 出门远行意味着离开家园和自己的安全居住范围，难免会让人产生一种离开家乡的失落感。
   - 许多禁忌都是为了避开不吉利的事情，所以如果不遵守禁忌习俗就会让人产生一种不安全感。

5. …，但是从另一方面来看，…都普遍存在

   … , but on the other hand, … is widespread

   - 在现代社会有很多人认为禁忌习俗就是一种陈旧古板的想法，或是不科学的迷信。但是从另一方面来看，禁忌习俗无论在西方还是东方社会，都普遍存在。
   - 随着中国经济的发展，贫富差距日益扩大，但是从另一方面来看，这个问题在世界各国都普遍存在。

6. ① **Subj. do sth.**是出于+N/NP（礼貌/…的原因/…的心理/…的考虑）

   Subj. does sth. stemming from good manners/the reason of … /the mindset of … /the consideration of …

   ② 出于+N/NP（…的原因/…的心理/…的考虑/礼貌），**subj. do sth.**

   Stemming from (good manners/the reason of … /the mindset of … / the consideration of …), subj. does sth.

   - 禁忌习俗不论在西方还是东方社会，都普遍存在，而且常常和占卜或风水等信仰相结合，这是出于避开不吉利的事物和追求平安的心理。
   - 出于语言发音特点的原因，华人在送礼方面有不少禁忌。

第三课　华人禁忌[1]
Chinese Taboos

（文本形式：杂志文章）

> ➢ 关键词：
>   禁忌、文化现象、习俗、送礼、吉利、谐音、风水、占卜
> ➢ 能力目标：
>   1. 学习者能列出至少5项华人禁忌并解释原因。
>   2. 学习者能说明美国社会的禁忌习俗。
>   3. 学习者能分享自己在生活中受到哪些禁忌的影响。
>   4. 学习者能表达自己对禁忌习俗的意见和看法。

---
[1] 禁忌　jìnjì　N.　taboo

课文节选版 (Abridged Version)

世界上几乎所有的民族[2]都有自己的禁忌习俗[3]，华人社区也不例外。那华人禁忌有哪些呢？

华人送礼[4]有一些禁忌，这往往和华人的语言发音特点相关。例如伞[5]和扇子[6]，跟"散[7]"的发音很相似，就是和亲友"散掉"的意思，所以作为礼物，伞和扇子都不合适。除此之外，华人不喜欢送别人时钟[8]，因为"送钟"与"送终[9]"同音，所以被当成[10]禁忌；送人刀或者剪刀也不合适，因为有句成语叫"一刀两断[11]"。据说[12]送别人刀[13]或剪刀[14]会导致分离。如果一定要送人刀或剪刀，可以向对方要一些零钱，变成买卖[15]就没关系了。送菊花[16]、剑兰[17]、手帕[18]也不吉利[19]，因为这些东西是华人办丧礼[20]时才会送的。如果朋友或情人分吃一个梨[21]，就代表"分离"。送水果可以考虑送苹果，象征[22]"平安[23]"，但是不能送四个，因为"四"与"死"发音相近，听起来不吉利。因此香港门牌[24]号码常常没有"四"号，车牌号[25]大多数也不以"四"开头；台湾医院里没有四楼或第四号病房，公共汽车也没有四路线[26]。不过，华人也有喜欢的数字，那就是"八"，因为"八"和"发"谐音[27]。比方说，香港过年时要吃发菜[28]，因为发菜是发财[29]的谐音。

[2]民族	mínzú	N.	ethnic group
[3]习俗	xísú	N.	custom
[4]送礼	sònglǐ	V.	to give sb. a present
[5]伞	sǎn	N.	umbrella
[6]扇子	shànzi	N.	fan
[7]散	sàn	V.	to disperse; to scatter
[8]时钟	shízhōng	N.	clock
[9]送终	sòngzhōng	V.	to attend to a dying parent or other senior member of one's family; to bury a parent
[10]当成	dāngchéng	V.	to regard as; treat as; take for
[11]一刀两断	yìdāoliǎngduàn	V.	to break with ... once and for all
[12]据说	jùshuō	Idiom	it is said
[13]刀	dāo	N.	knife
[14]剪刀	jiǎndāo	N.	scissors
[15]买卖	mǎimài	N.	business
[16]菊花	júhuā	N.	chrysanthemum
[17]剑兰	jiànlán	N.	gladiolus
[18]手帕	shǒupà	N.	handkerchief
[19]吉利	jílì	Adj.	lucky
[20](办)丧礼	(bàn)sānglǐ	V.	(to have) a funeral
[21]梨	lí	N.	pear
[22]象征	xiàngzhēng	V.	to symbolize
[23]平安	píng'ān	Adj.	safe and sound
[24]门牌	ménpái	N.	door plate
[25]车牌号	chēpáihào	N.	license plate
[26]路线	lùxiàn	N.	route
[27]谐音	xiéyīn	V./N.	similar sounding words
[28]发菜	fàcài	N.	hair weeds (*nostoc flagelliforme*)
[29]发财	fācái	V.	to make a fortune

在居住[30]环境和场所方面，华人非常相信住宅[31]室内的风水[32]。从住宅土地的选择到门、窗面对的方向，以及客厅[33]、卧室[34]、厨房[35]内各种物品的摆设[36]方法或方向，各方面都得考虑。此外，华人习惯以自己的住家为中心，这种思想观念使得人们在出门远行[37]时非常小心。每次出远门，都要经过占卜[38]或风水师，预测出门是否平安、顺利。这是因为出门远行意味着[39]离开家园[40]和自己的安全居住范围[41]。虽然许多禁忌都是为了避开[42]不吉利的事情，但偶尔[43]也有例外[44]，比方说，华人认为黑、白两色是不吉利的颜色，因而像结婚等喜庆[45]场合[46]多不喜欢看到黑或白色；而丧事则要求[47]戴黑色的纱[48]、白色的纸花[49]，或穿白色的孝服[50]等。

禁忌习俗无论在西方还是东方社会，都普遍存在，而且常常和占卜或风水等信仰[51]相结合，这是出于避开不吉利的事物和追求[52]平安的心理。因此，我们应该看到禁忌的深层意义[53]，而不只是禁忌本身所表现的行为。

[30]居住	jūzhù	V.	to live, to reside
[31]住宅	zhùzhái	N.	residence, dwelling
[32]风水	fēngshuǐ	N.	traditional Chinese practice of determining the location and orientation of a house, tomb, etc.
[33]客厅	kètīng	N.	parlour
[34]卧室	wòshì	N.	bedroom
[35]厨房	chúfáng	N.	kitchen
[36]摆设	bǎishè	V.	to furnish and decorate (a room)
[37]远行	yuǎnxíng	V.	to go on a long journey
[38]占卜	zhānbǔ	V.	fortune telling, divination
[39]意味着	yìwèizhe	V.	to signify; to mean; to imply
[40]家园	jiāyuán	N.	homeland
[41]安全居住范围	ānquánjūzhùfànwéi	NP.	safety zone
[42]避开	bìkāi	V.	to avoid, to evade, to keep away from
[43]偶尔	ǒu'ěr	Adv.	occasionally
[44]例外	lìwài	N./V.	exception; to be an exception
[45]喜庆	xǐqìng	Adj.	joyous
[46]场合	chǎnghé	N.	occasion
[47]要求	yāoqiú	N./V.	demand, request; to demand
[48]纱	shā	N.	band worn on the arm during a funeral
[49]纸花	zhǐhuā	N.	paper flower
[50]孝服	xiàofú	N.	mourning cloth
[51]信仰	xìnyǎng	N.	faith; belief
[52]追求	zhuīqiú	V.	to pursue
[53]深层意义	shēncéngyìyì	NP.	deeper meaning

语言重点：

1. **Subj.（禁忌/教育/成长）是一种…的现象/是一个…的问题（，几乎…都…），…也不例外**

   Subj. (taboo/education/growing up) is a ... phenomenon/problem (almost ...), and is no exception

   - 禁忌是人类社会特有的一种文化现象，世界上几乎所有的民族都有自己的禁忌习俗，华人社区也不例外。
   - 教育是一个一直被抨击的问题，几乎每个国家都存在一定程度的教育问题，美国也不例外。

2. ① **A象征（着）B（平安/和平/分离/不吉利），因此…（。除非…，否则…）**

   A symbolizes B (being safe and sound/peace/separation/unlucky), therefore ... (unless ... , otherwise ...)

   ② **A是B（平安/和平/分离/不吉利）的象征，因此…（。除非…，否则…）**

   A is a symbol of B (being safe and sound/peace/separation/unlucky), therefore ... (unless ... , otherwise ...)

   - 苹果象征"平安"，因此送水果可以考虑送苹果。
   - 刀或剪刀是分离的象征，因此送人这样的礼物不合适。除非送人刀或剪刀的时候，向对方拿取一些零钱，变成买卖关系，否则还是应该改送别的东西。

3. **Subj.以…（为）开头/中心/重点/标准**

   Take ... as the beginning/center/key point/standard

   - 香港门牌号码常常没有"四"号，车牌号大多数也没有以"四"开头的。
   - 中文教学的课堂应该以学生为中心，设计活动时要从学生的兴趣出发。

4. ① **Subj. do sth.是出于+N/NP（礼貌/…的原因/…的心理/…的考虑）**

   Subj. does sth. stemming from good manners/the reason of ... /the mindset of ... /the consideration of ...

   ② **出于+N/NP（…的原因/…的心理/…的考虑/礼貌），subj. do sth.**

   Stemming from (good manners/the reason of ... /the mindset of ... / the consideration of ...), subj. does sth.

   - 禁忌习俗不论在西方还是东方社会，都普遍存在，而且常常和占卜或风水等信仰相结合，这是出于避开不吉利的事物和追求平安的心理。
   - 出于语言发音特点的原因，华人在送礼方面有不少禁忌。

练习活动

理解诠释1：预习单

先看课文，然后完成下面的作业：

一、利用下面的表格采访五个中国人，了解下面禁忌的类别及文化意义，并通过采访举出其他相应例子。

类别		中国		其他例子
		禁忌内容	代表的意思	
谐音	物品	伞、扇		
		钟		
	食品	梨		
象征意义	物品	菊花、剑兰、手帕		
	颜色	白色、黑色		

二、比较中美文化中的禁忌，回答下面的问题：

1. 通过上表中禁忌文化分析，总结中国人的禁忌大多跟什么主题有关系？美国的禁忌与哪些方面有关系？中美文化中的禁忌有什么相同或不同之处？

2. 虽然因为谐音的关系，有些物品有不吉利的意思，但是如果真的需要以这些物品当作礼物时，中国人会用什么办法来避免不吉利？

3. 美国人一般认为哪些数字不吉利？请举两个例子说明生活中反映这种文化心理的现象。

理解诠释：中西数字、颜色禁忌比较

　　禁忌是世界各民族共有的文化现象，但是内容和形式各地都有所不同。从日常生活到政治经济，几乎各个领域都有特殊的禁忌文化。

　　在数字方面，4在中国被认为是一个不吉利的数字，原因是它的发音和"死"很相似。中国人特别不喜欢14(yāosì)，因为发音与"要死"相近。在西方文化里，星期五是个不吉利的日子，人们常说"黑色星期五"，因为星期五是耶稣的受难日。因此西方人认为在星期五结婚、出门远行、开始一个新的工作都是不吉利的。数字13在西方文化中也是一个禁忌，这已经有很长的历史了。至于原因究竟是什么，有很多不同的解释，

其中一种说法是耶稣是在13号星期五被钉在十字架上的；在最后的晚餐中，坐在第13位的人就是出卖耶稣的犹大，因此13就变成了不吉利的象征。在日常生活中，人们都尽量避开13。在一些西方的国家和地区，楼房和电梯一般没有13层；门牌号码和房间号常常没有13；航空公司没有13号班机；电影院没有13排、13座。

在颜色方面，中西文化也有差异。红色对中国人来说是一种传统的喜庆色彩，因此像结婚等场合，多用红色来象征喜庆欢乐。但是中国人忌用红色的笔写信，因为这是断绝来往，一刀两断的表示。在西方文化中，红色常常象征着残酷、狂热、灾祸等意思。在中国传统文化里，黑、白两色都是不吉利的颜色，常常和丧礼联系在一起。因此办丧事时，中国人常戴黑色的纱，或穿白色的孝服、戴白色的纸花。而在西方文化中，白色象征着欢乐、美好和希望，因此像结婚等喜庆场合多为白色。黑色象征着魔鬼、痛苦和不幸，因此黑色也叫做"死色"。在现代欧美国家，丧礼专有的色彩就是黑色。每逢丧事，人们穿黑色的西服，戴黑色的帽子。西方人认为黑色使人显得严肃，可以表达对死者的尊敬。但是，在西方人眼中，黑色同时也代表正式和庄重，因此，在正式的场合，人们也喜欢穿黑色的衣服。

1. 对中国人而言，哪个数字是不吉利的？
   A. 13　　　　B. 14　　　　C. 66　　　　D. 100

2. 在西方国家，星期五被视为不吉利的日子是出于哪方面的因素？
   A. 政治　　　B. 经济　　　C. 宗教　　　D. 谐音

3. 白色在中西方文化中有什么不同的象征意义？请你举出两个实际的例子。

4. 中国人喜欢红色，但并不是任何场合红色都合适。以下哪些时候应该避免：
   A. 给朋友写信祝他新年快乐　　B. 参加中国人的婚礼
   C. 春节去拜年的时候　　　　　D. 参加中国人的丧礼

人际交流1：课间谈话

你的一位美国朋友受邀到中国朋友家里吃饭。他想准备一份礼物感谢主人，但不知道送什么好，于是来请教你。

你的朋友：这是我第一次到中国人家里做客，希望准备的礼物他们会喜欢。因为你对中国文化有比较多的了解，我想事前问问你的意见。你觉得送花怎么样？

你的回答：【建议词汇和结构：对sb.而言，…；象征；不吉利；丧礼；出于+N/NP（…的原因/…的心理/…的考虑/礼貌），subj. do sth.】

你的朋友：原来送花还有这么一些禁忌，那就算了吧。中国人喜欢吃，送水果应该很安全吧？

你的回答： 也不一定。【建议词汇和结构：A是B（平安/和平/分离/不吉利）的象征，因此…；之所以…是因为…；平安；谐音；避开】
你的朋友： 我还以为什么水果都受欢迎，原来还有这些学问。哎，中国人的禁忌实在太多了，送礼真麻烦。
你的回答： 其实不同的文化或多或少都存在一些禁忌，…【建议词汇和结构：subj.（禁忌/教育/成长）是一种…的现象（，几乎…都…），…也不例外；避开；吉利；…，但是从另一方面来看，…都普遍存在；意味着；…让sb.1（对sb.2）产生一种…（失落/安全/信任）感；A对B有（很大/深刻的）影响】
你的朋友： 你说的一点儿都不错。幸好我先问过你，否则送错礼就闹笑话了。谢谢，我这两天再想想送什么好。

人际交流2：电子邮件

你的一位中国朋友最近要到美国来，他也正在烦恼送礼的问题，于是给你写信。请你读了之后给他回信。

新兰：
　　好久不见，近来一切都好吗？
　　下个月学校派我和几位同事到美国的几个中学进行交流，并讨论将来学校之间合作的可能。出国之前需要准备一些礼品，不知道你有什么建议？另外，其中一所学校的校长已邀请我们到他家晚餐，我正烦恼送什么礼物好，听说去西方人家做客，送酒最好，是吗？
　　祝　安康
　　　　　　　　　　　　　　　　　　　　　　　　　王丽文

【建议词汇和结构：送礼；subj.（禁忌/教育/成长）是一种…的现象（，几乎…都…），…也不例外；对sb.而言，…；象征；吉利；当成；…让sb.1（对sb.2）产生一种…（失落/安全/信任）感；…，但是从另一方面来看，…；场合；偶尔；subj.导致…；A跟B（之间）存在/有（着）（紧密/密切的）关系】

表达演说：外语学习与文化禁忌

请你准备一个3-5分钟的演讲，谈谈你认为外语学习者有没有必要遵从(zūncóng, follow)目标语国家文化中的禁忌，在外语教学中有没有必要融入这样的学习单元？

建议词汇和结构：subj.（禁忌/教育/成长）是一种…的现象（，几乎…都…），…也不例外；A对B有（很大/深刻的）影响；象征；导致…；当成；（…难免）让sb.1（对sb.2）产生一种…（失落/不安全/不信任）感；subj.以…（为）开头/中心/重点/标准；避开；吉利；…，但是从另一方面来看，…；意味着；迷信；民族；习俗；信仰；追求；综上所述，……

文化体验任务

通过采访分析比较中美的禁忌文化差异：

一、前期任务：
为了进一步了解中美禁忌文化的差异，找3–6个中国人进行采访。

- 采访要求：接受采访人来自三个不同年龄段，一半男性，一半女性
- 采访内容：
  1. 向中国人介绍三个美国禁忌（生活中、饭桌上、婚礼上、节日……）
  2. 请他们谈谈对这些美国禁忌的看法。
  3. 请他们介绍由这些美国禁忌想到的相关中国禁忌以及这些禁忌产生的原因。
  4. 请他们分享他们自己或朋友发生过的，跟禁忌有关的故事。

二、核心任务：
向其他学员报告你采访的结果，听完所有学员的采访结果以后，归纳总结中美的禁忌文化差异。

三、后期任务：
根据核心任务的讨论结果，给一位刚到中国留学的朋友写一封信，特别介绍几个重要的华人禁忌，建议他如何更快地适应当地的文化。

补充材料

[1] Cultural Taboos in China. (2007–2014). Retrieved from http://traditions.cultural-china.com/en/14Traditions5519.html
[2] 中国民间禁忌资料列表　网络链接　http://yw.eywedu.com/wenhua/ShowClass.asp?ClassID=130
[3] 万建中(2001)，《禁忌与中国文化》，北京：人民出版社
[4] 万建中(2010)，《中国民间禁忌风俗》，北京：中央编译出版社

第四课　流行新词
New and Popular Chinese Expressions

（文本形式：社会热点讨论）

> ➢ 关键词：
>   微博、用户、被自杀、被就业、弱势群体、社会文化现象
> ➢ 能力目标：
>   1. 学习者能理解诠释当前中国出现的流行新词。
>   2. 学习者能列举、介绍流行新词的意思及用法。
>   3. 学习者能讨论、分析流行新词所反映的社会文化现象。

课文全版 (Complete Version)

魏老师是一位K-12的中文老师。今年夏天,她带学生去了一趟中国,回美国以后,碰到了以前的同事杨老师,两人聊起了目前中国的一些流行新词的情况。

杨: 魏老师,我听说您最近去了一趟中国,感觉如何?

魏: 我觉得中国最近几年的变化挺大的,城市越来越现代化,人们的观念也越来越开放了。此外,我与当地年轻人交流的时候也发现如今出现了很多新的流行词,比方说,"微博[1]"、"土豪[2]"、"被自杀[3]"、"被就业"什么的,真是不胜枚举。

杨: 呵呵,您说的这些的确都是新颖[4]的流行词。像"微博"其实就是微型博客,现在在中国发展得非常迅速[5],据说目前中国的微博用户[6]已经达到5亿人了。

魏: 是吗?我没想到微博在中国居然这么受欢迎。

杨: 我觉得微博之所以能在中国迅速发展,其原因有两个,一是微博对使用者没有限制和规定,任何人都可以用它来记录自己的日常生活或者表达对时政[7]热点[8]的看法;二是微博非常方便快捷[9],用户通过它能及时了解到最新、最快的资讯[10],甚至是一些从其他媒体无法了解到的信息。

魏: 你说的对,现在微博的确已经成为信息表达和传播[11]的重要方式了,而且其社会影响力也越来越大。我身边年轻的中国朋友都有微博,在中国的时候我还在新浪上注册[12]了一个账户[13]呢。

杨: 哦,是吗?没想到,您还挺新潮[14]的。对了,您刚才还提到两个词,叫……,叫被什么来着?

魏: 你说的是"被自杀"和"被就业"吗?

杨: 对,对,对,就是"被自杀"和"被就业"。它们是什么意思?

[1]微博	wēibó	N.	weibo; Chinese term for microblog
[2]土豪	tǔháo	N.	upstart; local tyrant
[3]被自杀	bèizìshā	V.	"to be suicide" (a death claimed to be a suicide by the authorities)
[4]新颖	xīnyǐng	Adj.	[lit.] new bud, [fig.] new and original
[5]迅速	xùnsù	Adj.	rapid, speedy
[6]用户	yònghù	N.	user
[7]时政	shízhèng	N.	the political situation of the time
[8]热点	rèdiǎn	N.	hot spot
[9]快捷	kuàijié	Adj.	quick and convenient
[10]资讯	zīxùn	N.	information
[11]传播	chuánbō	V.	to spread
[12]注册	zhùcè	V.	to register
[13]账户	zhànghù	N.	(user) account
[14]新潮	xīncháo	Adj.	trendy, chic, fashionable

魏: "被自杀"的产生要追溯[15]到几年前在安徽[16]发生的一起死亡案件[17],当时一位政府职员检举[18]了当地政府的腐败[19]行为[20],不久以后便离奇[21]死亡[22],但随后[23]他的死被官方[24]归因于[25]自杀。之后,在各地又相继[26]出现了一系列[27]被有关部门认定[28]为自杀却疑点重重[29]的事件。公众质疑[30]这些事件,便开始在网上大量使用"被自杀"这个词,意思是一个人分明被别人杀害,但却说他是自杀。至于"被就业"也是最近几年比较流行的新词。目前,中国的高校[31]和教育部门[32]都需要体面[33]的就业率[34],所以很多高校规定[35]:毕业生不签[36]《就业协议[37]》就不发毕业证,这迫使[38]很多没有找到工作的毕业生自己找印章[39]盖[40]在《就业协议》上。有的学校甚至在学生毫不知情[41]的情况下,代替[42]没有找到工作的学生跟企业签署[43]虚假[44]的《就业协议》。教育部[45]每年公布[46]的高校就业率中,很多都是"被就业"的结果。现在你明白"被就业"的意思了吧?

[15]追溯	zhuīsù	V.	to track back to
[16]安徽	ānhuī	N.	a province in eastern China
[17]案件	ànjiàn	N.	case
[18]检举	jiǎnjǔ	V.	to report (an offence) to the authorities
[19]腐败	fǔbài	Adj.	corrupt; rotten
[20]行为	xíngwéi	N.	behavior
[21]离奇	líqí	Adj.	odd; extraordinary
[22]死亡	sǐwáng	V.	to die
[23]随后	suíhòu	Adv.	soon afterwards, thereafter
[24]官方	guānfāng	N.	(government) authority; official
[25]归因于	guīyīnyú	VP.	to attribute to; to credit with
[26]相继	xiāngjì	Adv.	one after another
[27]一系列	yíxìliè	Adj.	a series of
[28]认定	rèndìng	V.	to firmly believe, maintain, hold
[29]疑点重重	yídiǎnchóngchóng	Idiom	to be very suspicious
[30]质疑	zhìyí	V.	to question
[31]高校	gāoxiào	N.	institution of higher education; university; college
[32]教育部门	jiàoyùbùmén	NP.	Department of Education
[33]体面	tǐmiàn	Adj.	honorable; credible
[34]就业率	jiùyèlǜ	N.	employment rate
[35]规定	guīdìng	V./N.	to stipulate; rule; requirement
[36]签	qiān	V.	to sign
[37]协议	xiéyì	N.	agreement
[38]迫使	pòshǐ	V.	to force; to compel
[39]印章	yìnzhāng	N.	seal; stamp
[40]盖	gài	V.	to seal; to stamp
[41]毫不知情	háobùzhīqíng	Idiom	without the knowledge of
[42]代替	dàitì	V.	to substitute; to replace
[43]签署	qiānshǔ	V.	to sign (an agreement)
[44]虚假	xūjiǎ	Adj.	false; sham
[45]教育部	jiàoyùbù	N.	Ministry of Education
[46]公布	gōngbù	V.	to announce; to make public

杨： 听您这么一说，我觉得"被……"的人都是一些社会的弱势群体[47]。
魏： 你说的没错，在中国，这些弱势群体的权利常常受到强势[48]一方的侵犯[49]。而他们在强权[50]面前往往没有话语权[51]，所以只能通过像"被……"这样看似荒谬[52]的语法结构来表达自己的委屈[53]、无奈[54]和不满[55]。其实现在中国出现的很多流行新词背后都蕴含[56]着特定[57]的社会文化现象。了解这些流行新词将有助于我们更好地了解当代中国的社会文化。

 语言重点：

1. ① **Subj.**之所以…，其原因有…个，一是…，二是…，（…）

    There are … reasons why … , the first is … , the second is …

   ② **Subj.**之所以…，是因为…

    The reasons why … , include …

   - 中国社会之所以出现越来越多流行新词，其原因有两个，一是城市越来越现代化，二是人们的观念越来越开放。
   - 我觉得微博之所以能在中国迅速发展，是因为微博非常方便快捷，对使用者没有任何的限制和规定。

2. …来着？

    What is … again?

   - 对了，你先前是不是还提到别的词，叫……，叫什么来着？
   - 魏老师提到现在中国社会信息表达和传播的重要方式是什么来着？

---

[47]弱势群体	ruòshìqúntǐ	NP.	vulnerable group
[48]强势	qiángshì	Adj.	strong; powerful
[49]侵犯	qīnfàn	V.	to violate; encroach on
[50]强权	qiángquán	N.	(political) power
[51]话语权	huàyǔquán	N.	right of speech
[52]荒谬	huāngmiù	Adj.	ridiculous; absurd
[53]委屈	wěiqū	Adj.	aggrieved; feel wronged
[54]无奈	wúnài	Adj.	feel helpless
[55]不满	bùmǎn	Adj.	resentful; discontented
[56]蕴含	yùnhán	V.	to implicate
[57]特定	tèdìng	Adj.	special; particular

3. ① **A被sb.归因于B**（自杀/不断的创新/方便快捷/体面的就业率/坚定的信念）

   A is attributed to B (suicide/continuous/quick and convenient/reputable employment rate/steadfast belief) by sb.

   ② **Subj.把A归因于B**（自杀/不断的创新/方便快捷/体面的就业率/坚定的信念）

   Subj. attributes A to B (suicide/continuous/quick and convenient/reputable employment rate/steadfast belief).

   - 随后他的死被官方归因于自杀。
   - 很多人把微博的迅速发展归因于它的方便快捷。

4. **一系列+NP**（…的事件/…的任务/…的活动）

   a series of ... (incidents/tasks/activities)

   - 之后，在各地又相继出现了一系列被有关部门认定为自杀却疑点重重的事件。
   - 学生可以通过一系列真实的任务来学习如何使用第二语言跟别人交流。

5. **…迫使sb. do sth.**（签订…/签署…/承认…）

   ... forces sb. to ... (sign ... /admit ...)

   - 毕业生不签《就业协议》就不发毕业证，这迫使很多没有找到工作的毕业生自己找印章盖在《就业协议》上。
   - 人们不仅可以用微博来记录自己的日常生活或者表达对时政热点的看法，也可以通过微博揭露非法行为或事件，这可以迫使非法分子，特别是有权势的非法分子承认自己的罪行。

6. **Sb.通过…来表达+NP**（委屈/无奈/不满/愤怒）

   Sb. expresses (feeling wronged/feeling helpless/discontent/wrath) by means of ...

   - 但是在强权面前，他们没有话语权，只能通过"被……"这样一个看似荒谬的语法结构来表达自己的委屈、无奈和不满。
   - 微博实名制引起部分网友的不满，他们通过退出微博来表达自己的愤怒。

第四课　流行新词
New and Popular Chinese Expressions

（文本形式：社会热点讨论）

> ➤ 关键词：
>   微博、用户、被自杀、被就业、弱势群体、社会文化现象
> ➤ 能力目标：
>   1. 学习者能理解诠释当前中国出现的流行新词。
>   2. 学习者能列举、介绍流行新词的意思及用法。
>   3. 学习者能讨论、分析流行新词所反映的社会文化现象。

课文节选版 (Abridged Version)

魏老师是一位K-12的中文老师。今年夏天，她带学生去了一趟中国，回美国以后，碰到了以前的同事杨老师，两人聊起了目前中国的一些流行新词的情况。

杨：魏老师，我听说您最近去了一趟中国，感觉如何？
魏：我觉得中国最近几年的变化挺大的。城市越来越现代化，人们的观念也越来越开放了。此外，我与当地年轻人交流的时候也发现如今出现了很多新的流行词，比方说，"微博[1]"、"土豪[2]"、"被自杀[3]"、"被就业"什么的。
杨：呵呵，您说的这些的确都是新颖[4]的流行词。像"微博"其实就是微型博客，现在在中国发展得非常迅速，据说目前中国的微博用户[5]已经达到5亿人了。
魏：是吗？我真没有想到微博在中国这么受欢迎。
杨：我觉得微博之所以能在中国迅速发展，有两个原因，一是微博对使用者没有任何的限制[6]和规定[7]，任何人都可以用它来记录[8]自己的日常生活或者表达对时政[9]热点[10]的看法；二是微博非常方便快捷[11]，用户通过它能及时[12]了解到最新、最快的资讯[13]，甚至是一些从其他媒体无法了解到的信息。
魏：是呀，现在微博的确已经成为了信息表达和传播[14]的重要方式了，而且其社会影响力也越来越大。我身边年轻的中国朋友都有微博，在中国的时候我还在新浪上注册[15]了一个账户[16]呢。
杨：哦，是吗？没想到，您还挺新潮[17]的。对了，您刚才还提到一个词，叫……，叫被什么来着？
魏：你说的是"被自杀"吗？
杨：对，对，对，就是"被自杀"，这个结构[18]挺奇怪的，是什么意思？

[1] 微博	wēibó	N.	weibo; Chinese term for microblog
[2] 土豪	tǔháo	N.	upstart; local tyrant
[3] 被自杀	bèizìshā	V.	"to be suicide" (a death claimed to be a suicide by the authorities)
[4] 新颖	xīnyǐng	Adj.	[lit.] new bud, [fig.] new and original
[5] 用户	yònghù	N.	user
[6] 限制	xiànzhì	V.	to limit
[7] 规定	guīdìng	N./V.	regulation; to regulate
[8] 记录	jìlù	V.	to record
[9] 时政	shízhèng	N.	the political situation of the time
[10] 热点	rèdiǎn	N.	hot spot
[11] 快捷	kuàijié	Adj.	quick and convenient
[12] 及时	jíshí	Adj.	timely
[13] 资讯	zīxùn	N.	information
[14] 传播	chuánbō	V.	to spread
[15] 注册	zhùcè	V.	to register
[16] 账户	zhànghù	N.	(user) account
[17] 新潮	xīncháo	Adj.	trendy, chic, fashionable
[18] 结构	jiégòu	N.	structure

206 *New and Popular Chinese Expressions*

魏： 我听说这个词的产生和几年前在安徽[19]发生的一起死亡案件有关，当时一位政府职员检举[20]了当地政府的腐败[21]行为[22]，不久以后便离奇[23]死亡[24]，但官方[25]认定[26]他是自杀。之后，在各地又出现了一系列[27]被有关部门认定为自杀却疑点重重[28]的事件。公众质疑[29]这些事件，便开始在网上大量使用"被自杀"这个词，意思是一个人分明被别人杀害，但却说他是自杀。还有一个"被就业"也是最近几年比较流行的新词。目前，中国的高校[30]和教育部门[31]都需要体面[32]的就业率[33]，所以很多高校规定：毕业生不签[34]《就业协议[35]》就不发毕业证，这迫使[36]很多没有找到工作的毕业生都签虚假[37]的就业协议。现在你明白"被就业"的意思了吧？

杨： 听您这么一说，我觉得"被……"的人都是一些社会的弱势群体[38]。

魏： 你说的没错，在中国，这些弱势群体的权利常常受到强势[39]一方的侵犯[40]。而他们在强权[41]面前往往没有话语权[42]，所以只能通过"被……"这样看似荒谬[43]的语法结构来表达自己的委屈[44]、无奈[45]和不满[46]。其实现在中国出现的很多流行新词背后都蕴含[47]着特定[48]的社会文化现象。

[19]安徽	ānhuī	N.	a province in eastern China
[20]检举	jiǎnjǔ	V.	to report (an offence) to the authorities
[21]腐败	fǔbài	Adj.	corrupt; rotten
[22]行为	xíngwéi	N.	behavior
[23]离奇	líqí	Adj.	odd; extraordinary
[24]死亡	sǐwáng	V.	to die
[25]官方	guānfāng	N.	(government) authority; official
[26]认定	rèndìng	V.	firmly believe, maintain, hold
[27]一系列	yíxìliè	Adj.	a series of
[28]疑点重重	yídiǎnchóngchóng	Idiom	to be very suspicious
[29]质疑	zhìyí	V.	to question
[30]高校	gāoxiào	N.	institution of higher education; university; college
[31]教育部门	jiàoyùbùmén	NP.	Department of Education
[32]体面	tǐmiàn	Adj.	honorable; creditable
[33]就业率	jiùyèlǜ	N.	employment rate
[34]签	qiān	V.	to sign
[35]协议	xiéyì	N.	agreement
[36]迫使	pòshǐ	V.	to force; to compel
[37]虚假	xūjiǎ	Adj.	false; sham
[38]弱势群体	ruòshìqúntǐ	NP.	vulnerable group
[39]强势	qiángshì	Adj.	strong; powerful
[40]侵犯	qīnfàn	V.	to violate; encroach on
[41]强权	qiángquán	N.	(political) power
[42]话语权	huàyǔquán	N.	right of speech
[43]荒谬	huāngmiù	Adj.	ridiculous; absurd
[44]委屈	wěiqū	Adj.	aggrieved; feel wronged
[45]无奈	wúnài	Adj.	feel helpless
[46]不满	bùmǎn	Adj.	resentful; discontented
[47]蕴含	yùnhán	V.	to implicate
[48]特定	tèdìng	Adj.	special, particular

语言重点：

1. ① **Subj.之所以…，是因为…**

   The reasons why ... , include ...

   ② **Subj.之所以…，其原因有…个，一是…，二是…，（…）**

   There are ... reasons why ... , the first is ... , the second is ...

   - 我觉得微博之所以能在中国迅速发展，其原因有两个，一是微博对使用者没有任何的限制和规定，二是微博非常方便快捷。
   - 中国社会出现越来越多流行新词，其原因有两个，一是城市越来越现代化，二是人们的观念越来越开放。

2. **…来着？**

   What is ... again?

   - 对了，你先前是不是还提到别的词，叫……，叫什么来着？
   - 魏老师提到现在中国社会信息表达和传播的重要方式是什么来着？

3. **一系列+NP（…的事件/…的任务/…的活动）**

   a series of ... (incidents/tasks/activities)

   - 之后，在各地又相继出现了一系列被有关部门认定为自杀却疑点重重的事件。
   - 学生可以通过一系列真实的任务来学习如何使用第二语言跟别人交流。

4. **…迫使sb. do sth.（签订…/签署…/承认…）**

   ... forces sb. to ... (sign ... /admit ...)

   - 毕业生不签《就业协议》就不发毕业证，这迫使很多没有找到工作的毕业生都签虚假的就业协议。
   - 人们不仅可以用微博来记录自己的日常生活或者表达对时政热点的看法，也可以通过微博揭露非法行为或事件，这可以迫使非法分子，特别是有权势的非法分子承认自己的罪行。

5. **Sb.通过…来表达+NP（委屈/无奈/不满/愤怒）**

   Sb. expresses (feeling wronged/feeling helpless/discontent/wrath) by means of ...

   - 但是在强权面前，他们没有话语权，只能通过"被……"这样一个看似荒谬的语法结构来表达自己的委屈、无奈和不满。
   - 微博实名制引起部分网友的不满，他们通过退出微博来表达自己的愤怒。

练习活动

理解诠释1：预习单

先看课文，然后完成下面的作业：

一、说明微博在中国发展迅速的两个原因。
1、
2、

二、在下面4个选项中，选出与课文描述不符的一项。
A. 在微博上能看到一些电视上看不到的新闻。
B. 在中国已经有很多人注册了微博账户。
C. 高校公布的就业率往往是真实的。
D. 人们会通过创造新词来表达对不公平现象的不满。

三、根据课文中对"被"字结构的介绍，阐述你对"被幸福"和"被捐款"的理解。

理解诠释2：扩展阅读

选自《改革开放30年来社会流行的新词新语及其规范化》
作者：黄芳

　　在人们的日常生活中，在每一个特定的历史阶段都会出现一些反映当时事物与现象的词语，这些词语在当时特定的阶段都曾被列为流行新词。新词汇的来源很广泛，基本包括下面几个方面：

　　1. 外借词。改革开放30多年以来，随着中国与国外联系的日益频繁，汉语也在不断地从外族语言中吸收有生命力的成分来丰富自己。例如，克隆、托福、卡通等等。以往借用外来词语，大体分为意译（如"人权(human right)"、"软饮料(soft drink)"）、音译（如"克隆(clone)"、"伊妹儿(E-mail)"）、音译兼意译（如"因特网(Internet)"、"迷你裙(mini skirt)"、"T恤衫(T shirt)"）几类。

　　2. 方言词及港台词。多种方言并存是汉语言文化的重要特色，方言词除了能带给人新颖之感，有时表达更经济简洁、清楚生动，因而受到社会各阶级的普遍认可，如"打的"一词源于香港，在普通话中，与之对应的概念是"坐出租汽车"。可以看出"打的"较"坐出租汽车"更加具有新鲜感、时尚感。

　　3. 旧词新用。旧词新用指的是一些已经不在交际场所使用，成为"历史性词语"的词，又被赋予新的意义或扩大其使用范围，重新活跃起来。比如"下课"原指上课时间结束了，现在的意义还指辞职或被撤换。

　　4. 新生词语。这里是指随着新事物的产生，人们依照汉语构词法而创造出的新的词或短语。这类新生词语的寿命不等，有的会随着社会的演变、新事物现象新颖色彩的退化而退出交际场合，如"PK"、"驴友"、"秀"等；但有的具有较强生命力，在发展过程中逐渐深化词义内涵或转变词义，而被保留在共同语中，如"转基因"、"知识产权"等。

5. 缩略词。缩略词一般是把音节较长的词或词组缩简为双音节词。例如，审批（审查批示）、消协（消费者权益保护协会）等等。这些新构成的缩略词既顺应了汉语词汇双音节化的主流趋势，也符合语言表达的经济原则。随着英语成为国际通用语言，很多英语缩写也直接进入汉语中来，例如，CT（X射线电子计算机断层扫描）、TV（电视）、WTO（世贸组织）等。

1. 关于流行词语，哪一个叙述是不对的？
   A. 每个历史阶段都有可能产生新的词语
   B. 流行词语的来源不是只有一种
   C. 流行词语不一定会被人长期使用
   D. 流行词语跟汉语的结构毫无关系

2. Starbucks咖啡中文的翻译为"星巴克"。根据你的理解，这个词的来源和下列哪个词一样？
   A. 电脑　　B. 因特网　　C. 北大（北京大学）　　D. 卡通

3. 人们喜欢用"打的"来代替"坐出租汽车"，原因有哪些：（多选）
   A. 更简单　　　　　　B. 重视方言
   C. 有新鲜感　　　　　D. "打的"的历史比较长

4. 最近几年有哪些词是英语的流行新词？请你举出1–2个，并且说明该词语是属于外借词、方言词、旧词新用、新生词语，还是缩略词。

人际交流1：访谈

为了让全校的师生对不同的国家有更多的了解，学校每个星期都在校刊上刊登一则关于某个国家的专栏(column)。这一个星期是"中国周"，学校的小记者来访问你，希望你给同学们介绍一下"Weibo"的情况。

小记者：	老师好，我们都知道近年来网络在中国发展得特别迅速。能不能请您给我们介绍一下什么是Weibo？
你的回答：	【建议词汇和结构：用户；热点；资讯；传播；时政；sb.通过…来表达+NP（无奈/不满/委屈/看法）】
小记者：	微博为什么受到中国人的欢迎？使用微博容易吗？
你的回答：	【建议词汇和结构：subj.之所以…，其原因有…个，一是…，二是…；规定；注册；帐户】
小记者：	您认为微博的发展对社会可能有哪些影响？
你的回答：	【建议词汇和结构：弱势群体；话语权；官方；腐败；质疑；案件；侵犯；A被sb.归因于B（自杀/不断的创新/方便快捷/体面的就业率/坚定的信念）；…迫使sb.+do sth.（承认/签订/公布）；一系列+NP（…的事件/…的活动/…的任务）；虚假】
小记者：	老师，对了，我好像还听同学提过一个叫微什么来着的APP，好像现在也很受中国年轻人的欢迎。
你的回答：	哦，你说的是微信，也就是WeChat。

小记者： 对对对，就是微信。啊，时间不早了，谢谢老师今天抽空接受我们的访谈，我们下次再来请教您关于微信的事。

人际交流2：短信

你的朋友用手机给你发来信息，希望跟你讨论一下流行新词教学的问题。

> 小林，我的学生对中文网络的流行词语很感兴趣。您觉得学生有没有需要在课堂上学习这些新颖的词语？如果要教，你有什么建议吗？

【建议词汇和结构：不胜枚举；subj.之所以…，其原因有…个，一是…，二是…；热点；新潮；蕴含；特定；sb.通过…来表达+NP（无奈/不满/委屈/看法）；A跟B（之间）有（着）（密切的）关系；…，但是从另一方面来看，…；价值观念；新颖；规定；…迫使sb.+do sth.】

表达演说：对流行新词的看法

请你准备一个5分钟的演讲，谈谈你是否同意下列看法？

> 大多数的流行新词或者不符合语言本身的结构，破坏了语言的"纯正性"；或者用字粗俗不雅，听起来没有礼貌；有时甚至成为人们沟通的障碍。而且，流行词汇往往是短暂的，不久就会消失。因此，我们没有必要重视这些新词汇，更没有必要特别花时间去学习。

发表演说时，你可以从以下几个方面谈起：

(1) 对人们生活的影响；(2) 对语言发展的影响；(3) 对文化发展的影响等等。

建议词汇和结构：不胜枚举；资讯；传播；subj.之所以…，其原因有…个，一是…，二是…；新潮；特定；sb.通过…来表达+NP（无奈/不满/委屈/看法）；新颖；…迫使sb.+do sth.；一系列+NP（…的事件/…的活动/…的任务）；限制；及时；荒谬；归因于；具有…的特性/优势；毫无+N（疑问/希望/关系）；价值观念

反思任务
通过采访了解流行新词的用法以及这些词产生的文化背景:

一、前期任务:
为了进一步了解中国流行新词的情况,对中国人进行采访。

- 采访要求:至少采访四位陌生的中国人,两个年轻人,两个中年人。
- 采访内容:
  1. 让中国人在下列的流行新词中选择出他/她认为最流行的三个,并让他/她说明该词的词义、使用的语境和具体用法,以及这个词产生的文化背景。
  2. 让他/她介绍一个他/她觉得有意思的流行新词。

雷人	秒杀
房奴	高大上
坑爹、拼爹	奇葩
裸婚	伤不起
HOLD不住/HOLD得住	官二代
屌丝	女汉子
高富帅、白富美	土豪

二、核心任务:
给其他学员介绍,通过采访你所了解到的十个流行新词以及这些新词产生的文化背景,并且教会其他学员如何正确使用这些流行新词。

三、后期任务:
在其他学员教你的流行新词中选择至少三个流行新词创作一个小故事。

补充材料
[1]《网络汉语"入侵"纯正英语?》网络连接 http://news.sina.com.cn/c/2013-11-25/070128800997.shtml
[2]《微博的社会文化传统分析》网络连接 http://media.people.com.cn/GB/22114/52789/205663/13015452.html
[3]《年度汉语突出时尚鲜活 流行语记录时代生活》(视频文件)网络连接 http://v.ifeng.com/history/wenhuashidian/201312/0197d48a-d898-4de4-a66e-0a421d5d61b7.shtml
[4] 刘德联(2006),《时尚汉语》,北京:世界图书出版公司

第五课　现代科技：微信[1]
Modern Technology: WeChat

（文本形式：科技说明）

- ➤ 关键词：
  应用软件、操作、社交、用户、上传、发送、添加、删除
- ➤ 能力目标：
  1. 学习者能阅读理解科技应用软件的使用说明。
  2. 学习者能说明、讨论现代科技的不同特点。
  3. 学习者能口述、演示现代科技应用软件的功能及方法。
  4. 学习者能讨论、比较不同社交类科技应用软件的异同。

---

[1] 微信　wēixin　N.　WeChat (social media platform)

Modern Technology: WeChat   213

课文全版 (Complete Version)

微信是中国一家电脑公司于2011年初推出[2]的一款[3]手机聊天软件[4]，该软件不但能快速收发语音短信[5]和图片，而且支持多人语音对话。要想使用微信，用户只要在智能手机[6]上下载[7]并安装[8]这款应用软件[9]就可以了。微信具有三个吸引人的特点：一是可以免费使用。用户在手机上使用微信不用支付[10]任何通讯[11]费用，只需消耗[12]少量的流量[13]。二是多功能[14]。微信除了具有通过网络收发语音、视频、图片和文字等功能以外，还提供"摇一摇"、"附近的人"等社交[15]插件[16]，帮助用户在网络上广交朋友。三是应用广泛。微信在苹果、安卓[17]等手机操作系统[18]上都可以使用，并提供多国语言界面[19]。凭借[20]这三大特点，微信一经推出就受到了广大用户的欢迎，截止[21]到2013年1月，微信的注册用户量已经突破[22]了3亿，成为亚洲地区用户群体最大的移动即时[23]通讯软件。

用户要想使用微信，首先需要登录[24]微信官方网站[25]http://weixin.qq.com下载适合自己手机操作系统的应用软件并进行安装，然后就可以注册了。注册时，用户可以使用手机号进行快速注册，只需要选择所在国家和地区，输入手机号及密码[26]即可。

[2]推出	tuīchū	V.	to launch; release
[3]款	kuǎn	Classifier	classifier for software
[4]软件	ruǎnjiàn	N.	software
[5]短信	duǎnxìn	N.	text, message
[6]智能手机	zhìnéngshǒujī	NP.	smartphone
[7]下载	xiàzài	V.	to download
[8]安装	ānzhuāng	V.	to install
[9]应用软件	yìngyòngruǎnjiàn	N.	app (for smartphones, tablets or computers)
[10]支付	zhīfù	V.	to pay
[11]通讯	tōngxùn	N.	communications
[12]消耗	xiāohào	V.	to consume
[13]流量	liúliàng	N.	data
[14]功能	gōngnéng	N.	function
[15]社交	shèjiāo	N.	social contact
[16]插件	chājiàn	N.	plug-in (software component)
[17]安卓	ānzhuó	N.	Android
[18]操作系统	cāozuòxìtǒng	NP.	operating system
[19]界面	jièmiàn	N.	interface
[20]凭借	píngjiè	V.	by means of
[21]截止	jiézhǐ	V.	by the end of, with the stopping point
[22]突破	tūpò	V.	to break through
[23]即时	jíshí	Adv.	immediately
[24]登录	dēnglù	V.	to log in
[25]官方网站	guānfāngwǎngzhàn	NP.	official website
[26]密码	mìmǎ	N.	password, PIN

登录微信以后，主界面下方有四个选项[27]，分别是："微信"、"通讯录[28]"、"发现"和"我"。点击[29]选项"我"，用户可以进入"个人信息"界面填写[30]个人资料，上传[31]个人照片，或者修改[32]个人情况介绍等。

要想添加[33]或删除[34]好友的话，需要进入"通讯录"选项，点击"添加"或"删除"键，要想利用"QQ好友"或者"手机联系人[35]"来查找[36]好友，可以输入好友的QQ号、手机号或者微信号来搜索[37]添加好友。添加以后，点击朋友的头像[38]，就可以开始与微信好友进行对话了。与好友对话时，可以发送[39]文字短信，也可以发送语音短信。要想发送语音短信，需按下"按住说话"键[40]，开始录音[41]说话，录音完毕[42]后松开[43]按钮[44]，语音信息会自动[45]发送到对方手机。在北京街头，随处都能看到用嘴对着手机说话的人，他们就是在利用微信免费发送语音短信呢。

如果想给好友发送照片或者视频，可以点击对话框[46]右下方的加号[47]键 ➕，选中[48]"照片"图标[49]，然后选择保存[50]在手机相册[51]里的照片或者视频，最后按"发送"键。如果用户想要拍摄[52]实时视频，就点击"拍摄"键开始录制[53]，结束录制并压缩[54]完毕以后，点击"播放[55]"键进行预览[56]，或点击"发送"发出视频。

[27]选项	xuǎnxiàng	N.	options
[28]通讯录	tōngxùnlù	N.	address book
[29]点击	diǎnjī	V.	to click
[30]填写	tiánxiě	V.	to fill in
[31]上传	shàngchuán	V.	to upload
[32]修改	xiūgǎi	V.	to correct
[33]添加	tiānjiā	V.	to add
[34]删除	shānchú	V.	to delete
[35]联系人	liánxìrén	N.	contact person
[36]查找	cházhǎo	V	to search for
[37]搜索	sōusuǒ	V	to search via internet or database
[38]头像	tóuxiàng	N.	profile picture
[39]发送	fāsòng	V.	to transmit; dispatch; send
[40]键	jiàn	N.	key (on computer's keyboard, piano)
[41]录音	lùyīn	V./N.	to record sound; sound recording
[42]完毕	wánbì	V.	to finish; complete
[43]松开	sōngkāi	V.	to release; let go
[44]按钮	ànniǔ	N.	button
[45]自动	zìdòng	Adv.	automatic
[46]对话框	duìhuàkuàng	N.	conversation box (computing)
[47]加号	jiāhào	N.	plus sign
[48]选中	xuǎnzhòng	V.	to select; decide upon
[49]图标	túbiāo	N.	icon (computing)
[50]保存	bǎocún	V.	to save (computing)
[51]相册	xiàngcè	N.	photo album
[52]拍摄	pāishè	V.	to take (a picture); to record (radio)
[53]录制	lùzhì	V.	to record (video/audio, etc.)
[54]压缩	yāsuō	V.	to compress (into a zip file)
[55]播放	bōfàng	V.	to play; broadcast
[56]预览	yùlǎn	V.	to preview

总而言之[57]，微信的设计以用户为中心，各项操作非常灵活[58]、智能，是一款集多项功能于一身的社交应用软件。你还在等什么？现在就赶紧尝试一下吧，相信它一定会为你的生活带来无限乐趣！

 语言重点：

1. **Subj.于point in time推出…（产品/游戏/软件）**

   At (point in time) subj. launches/comes out with … (product/game/software)

   - 微信是中国一家电脑公司于2011年初推出的一款手机聊天软件。
   - 苹果公司将于今年下半年推出第六代苹果手机。

2. **Subj. +凭借+NP（…的功能）+VP（受到欢迎/成为…）**

   Subj. + by means of/thanks to + … functions + VP (is very popular/becomes …)

   - 微信凭借这三大特点，一经推出就受到了广大用户的欢迎。
   - 该电脑公司凭借微信这一产品，再次成为中国国内最受欢迎的社交电脑公司。

3. **Subj.一经+VP（推出/采用/发现）+就/便…**

   Subj. + once/as soon as/immediately after + VP (launching/adopting/discovering)

   - 微信凭借这三大特点，一经推出就受到了广大用户的欢迎.
   - 发送语音消息这一通讯方式一经推出，便受到全国用户，尤其是一线大城市白领和高校学生的欢迎。

4. **截止到+point in time, subj. …**

   By the end of/with the stopping point of + point in time, subj. …

   - 截止到2013年1月，微信的注册用户量已经突破了3亿，成为亚洲地区用户群体最大的移动即时通讯软件。
   - 我上传了新的微信头像后，截止到昨晚，已经有五十多人要求添加我为好友了。

5. **Subj.集+NP（各项功能/美貌与智慧/万千宠爱）于一身**

   Subj. focuses/gathers + NP (every function/beauty and intelligence/love) into one object.

   - 微信以用户体验为中心，各项操作非常灵活、智能，是一款集多项功能于一身的应用软件。
   - 要想成为一个集美貌与智慧于一身的女人，除了要有漂亮的外表以外，还应该有丰富的内涵。

---

[57] 总而言之　zǒngéryánzhī　Idiom　in a word; in short; in brief
[58] 灵活　línghuó　Adj.　flexible

第五课　现代科技：微信[1]
Modern Technology: WeChat

（文本形式：科技说明）

> 关键词：
> 应用软件、操作、社交、用户、上传、发送、添加、删除
> 能力目标：
> 1. 学习者能阅读理解科技应用软件的使用说明。
> 2. 学习者能说明、讨论现代科技的不同特点。
> 3. 学习者能口述、演示现代科技应用软件的功能及方法。
> 4. 学习者能讨论、比较不同社交类科技应用软件的异同。

---

[1] 微信　wēixin　N.　WeChat (social media platform)

课文节选版 (Edited Version)

微信是一款[2]手机聊天软件[3]，用户只要在智能手机[4]上下载[5]并安装[6]这款应用软件[7]就可以快速收发[8]语音短信[9]和图片，和很多人同时进行语音对话。微信具有三个吸引人的特点：一是可以免费使用。用户在手机上使用微信不用支付[10]任何通讯[11]费用，只需消耗[12]少量的流量[13]。二是多功能[14]。微信除了可以让用户通过网络收发语音、视频[15]、图片和文字，还提供很多社交[16]插件[17]帮助用户在网络上广交朋友。三是应用广泛。微信在不同的手机操作系统[18]上都可以使用，并提供多国语言界面[19]。凭借[20]这三大特点，微信一经推出[21]就受到了广大用户的欢迎，成为现在最流行的移动即时[22]通讯软件。

用户要想使用微信，可以登录[23]微信官方网站[24]http://weixin.qq.com下载适合自己手机操作系统的应用软件并进行安装，然后就可以注册了。注册时，用户可以使用手机号进行快速注册，只需要输入[25]手机号和密码[26]就可以了。

[2]款	kuǎn	Classifier	classifier for software
[3]软件	ruǎnjiàn	N.	software
[4]智能手机	zhìnéngshǒujī	NP.	smartphone
[5]下载	xiàzài	V.	to download
[6]安装	ānzhuāng	V.	to install
[7]应用软件	yìngyòngruǎnjiàn	N.	app (for smartphones, tablets or computers)
[8]收发	shōufā	V.	send and receive
[9]短信	duǎnxìn	N.	text, message
[10]支付	zhīfù	V.	to pay
[11]通讯	tōngxùn	N.	communications
[12]消耗	xiāohào	V.	to consume
[13]流量	liúliàng	N.	data
[14]功能	gōngnéng	N.	function
[15]视频	shìpín	N.	video
[16]社交	shèjiāo	N.	social contact
[17]插件	chājiàn	N.	plug-in (software component)
[18]操作系统	cāozuòxìtǒng	NP.	operating system
[19]界面	jièmiàn	N.	interface
[20]凭借	píngjiè	V.	by means of
[21]推出	tuīchū	V.	to launch; release
[22]即时	jíshí	Adv.	immediately
[23]登录	dēnglù	V.	to log in
[24]官方网站	guānfāngwǎngzhàn	NP.	official website
[25]输入	shūrù	V.	to input
[26]密码	mìmǎ	N.	password, PIN

Modern Technology: WeChat

  登录微信以后，主界面下方有四个选项[27]，分别是："微信"、"通讯录[28]"、"发现"和"我"。点击[29]选项"我"，用户可以进入"个人信息"界面填写[30]个人资料，上传[31]个人照片，或者修改[32]个人情况介绍等。

  要想添加[33]好友的话，需要进入"通讯录"选项，点击"添加"键，输入好友的QQ号、手机号或者微信号来搜索[34]添加好友。添加完以后，就可以与微信好友进行对话了。与好友对话时，要想发送语音短信，需按下[35]"按住说话"键[36]，开始录音[37]，录完音松开[38]按钮[39]，语音信息会自动发送到对方手机。在北京街头，随处都能看到用嘴对着手机说话的人，他们就是在利用微信免费发送语音短信呢。

  如果想给好友发送照片或者视频，可以点击对话框[40]右下方的加号[41]键➕，选中[42]"照片"图标[43]，然后选择保存[44]在手机相册里的照片或者视频，最后按"发送"键。如果用户想要拍摄[45]实时视频，就点击"拍摄"键开始录制[46]，结束录制并压缩[47]完毕以后，点击"播放"[48]键进行预览[49]，或点击"发送"发出视频。

  总而言之[50]，微信的设计以用户为中心，各项操作非常灵活[51]、智能，是一款集多项功能于一身的社交应用软件。你还在等什么？现在就赶紧尝试一下吧，相信它一定会为你的生活带来无限乐趣！

---

[27]选项	xuǎnxiàng	N.	options
[28]通讯录	tōngxùnlù	N.	address book
[29]点击	diǎnjī	V.	to click
[30]填写	tiánxiě	V.	to fill in
[31]上传	shàngchuán	V.	to upload
[32]修改	xiūgǎi	V.	to correct
[33]添加	tiānjiā	V.	to add
[34]搜索	sōusuǒ	V	to search via internet or database
[35]按下	ànxià	V.	to press
[36]键	jiàn	N.	key (on computer's keyboard, piano)
[37]录音	lùyīn	V./N.	to record sound; sound recording
[38]松开	sōngkāi	V.	to release; let go
[39]按钮	ànniǔ	N.	button
[40]对话框	duìhuàkuàng	N.	conversation box (computing)
[41]加号	jiāhào	N.	plus sign
[42]选中	xuǎnzhòng	V.	to select; decide upon
[43]图标	túbiāo	N.	icon (computing)
[44]保存	bǎocún	V.	to save (computing)
[45]拍摄	pāishè	V.	to take (a picture); to record (radio)
[46]录制	lùzhì	V.	to record (video/audio etc.)
[47]压缩	yāsuō	V.	to compress (into a zip file)
[48]播放	bōfàng	V.	to play; broadcast
[49]预览	yùlǎn	V.	to preview
[50]总而言之	zǒngéryánzhī	Idiom	in a word; in short; in brief
[51]灵活	línghuó	Adj.	flexible

语言重点：

1. **Subj. +凭借+NP（…的功能）+VP（受到欢迎/成为…）**

    Subj. + by means of/thanks to + … functions + VP (is very popular/becomes …)

    - 微信凭借这三大特点，一经推出就受到了广大用户的欢迎。
    - 该电脑公司凭借微信这一产品，再次成为中国国内最受欢迎的社交电脑公司。

2. **Subj.一经+VP（推出/采用/发现）+就/便…**

    Subj. + once/as soon as/immediately after + VP (launching/adopting/discovering)

    - 微信凭借这三大特点，一经推出就受到了广大用户的欢迎。
    - 发送语音消息这一通讯方式一经推出，便受到全国用户，尤其是一线大城市白领和高校学生的欢迎。

3. **Subj.集+NP（各项功能/美貌与智慧/万千宠爱）于一身**

    Subj. focuses/gathers + NP (every function/beauty and intelligence/love) into one object.

    - 微信以用户体验为中心，各项操作非常灵活、智能，是一款集多项功能于一身的应用软件。
    - 要想成为一个集美貌与智慧于一身的女人，除了要有漂亮的外表以外，还应该有丰富的内涵。

练习活动

 理解诠释1：预习单

先看课文，然后完成下面的作业：

一、根据课文，填写下面的"微信"使用说明。
1、"微信"用户注册说明：

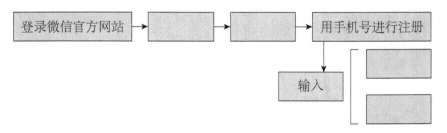

2、"微信"用户使用说明：

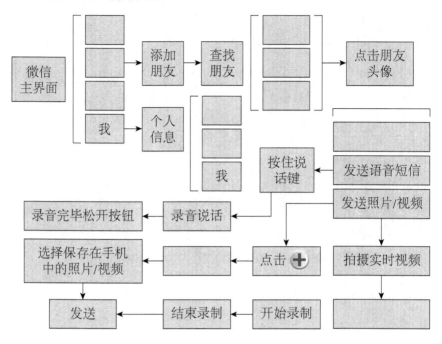

📖 **理解诠释2：扩展阅读**

在线汉语教学和资源系统

——截选自《在线汉语教学和资源系统建设的问题与改进》笪骏

1. 通用型教学管理平台

   这类教学平台[52]为各个科目的教学和课程管理提供相应的工具，比如：用户管理、在线作业和测试、教学文件管理、用户交流和日历等，教师可以在这类教学平台上上传自己的教案。

   美国大学常用的平台包括 Blackboard Learning System、Desire2Learn Learning Environment和Moodle，它们一般由学校统一提供和管理。

   优点：　系统功能相对稳定和成熟。
   缺点：　并非为（汉语）语言教学所专门设计，缺少一些语言教学特需的工具和功能。

---

[52]平台　píngtái　N.　platform

2. 专用汉语教学平台

   这类平台专为汉语学习者所设计，提供了（相对）完整的在线汉语课程和其他教学内容。在美国制作和出版的专用汉语教学平台包括：MyChineseLab、ActiveChinese[53]和IQChinese[54]。

   优点： 汉语课程和汉语教学解决办法比较系统。
   缺点： 用户无法选择其内容配合其他教材或者课程的使用。

3. 通用型辅助教学平台

   这类平台主要是提供在线教学环境和工具以方便教师创建和分享教学资源，给学习者提供（互动）学习内容，如在线互动练习、问卷调查和在线测试等功能。同时，它们会提供由第三方（如出版社）开发的教学资源。

   这类平台如：Quia[55]，上面有《Integrated Chinese》的学生练习册。

   优点： 提供的教学资源可以由教师自己创建和分享，第三方提供的资源多为配合现在的教材。
   缺点： 不提供完整的教学管理环境和功能以及完整的课程学习内容。

4. 语言教学在线工具

   这类平台为满足（汉）语言教学的特殊需求提供一种或有限的几种语言学习工具。

   比如在美国出版的Lingt[56]和《线上中文工具》[57]。

   优点： Lingt提供的在线多媒体口语作业系统可以很方便地让教师上传和批改带有口语练习的作业。

5. 汉语教师和学习者社区平台

   这类平台主要通过如论坛、博客、微博和短信等工具为教师和学习者提供互动社区。

   比如：国内开发的如《易校园》和《网络孔子学院》的用户社区。

   优点： 话题集中于汉语学习，对参与者没有严格的限制，提供的互助工具也更丰富。

1. 该阅读文章介绍了几类在线教学平台？其各自的优点分别是什么？

2. 下面哪些教学平台可以由教师自己创建和分享教学资源？（可多选）
   A. My Chinese Lab   B. Quia   C. Lingt   D. 《易校园》

---

[53] 参见http://www.activechinese.com/
[54] 参见http://www.iqchinese.com/
[55] 参见http://www.quia.com/
[56] 参见http://lingt.com
[57] 参见http://www.mandarintools.com

3. 下列哪些事情可以在通用型辅助教学平台上完成？
   A. 在线互动练习
   B. 在线测试
   C. 教师分享教学资源
   D. 提供完整的教学文件管理

4. 利用Lingt，教师可以做下列哪些事情？（可多选）
   A. 教师上传录音
   B. 学生利用Lingt完成口语作业
   C. 教师在Lingt上批改学生的口语作业
   D. 教师利用Lingt创建教学论坛

人际交流1：采访调查

目前一家用户体验调查网站想对微信用户进行一项调查，作为其中一位被调查者，请你回答以下的问题。

调查人员：	您好，您是从什么时候开始，因为什么原因使用微信的呢？
你的回答：	【建议词汇和结构：新颖；流量；用户；及时；快捷；新潮；应用软件；社交；灵活；之所以…，其原因有…个，一是…，二是…；总而言之；subj.集…（各项功能/很多优点）于一身】
调查者：	您最喜欢使用微信的什么功能？为什么？
你的回答：	【建议词汇和结构：及时；登录；下载；通讯录；上传；修改；添加；删除；搜索；查找；发送；按钮；之所以…，其原因有…个，一是…，二是…；总而言之；subj.集…（各项功能/很多优点）于一身】
调查者：	您刚才谈了很多微信的优点，那您觉得微信还有没有什么方面需要改进？
你的回答：	【建议词汇和结构：subj.以…为中心；限制；规定；记录；传播；及时；登录；下载；上传；修改；添加；删除；搜索；查找；发送；按钮；subj.凭借+NP（..的功能）+VP.】
调查人员：	非常谢谢您今天接受我们的调查采访。

人际交流2：回复微信留言

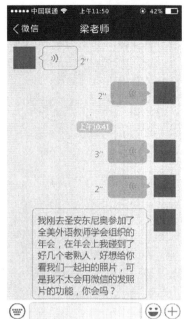

你的朋友周老师在微信上请教你一个关于微信操作的问题，请你回复她的留言。

【建议词汇和结构：发送；点击；保存；相册；选中；加号；拍摄；松开；完毕；查找；搜索；上传；下载】

 表达演说：用户体验报告

根据下面的采访单，采访最少3位微信用户，了解他们使用微信的情况，并根据采访结果，归纳总结出微信用户对微信这款应用软件的使用情况以及评价，最后完成一篇800字的微信用户体验报告。

1.	使用微信的频率：A 每天　B 每周1–3次　C 每月1–3次
2.	在什么情况下使用微信？
3.	最喜欢使用微信的什么功能？为什么？
4.	对微信操作便利性的评价：
5.	希望微信在什么方面进行改善或者增加什么服务？
6.	其他

文化体验任务

一、前期任务：

三位成员一组，每位成员分别了解一款社交软件（这些软件包括：QQ、人人以及微博），小组成员可以通过以下两种形式了解软件的情况

1. 通过采访该款社交软件的用户，了解软件的情况，采访内容包括以下的方面：
   - 被采访者什么时候使用这款软件？跟谁用？用来做什么？
   - 被采访者认为这款社交软件有什么优点和缺点？
   - 请被采访者详细介绍这款社交软件应该如何操作。

2. 通过上网了解该款社交软件的情况。了解的情况应该包括以下的方面：
   - 用户什么时候用这款软件？跟谁用？用来做什么？
   - 这款社交软件有什么优点和缺点？
   - 这款社交软件应该如何操作？

二、核心任务：

1. 小组成员根据了解到的情况，给别的成员介绍自己了解的社交软件，并且把该款软件跟一个别的社交软件（可以是中国的也可以是美国的）做简单的比较。
2. 每位成员都介绍完以后，大家一起讨论如何在中文教学的课堂有效地使用这些社交软件。

三、后期任务：

根据前期了解到的情况以及中期任务讨论的结果，写一篇"如何在中文教学课堂使用社交软件"的总结报告。

补充材料

[1] Duckworth, S. (2012, December 27). How to use social media in the foreign language class: A primer. *E-Tools for Language Teachers*. Retrieved from http://mmeduckworth.blogspot.ca/2012/12/how-to-use-social-media-in-foreign.html
[2] Deyamport, E. (2010, July 8). Technology in the foreign language classroom. *Edutopia*. Retrieved from http://www.edutopia.org/groups/foreign-language/26816
[3] Edutopia. (2014). *Technology Integration in Education*. Retrieved from http://www.edutopia.org/technology-integration
[4] *Journal of Technology and Chinese Language Teaching*. http://www.tclt.us/journal

第六课　纪录片[1]讨论《请投我一票》
A Chinese Documentary—
Please Vote For Me

（文本形式：影评会）

> 关键词：
> 纪录片、民主选举、投票、拉票、才艺、辩论、演讲
> 能力目标：
> 1. 学习者能理解诠释纪录片的内容及其文化内涵。
> 2. 学习者能说明纪录片中的主题以及所反映的社会问题。
> 3. 学习者能介绍、描述纪录片中的人物特点及故事内容。
> 4. 学习者能使用专业套语主持正式的讨论会。

---

[1] 纪录片　jìlùpiān　N.　documentary

课文全版 (Complete Version)

语言大学暑期中文培训班的学员们在观看完纪录片《请投我一票》(Please Vote For Me) http://v.youku.com/v_show/id_XMTEwNjc1NjU2.html 之后，组织了一场影评[2]会。

主持人： 欢迎大家来参加影评会。今天我们要讨论的是一部纪录片，叫做《请投我一票》。这部纪录片通过一个小学选举[3]班长[4]的活动来反映中国社会的民主现状和民主意识，希望通过今天的讨论，大家对中国的民主过程和社会发展有进一步的了解。请大家在讨论中积极[5]发言，主动分享自己的看法。首先，请何老师简单介绍一下这部纪录片的相关背景。

何老师： 《请投我一票》是中国武汉电视台制作人[6]陈为军在2007年执导[7]的一部纪录片。影片记录了当地一所小学三年级的学生民主选举班长的过程。三位班长候选人[8]分别是：性格腼腆[9]的徐晓菲、能说会道[10]的成成、已经当了两年班长的罗雷。由于涉及[11]敏感[12]题材[13]，这部纪录片未能在中国大陆上映[14]，然而在海外却连连获奖[15]，引起了广泛的关注。

李老师： 我认为这部纪录片之所以引人关注，是因为这场民主选举本身存在一定的争议性[16]。在影片一开始，摄影[17]的工作人员问那些8岁大的孩子"什么叫民主？"孩子的回答是"不知道。什么意思啊？"这些孩子连"民主"这个简单的日常词汇都没听说过，可见在家庭以及学校教育中，从未有人告诉过他们有关民主的概念[18]。在这样的情况下进行所谓的民主选举不是很具有讽刺[19]意义吗？

[2]影评	yǐngpíng	N.	film review
[3]选举	xuǎnjǔ	V.	to elect
[4]班长	bānzhǎng	N.	class monitor
[5]积极	jījí	Adj.	active; energetic; positive
[6]制作人	zhìzuòrén	N.	producer
[7]执导	zhídǎo	V.	to direct
[8]候选人	hòuxuǎnrén	N.	candidate
[9]腼腆	miǎntiǎn	Adj.	shy; timid; bashful
[10]能说会道	néngshuōhuìdào	Adj.	good at expressing oneself
[11]涉及	shèjí	V.	to involve; to touch upon
[12]敏感	mǐngǎn	Adj.	sensitive
[13]题材	tícái	N.	subject; theme
[14]上映	shàngyìng	V.	to show (a film)
[15]获奖	huòjiǎng	V.	to win an award
[16]争议性	zhēngyìxìng	N.	controversial
[17]摄影	shèyǐng	V.	to take a photograph; to shoot a film
[18]概念	gàiniàn	N.	concept
[19]讽刺	fěngcì	Adj./V.	satire; to mock; ironic

孙老师：我也有同感。开始民主选举之前，班主任告诉孩子"民主就是你可以自己决定班长是谁，而不是老师指派[20]。"首先，民主的定义[21]似乎过于简单了一点儿，其次，事实上，三位班长的候选人都是由老师指派的！依我之见，这场民主选举从一开始就已经不"民主"了。

陈老师：我来说两句。这场民主选举由才艺[22]表演、辩论、演讲和投票四个环节[23]组成。我个人认为，就活动环节本身而言还是值得肯定的。根据活动要求，候选人可以选择两个学生作为自己的选举小助手；通过才艺表演、辩论和演讲等方式充分展示自己的能力和特点；最后再进行全班投票。

主持人：不可否认，这样的活动设计有一定的道理，但是接下来发生的事情却让人震惊[24]。哪位老师可以介绍一下三位候选人在选举中的表现呢？

李老师：我先来谈一下才艺表演的环节吧。尽管展示才艺能反映候选人的领导才能，可是在这个过程中却出现了完全不符合[25]民主选举程序[26]的情况。比方说，徐晓菲吹笛子[27]的时候，成成和他的两个小助手在台下[28]不停地起哄[29]，这直接导致了徐晓菲才艺表演的失败。成成自己唱歌的时候，安排两个助手在台下鼓掌[30]。可是到罗雷唱的时候，成成却和助手再一次在台下起哄。成成的种种做法完全来自母亲的背后[31]指点[32]。很明显，母亲的"策略"使成成在才艺展示中占了上风[33]，这使罗雷失去了信心，从而产生了退出选举的念头[34]。

孙老师：罗雷的闷闷不乐[35]引起了父亲的注意。父亲决定通过请全班学生坐轻轨[36]的方式来为罗雷拉票[37]。于是在电影中，我们看到一群孩子去坐轻轨。这种大人每天必坐的交通工具，对孩子而言，恰

[20]指派	zhǐpài	V.	to designate; to appoint
[21]定义	dìngyì	N./V.	definition; to define
[22]才艺	cáiyì	N.	talent and skill
[23]环节	huánjié	N.	segment; link; sector
[24]震惊	zhènjīng	Adj./V.	astounded; to shock
[25]符合	fúhé	V.	to conform; in accordance with
[26]程序	chéngxù	N.	procedure; routine
[27]笛子	dízi	N.	flute
[28]台下	táixià	N.	off the stage
[29]起哄	qǐhòng	V.	to create a disturbance; to jeer
[30]鼓掌	gǔzhǎng	V.	to applaud
[31]背后	bèihòu	N.	behind; behind one's back
[32]指点	zhǐdiǎn	V.	to give advice; to show how to do sth.
[33]占上风	zhànshàngfēng	VP.	to take the lead; gain the upper hand
[34]念头	niàntóu	N.	thought; idea; intention
[35]闷闷不乐	mènmènbúlè	Idiom.	be depressed; be in low spirits
[36]轻轨	qīngguǐ	N.	light rail
[37]拉票	lāpiào	V.	to campaign for votes; to solicit votes

228　*Please Vote For Me*

恰[38]是新奇好玩的事物。因此，经过这一次的"贿赂[39]"，原本支持成成的学生，开始倾向于[40]支持罗雷，连成成的小助手也不例外。从以上的例子我们可以发现，这个所谓的选举环节存在很大的问题。

何老师：　我来接着说第二个环节——辩论的情况吧。在辩论以前，三位候选人都分别得到了父母的指点。成成的母亲甚至帮他准备了辩论词。第一次辩论是徐晓菲对成成。成成直接指出徐晓菲挑食[41]、爱讲话的缺点[42]，而且特别强调[43]"你第一天才艺表演的时候就哭了，动不动就哭，怎么管理得好同学？"徐晓菲被问得哑口无言[44]。

陈老师：　我来介绍第二次辩论：罗雷对成成。成成几乎一字不差[45]地背出了母亲为他准备好的攻击[46]罗雷的辩论词："罗雷，你是班级的统治者[47]，而不是管理者。因为你打同学，你高高在上[48]！而我会和同学搞好关系，不会打同学。我不会做统治者，而会做管理者！"成成用这几句保证[49]，将自己和罗雷形成了鲜明[50]的对比。紧接着，成成还采用了母亲的建议，让被罗雷打过的学生举手[51]。面对学生们纷纷[52]举手的情况，罗雷使用了同样的策略，他用了父亲为他准备好的问题，当着全班问成成："如果投票，你会选谁？"当成成表示会选自己时，罗雷用手指着成成大声地说："你骗人！你是个骗子！你当众说你选自己，可是在下面说会选我！你是个骗子。"这一次的辩论，成成哑口无言。很明显，辩论环节实际上是家长之间的竞争。

孙老师：　最后的演讲环节也完全是家长们的竞争，从演讲稿[53]的准备到演讲时的语气和眼神，无一不是竞争的方面。孩子唯一的任务就是死记硬背[54]，反复练习，完全没有行使[55]自己的民主权利。在这个环节，罗雷在父亲的指点下，送给每位学生一个小礼物。依我之见，这是再一次的贿赂！这也是他最终赢得选举的关键因素。

[38]恰恰	qiàqià	Adv.	exactly; just
[39]贿赂	huìlù	V.	to bribe
[40]倾向于	qīngxiàngyú	VP.	to be inclined to
[41]挑食	tiāoshí	V.	to be fastidious about one's food
[42]缺点	quēdiǎn	N.	shortcoming; defect; weakness
[43]强调	qiángdiào	V.	to stress; to emphasize
[44]哑口无言	yǎkǒuwúyán	Idiom.	be rendered speechless
[45]一字不差	yízìbùchā	Idiom.	verbatim
[46]攻击	gōngjī	V.	to attack
[47]统治者	tǒngzhìzhě	N.	ruler
[48]高高在上	gāogāozàishàng	Idiom.	be far removed from the masses and reality
[49]保证	bǎozhèng	V./N.	to assure; to pledge; pledge
[50]鲜明	xiānmíng	Adj.	distinct
[51]举手	jǔshǒu	V.	to raise one's hand
[52]纷纷	fēnfēn	Adv.	one after another
[53]演讲稿	yǎnjiǎnggǎo	N.	written text of a speech
[54]死记硬背	sǐjiyìngbèi	Idiom.	memorize by rote
[55]行使	xíngshǐ	V.	to exercise; to perform

主持人：这部纪录片反映的是民主的主题，反映了中国人对民主的理解。而在这一场民主选举中，除最后的投票环节以外，前三个拉票环节——才艺表演、辩论和演讲都存在很大的问题，不符合民主选举的程序。小学生们在选举中说着成人式的语言，在家长的大力帮助下不惜[56]采用贿赂选民[57]、打击[58]对手的手段，这一过程非常引人深思[59]，值得进一步讨论。在结束今天的讨论之前，我想提出两个值得思考的问题：(1)什么是民主？(2)如何教育下一代明白"民主"这两个字？

好，由于时间的关系，今天的影评会到此结束。谢谢大家。

 语言重点：

1. 由于涉及（敏感/政治/民主/争议性）题材，（纪录片/影片/电影/小说）未能在**Place1**上映/发表，然而在**Place2**（海外/国际上）却连连获奖/引起了广泛的关注。

   As a result of touching upon + (sensitive/political/democratic/controversial) subject matter, (the documentary/film/movie/novel) still cannot be shown/published in + Place1; however, in + Place2 (abroad/internationally) + it repeatedly receives awards/attracts wide-ranging attention.

   - 由于涉及敏感题材，这部纪录片未能在中国大陆上映，然而在海外却连连获奖，引起了广泛的关注。
   - 由于涉及争议性题材，很多第六代导演的电影未能在中国地区上映，然而在国际上却引起了广泛的关注。

2. **Subj.**连+NP（民主/投票/选举/三种沟通模式）都+negative+verb，可见在（家庭教育/学校教育/日常生活）中，从未+verb。在这样的情况下，（进行民主选举/讨论以标准为本的语言教学）不是很具有讽刺意义吗？

   Subj. + negative + even + verb + (democracy/voting/elections/3 Modes of Communication), so it can be seen that (at home/in education/in school/in everyday life), they have never + verb. Under these circumstances, isn't (practicing a democratic election/discussing standards-centered education) ironic/satirical?

   - 这些孩子连"民主"这个简单的日常词汇都没听说过，可见在家庭以及学校教育中，从未有人告诉过他们有关民主的基本常识。在这样的情况下进行所谓的民主选举不是很具有讽刺意义吗？
   - 这些暑期中文培训班的学员连三种沟通模式都不知道，可见在课堂教学中，从未涉及过与能力标准相关的知识。在这样的情况下讨论以标准为本的语言教学不是很具有讽刺意义吗？

---

[56]不惜	bùxī	Adv./V.	regardless of; not hesitate to
[57]选民	xuǎnmín	N.	voter; elector
[58]打击	dǎjī	V.	to hit; to strike; to attack
[59]深思	shēnsī	V.	to think deeply about

3. **Sb.**通过（才艺表演/辩论/演讲）的方式+充分+**VP**（展示/说明/表达）

   Sb. + by means of (talent show/debate/speeches) + fully + Verb Phrase (displayed/explained/expressed)

   - 候选人通过才艺表演、辩论和演讲等方式充分展示自己的能力和特点。
   - 作者通过创作励志歌曲的方式充分表达自己不愿意放弃，坚持追求自己梦想的信念。

4. 不可否认，**subj.**+有一定的道理，但是在…+的过程中却出现了不符合+程序/要求/规定+的情况。

   It cannot be denied, subj. is certainly reasonable, but during the process of … + emerged a situation that was not in accordance with + the procedure/requirements/rules.

   - 不可否认，这样的活动设计有一定的道理，但是在这个过程中却出现了完全不符合民主选举程序的情况。
   - 不可否认，高校和教育部门追求体面的就业率有一定的道理，但是在这些措施实行的过程中却出现了不符合国家规定的情况。比方说，有的高校迫使很多没有找到工作的毕业生自己找印章盖在《就业协议》上。

5. **Sb.1**+在（才艺展示/辩论/演讲/比赛）中占了上风，这使+**sb.2**+失去了信心，从而产生了退出（才艺展示/辩论/演讲/比赛）的念头。

   Sb.1 + during (the talent show/debate/speech/competition) took the upper hand. This caused + sb.2 + to lose confidence, and from this produced thoughts about pulling out of the (talent show/debate/speech/competition).

   - 成成在才艺展示中占了上风，这使罗雷失去了信心，从而产生了退出选举的念头。
   - 罗雷通过请同学们坐轻轨的方式在前期选举中占了上风，这使成成和徐晓菲失去了信心，从而产生了退出班长选举的念头。

6. （对+**sb.**+而言，…。因此+）经过/通过+**NP**（这一次的贿赂/拉票），原本支持/同情/欣赏**A**的人开始倾向于**B**，连+**sb.2**+也不例外。

   (In regard to sb., ….) Thus, by means of (this bribe/solicitation of votes), those who originally supported/sympathized with/admired A started to lean towards B, even though sb.2 was not an exception.

   - 对孩子而言，这种大人每天必坐的交通工具，恰恰是新奇好玩的事物。因此经过这一次的"贿赂"，原本支持成成的学生开始倾向于罗雷，连成成的小助手也不例外。
   - 对选民而言，领导才能是成为班长的关键因素。因此通过辩论和演讲，原本欣赏能说会道的男候选人的选民开始倾向于有过三年领导经验的女候选人，连组织这场民主选举的老师也不例外。

7. …，从A到B，无一不是（竞争/考虑/评估/检查）的方面

   … , from A to B, everything is an aspect of (competition/consideration/evaluation/inspection)

   - 最后的演讲环节也完全是家长们的竞争，从演讲稿的准备到演讲时的语气和眼神，无一不是竞争的方面。
   - 教师应该利用主题单元设计的方法来设计课程，从五大教学内容到三种沟通模式，无一不是考虑的方面。

8. Sb.（为了+purpose）（在sb.的大力+帮助/支持+下）不惜+do sth.（采用…的手段/方式），这一过程（非常/十分）引人+深思/关注/注意…

   Sb. (in order to + purpose) (under sb.'s great effort + help/support +) does not hesitate to + do sth. (adopt tricks/methods). This process (extremely) leads one to ponder/focus on/pay attention to …

   - 小学生们在家长的大力帮助下不惜采用贿赂选民、打击对手的手段，这一过程非常引人深思。
   - 高校和教育部门为了追求体面的就业率不惜采用迫使没有找到工作的毕业生在《就业协议》上签字的手段，这一过程非常引人关注。

第六课　纪录片[1]讨论《请投我一票》
A Chinese Documentary—
Please Vote For Me

（文本形式：影评会）

> ➢ 关键词：
>   纪录片、民主选举、投票、拉票、才艺、辩论、演讲
> ➢ 能力目标：
>   1. 学习者能理解诠释纪录片的内容及其文化内涵。
>   2. 学习者能说明纪录片中的主题以及所反映的社会问题。
>   3. 学习者能介绍、描述纪录片中的人物特点及故事内容。
>   4. 学习者能使用专业套语主持正式的讨论会。

---

[1] 纪录片　jìlùpiān　N.　documentary

课文节选版 (Edited Version)

语言大学暑期中文培训班的学员们在观看完纪录片《请投我一票》(Please Vote For Me) http://v.youku.com/v_show/id_XMTEwNjc1NjU2.html 之后，组织了一场影评[2]会。

主持人： 欢迎大家来参加影评会。今天我们要讨论的是一部纪录片，叫做《请投我一票》。这部纪录片通过一个小学选举[3]班长[4]的活动来反映中国社会的民主现状和民主意识，希望通过今天的讨论，大家对中国的民主过程和社会发展有进一步的了解。请大家在讨论中积极[5]发言，主动分享自己的看法。首先，请何老师简单介绍一下这部纪录片的相关背景。

何老师： 《请投我一票》是中国武汉电视台制作人[6]陈为军在2007年执导[7]的一部纪录片。影片记录了当地一所小学三年级的学生民主选举班长的过程。三位班长候选人[8]分别是：徐晓菲、成成和罗雷。由于涉及[9]敏感[10]题材[11]，这部纪录片未能在中国大陆上映[12]，然而在海外却连连获奖[13]，引起了广泛的关注。

李老师： 我认为这部纪录片之所以引人关注，是因为这场民主选举本身存在一定的争议性[14]。开始民主选举之前，班主任告诉孩子"民主就是你可以自己决定班长是谁，而不是老师指派[15]。"首先，民主的定义[16]似乎过于简单了一点儿，其次，事实上，三位班长的候选人都是由老师指派的！依我之见，这场民主选举从一开始就已经不"民主"了。

陈老师： 我来说两句。这场民主选举由才艺[17]表演、辩论、演讲和投票四个环节[18]组成。我个人认为，就活动环节本身而言还是值得肯定的。根据活动要求，候选人可以选择两个学生作为自己的选举小

[2]影评	yǐngpíng	N.	film review
[3]选举	xuǎnjǔ	V.	to elect
[4]班长	bānzhǎng	N.	class monitor
[5]积极	jījí	Adj.	active; energetic; positive
[6]制作人	zhìzuòrén	N.	producer
[7]执导	zhídǎo	V.	to direct
[8]候选人	hòuxuǎnrén	N.	candidate
[9]涉及	shèjí	V.	to involve; to touch upon
[10]敏感	mǐngǎn	Adj.	sensitive
[11]题材	tícái	N.	subject; theme
[12]上映	shàngyìng	V.	to show (a film)
[13]获奖	huòjiǎng	V.	to win an award
[14]争议性	zhēngyìxìng	N.	controversial
[15]指派	zhǐpài	V.	to designate; to appoint
[16]定义	dìngyì	N./V.	definition; to define
[17]才艺	cáiyì	N.	talent and skill
[18]环节	huánjié	N.	segment; link; sector

助手；通过才艺表演、辩论和演讲等方式充分展示自己的能力和特点；最后再进行全班投票。

主持人：不可否认，这样的活动设计有一定的道理，但是接下来发生的事情却让人震惊[19]。哪位老师可以介绍一下三位候选人在选举中的表现呢？

李老师：我先来谈一下才艺表演的环节吧。尽管展示才艺能反映候选人的领导才能，可是在这个过程中却出现了完全不符合[20]民主选举程序[21]的情况。比方说，成成自己唱歌的时候，安排两个小助手在台下鼓掌[22]。可是在别人表演的时候，却和助手在台下[23]不停地起哄[24]。成成的种种做法完全来自母亲的背后[25]指点[26]。

孙老师：罗雷的父亲决定通过请全班学生坐轻轨[27]的方式来为他拉票[28]。于是在电影中，我们看到一群孩子去坐轻轨。经过这一次的"贿赂[29]"，原本支持成成的学生，开始倾向于[30]罗雷，连成成的小助手也不例外。从以上的例子我们可以发现，这个所谓的选举环节存在很大的问题。

何老师：我来接着说第二个环节——辩论的情况吧。在辩论以前，三位候选人都分别得到了父母的指点。成成的母亲甚至帮他准备了辩论词。第一次辩论是徐晓菲对成成。成成直接指出徐晓菲的缺点[31]，让徐晓菲哑口无言[32]。

陈老师：我来介绍第二次辩论：罗雷对成成。成成背出了母亲为他准备好的攻击[33]罗雷的辩论词："罗雷，你是班级的统治者[34]，而不是管理者。因为你打同学，你高高在上[35]！而我会和同学搞好关系，不会打同学。我不会做统治者，而会做管理者！"紧接着，成成还采用了母亲的建议，让被罗雷打过的学生举手[36]。而罗雷使用了同样的策略，也用了父亲为他准备好的问题，当着全班问

[19]震惊	zhènjīng	Adj./V.	astounded; to shock
[20]符合	fúhé	V.	to conform; in accordance with
[21]程序	chéngxù	N.	procedure; routine
[22]鼓掌	gǔzhǎng	V.	to applaud
[23]台下	táixià	N.	off the stage
[24]起哄	qǐhòng	V.	to create a disturbance; to jeer
[25]背后	bèihòu	N.	behind; behind one's back
[26]指点	zhǐdiǎn	V.	to give advice; to show how to do sth.
[27]轻轨	qīngguǐ	N.	light rail
[28]拉票	lāpiào	V.	to campaign for votes; to solicit votes
[29]贿赂	huìlù	V.	to bribe
[30]倾向于	qīngxiàngyú	VP.	to be inclined to
[31]缺点	quēdiǎn	N.	shortcoming; defect; weakness
[32]哑口无言	yǎkǒuwúyán	Idiom.	be rendered speechless
[33]攻击	gōngjī	V.	to attack
[34]统治者	tǒngzhìzhě	N.	ruler
[35]高高在上	gāogāozàishàng	Idiom.	be far removed from the masses and reality
[36]举手	jǔshǒu	V.	to raise one's hand

	成成："如果投票，你会选谁？"当成成表示会选自己时，罗雷用手指着成成大声地说："你骗人！你是个骗子！你当众说你选自己，可是在下面说会选我！你是个骗子。"这一次的辩论，成成哑口无言。很明显，辩论环节实际上是家长之间的竞争。
孙老师：	最后的演讲环节也完全是家长们的竞争，从演讲稿[37]的准备到演讲时的语气和眼神，无一不是竞争的方面。孩子唯一的任务就是死记硬背[38]，反复练习，完全没有行使[39]自己的民主权利。在这个环节，罗雷在父亲的指点下，送给每位学生一个小礼物。依我之见，这是再一次的贿赂！这也是他最终赢得选举的关键因素。
主持人：	这部纪录片反映的是民主的主题，反映了中国人对民主的理解。而在这一场民主选举中，除最后的投票环节以外，前三个拉票环节——才艺表演、辩论和演讲都存在很大的问题，不符合民主选举的程序。小学生们在家长的帮助下不惜[40]采用贿赂选民[41]、打击[42]对手的手段，这一过程非常引人深思[43]，值得进一步讨论。在结束今天的讨论之前，我想提出两个值得思考的问题：（1）什么是民主？（2）如何教育下一代明白"民主"这两个字？ 好，由于时间的关系，今天的影评会到此结束。谢谢大家。

 语言重点：

1. 由于涉及（敏感/政治/民主/争议性）题材，（纪录片/影片/电影/小说）未能在Place1上映/发表，然而在Place2（海外/国际上）却连连获奖/引起了广泛的关注。

   As a result of touching upon + (sensitive/political/democratic/controversial) subject matter, (the documentary/film/movie/novel) still cannot be shown/published in + Place1; however, in + Place2 (abroad/internationally) + it repeatedly receives awards/attracts wide-ranging attention.

   - 由于涉及敏感题材，这部纪录片未能在中国大陆上映，然而在海外却连连获奖，引起了广泛的关注。
   - 由于涉及争议性题材，很多第六代导演的电影未能在中国地区上映，然而在国际上却引起了广泛的关注。

---

[37]演讲稿	yǎnjiǎnggǎo	N.	written text of a speech
[38]死记硬背	sǐjìyìngbèi	Idiom.	memorize by rote
[39]行使	xíngshǐ	V.	to exercise; to perform
[40]不惜	bùxī	Adv./V.	regardless of; not hesitate to
[41]选民	xuǎnmín	N.	voter; elector
[42]打击	dǎjī	V.	to hit; to strike; to attack
[43]深思	shēnsī	V.	to think deeply about

2. **Sb.通过（才艺表演/辩论/演讲）方式+充分+VP（展示/说明/表达）**

    Sb. + by means of (talent show/debate/speeches) + fully + Verb Phrase (displayed/explained/expressed)

    - 候选人通过才艺表演、辩论和演讲等方式充分展示自己的能力和特点。
    - 作者通过创作励志歌曲的方式充分表达自己不愿意放弃，坚持追求自己梦想的信念。

3. **不可否认，subj.+有一定的道理，但是…**

    It cannot be denied, subj. is certainly reasonable, but …

    - 不可否认，这样的活动设计有一定的道理，但是接下来发生的事情却让人震惊。
    - 不可否认，高校和教育部门追求体面的就业率有一定的道理，但是在这个过程中却出现了不符合国家规定的情况。比方说，有的高校迫使很多没有找到工作的毕业生自己找印章盖在《就业协议》上。

4. **经过/通过+NP（这一次的贿赂/拉票），原本支持/同情/欣赏A的人开始倾向于B，连+sb.2 +也不例外。**

    (In regard to sb., ….) Thus, by means of (this bribe/solicitation of votes), those who originally supported/sympathized with/admired A started to lean towards B, even though sb.2 was not an exception.

    - 于是在电影中，我们看到一群孩子去坐轻轨。经过这一次的"贿赂"，原本支持成成的学生，开始倾向于罗雷，连成成的小助手也不例外。
    - 领导才能是成为班长的重要因素。因此通过辩论和演讲，原本欣赏男候选人的同学开始倾向于有过三年领导经验的女候选人，连老师也不例外。

5. **…，从A到B，无一不是（竞争/考虑/评估/检查）的方面**

    … , from A to B, everything is an aspect of (competition/consideration/evaluation/inspection)

    - 最后的演讲环节也完全是家长们的竞争，从演讲稿的准备到演讲时的语气和眼神，无一不是竞争的方面。
    - 教师应该利用主题单元设计的方法来设计课程，从五大教学内容到三种沟通模式，无一不是考虑的方面。

6. **Sb.**（为了+purpose）（在sb.的+帮助/支持+下）不惜+**do sth.**（采用…的手段/方式），这一过程（非常/十分）引人+深思/关注/注意…

   Sb. (in order to + purpose) (under sb.'s great effort + help/support +) does not hesitate to + do sth. (adopt tricks/methods). This process (extremely) leads one to ponder/focus/pay attention to …

   - 小学生们在家长的帮助下不惜采用贿赂选民、打击对手的手段，这一过程非常引人深思。
   - 高校和教育部门为了追求体面的就业率不惜采用迫使没有找到工作的毕业生在《就业协议》上签字的手段，这一过程非常引人关注。

练习活动

 理解诠释1：预习单

先看课文，然后完成下面的作业：

一、根据课文介绍，把三位班长候选人与他们的性格和拉票方式进行连连看。

班长候选人	性格	拉票方式
成成	能说会道	展示吹笛子的才艺
罗雷	喜欢使用暴力	
徐晓菲	腼腆	在才艺展示的环节打击对手
	爱哭	
	不诚实	贿赂选民

二、以下是《请投我一票》中某小学班长选举活动的各个环节，请把这些环节按照选举的正确顺序进行排列。

a. 候选人通过才艺展示拉票。
b. 由老师指派出三位班长候选人。
c. 候选人通过辩论打击对手。
d. 全班投票选举出班长。
e. 候选人在家长的帮助下通过演讲展示自己的能力。
f. 候选人选择出两位学生作为自己的选举小助手。

☐ ⇨ ☐ ⇨ ☐ ⇨ ☐ ⇨ ☐ ⇨ ☐

理解诠释2：扩展阅读

改编自豆瓣电影影评

《民主的不可承受之重》
作者：1900顽石

故事发生在中国武汉，导演把西方的一套民主模式放置在一所小学中。片中三位班长候选人，一个具有一定的管理能力且有竞选小手段，一个为现任班长，拥有令人羡慕的家庭背景，一个则是成绩优秀的单亲家庭女生。三个人的竞选围绕着寻找竞选搭档、才艺表演、辩论及演讲展开。

竞选中，三个孩子组织了自己的团队为之出谋划策，但孩子们是善变的，于是上演了一场场挖墙脚[44]的好戏。在辩论这个很关键的环节中竞争者们很少围绕"班长职责"展开讨论，而是转到了相互揭露，相互诋毁[45]的路子上，吃饭吃得慢、爱哭闹成了打击对手的策略。这些办法或行为来自于孩子父母的"智慧"，也源于社会所带来的影响。可以说这场民主的竞选中孩子们的民主概念是建立在中国父母和社会对民主的理解之上的。于是我们听到了小学三年级的学生会用"统治者""法西斯"这样的词语攻击对方，也会想到用对方曾经的许诺来作为指责对方的凭据。竞选的结局也很戏剧化，中秋节的小礼品扭转了本来势均力敌[46]的选情，罗雷的贿赂成就了最后压倒性的胜利。

这场民主游戏不禁让人想到目前中国的"民主"教育。民主，是一种形式，但也是一种思想。然而，在中国，"民主"一直都是个敏感的词汇。在中国近百年的民主进程中，民主的形式和结果一再被强调，而我们的社会却一直缺乏着民主的根基，于是我们看到电影开头当小学生们被问到"民主是什么？"时，大家茫然的眼神。大家对"班长"的理解，也是"让他站着，就不能坐着"，而在竞选还没结束前，小竞选者们就已经开始品尝"民主"所带来的权力感了。

现代民主的意义在于其是制衡[47]权力的手段，而不是成就权力的捷径[48]。中国的民主之路还在摸索的过程中，民主是否有模式，是否能带来国强民富，是否能化解社会矛盾，中国的"民主"，责任太重了。

1. 片中三位班长候选人分别有什么特点？
2. 在竞选中，孩子们的民主概念来自于哪些方面？（可多选）
   A. 父母对民主的理解　　B. 社会对民主的理解　　C. 学校教育
3. 孩子们在这次民主选举中学会了什么？（可多选）
   A. 班长的职责　　B. 打击对手　　C. 民主的意义　　D. 贿赂方式
4. 作者对"中国的民主之路"持什么样的态度？
   A. 乐观　　　　　B. 中立　　　　　C. 不容乐观

---

[44]挖墙脚　　wāqiángjiǎo　　VP.　　undermining a competitor's ability to succeed by taking a key element away from the competitor (i.e. by bribing a competitor's business partner, stealing trade secrets etc.)

[45]诋毁　　dǐhuǐ　　V.　　to defame, to slander

[46]势均力敌　　shìjūnlìdí　　Idiom.　　to be well-matched in strength

[47]制衡　　zhìhéng　　V.　　to check and balance

[48]捷径　　jiéjìng　　N.　　shortcut

Please Vote For Me 239

人际交流1：面对面讨论

你和同事王老师一起坐飞机去外地开会。在飞机上，你们谈到了《请投我一票》这部纪录片。

王老师：　徐老师，刚才您提到的《请投我一票》这部纪录片，我还没看过。这部影片记录了什么内容呢？
你的回答：　【建议词汇和结构：涉及…（敏感/政治/争议性）题材；引起广泛的关注；腼腆；能说会道】
王老师：　这场民主选举由哪几个环节组成？是如何进行的呢？
你的回答：　【建议词汇和结构：subj.由…组成；sb.通过（才艺表演/辩论/演讲）方式+充分+VP（展示/说明/表达）；候选人；助手；投票】
王老师：　在你看来，为什么这部纪录片能引起广泛的关注呢？
你的回答：　【建议词汇和结构：不可否认，subj.有一定的道理，但是在…的过程中却出现了不符合+要求/规定+的情况；sb.（为了+purpose）不惜+do sth.；采用…的手段/方式；争议性；基本常识；所谓的+N；讽刺】

人际交流2：回复微信朋友圈

王老师在网上看完《请投我一票》这部纪录片以后，在微信的"朋友圈"发了一条信息，请给他回复。【建议词汇和结构：之所以…，其原因有…个，一是…，二是…；争议性；基本常识；讽刺；指派；依我之见，…；sb.通过（才艺表演/辩论/演讲）方式+充分+VP（展示/说明/表达）；sb.（为了+purpose）不惜+do sth.；采用…的手段/方式；起哄；背后指点；拉票；攻击；死记硬背；贿赂选民；打击对手；…引人+深思/关注/注意；…，从A到B，无一不是（竞争/考虑/评估）的方面；综上所述，…】

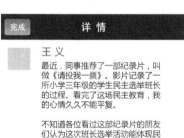

表达演说：观后感

请你写一篇400–500字的读后感，谈谈你看完《请投我一票》这部纪录片以后的感想。请包括以下内容：

1. 评价这次民主选举活动。
2. 在你看来什么是民主？
3. 如何教育下一代明白"民主"这两个字？结合自己受教育的亲身经历进行说明。
4. 其他：你自己想讨论的角度。

建议词汇和结构：subj.由…组成；sb.通过（才艺表演/辩论/演讲）方式+充分+VP（展示/说明/表达）；候选人；投票；拉票；环节；sb.（为了+purpose）不惜+do sth.；采用…的手段/方式；背后指点；攻击；死记硬背；贿赂选民；打击对手；…引人+深思/关注/注意；…，从A到B，无一不是（竞争/考虑/评估）的方面；总而言之，…；综上所述，…；符合…的程序/要求/规定

反思任务

一、前期任务：

为了了解中国式民主的情况，你和小组成员需要对中国人进行采访。

- 采访以前，和小组成员讨论并设计一个采访问题单。问题单可以包括：你觉得中国有没有民主？中国的民主体现在哪些方面？请介绍你参加过的一次选举经历等这样的问题，你们也可以完全按照自己的想法来设计采访问题单。
- 小组成员根据采访问题单分别对两位中国的年轻人、中年人和老年人进行采访。

二、核心任务：

- 小组成员分享采访结果。
- 根据采访结果，讨论比较中国年轻人、中年人和老年人对于民主的看法有什么不同。
- 小组成员一起讨论中国的民主和西方民主的异同。

三、后期任务：

- 根据前期任务和核心任务中你对中国式民主的理解，写一篇关于"中国式民主"的文章。

补充材料

[1] Couet, R. (n.d.). Authentic materials: Where to find them, how to use them [PowerPoint slides]. Retrieved from https://ed.sc.gov/agency/se/Instructional-Practices-and-Evaluations/documents/AuthenticMaterials.pdf

[2] United States Copyright Office. (2009, November). Reproduction of copyrighted works by educators and librarians. Circular 21. Retrieved from http://www.copyright.gov/circs/circ21.pdf

[3] Collard, L. (2013). How to avoid copyright infringement. Wikihow. Retrieved from http://www.wikihow.com/Avoid-Copyright-Infringement

[4] 看电影学汉语《非诚勿扰》（视频文件）网络链接 http://video.chinese.cn/article/2011-03/10/content_233825.htm

看电影学汉语《非诚勿扰 II》（视频文件）网络链接 http://video.chinese.cn/article/2011-03/10/content_233824.htm

附录一：教学论坛演讲模板

如何提高中级汉语学生的阅读能力
ACCK-12项目学员：陈美安

大家好，我今天演讲的题目是如何提高中级汉语水平学生的阅读能力。

提高自己的阅读能力对中级汉语水平的学生来说是一种挑战。一般来说，中级汉语水平的学生能看懂很多和汉语口语有关的句子。但是，比较书面的文字他们还是看不懂，其中的原因包括书面语比口语复杂，词汇也更丰富。我这次报告会提到三种和中级汉语水平学生的阅读能力有关的教学方法。

第一种教学法是主题单元设计，确立主题单元设计会帮助学生积累词汇和掌握语法。在学习主题的时候，他们会在一个有意义的语境下学习生词，然后用新的生词和语法来建立他们的背景知识。此外，在学习这个主题单元的过程中，学生会重复见到这些汉字和句型。这样一来，学生会开始理解这些汉字的意思和用法。我给大家举一个例子。比方说学习如何保护环境的时候，学生能用到很多跟环保有关的生词，例如"回收"、"垃圾"、"垃圾桶"、"瓶子"等等。他们也会用到"把"这个语法点。老师给他们安排的活动会包括这些生词与语法。学生参加活动的时候能多次重复生词和句型，于是他们会加深对生词与句型的了解。此外他们能在讨论环保这个话题时，达到语言使用的自动化。

不过，在给学生上课的时候，大部分的老师会面临一个同样的问题：学生的阅读能力有所不同。老师们要想如何给所有的学生适合他们阅读能力的作品，同时不要让学生感觉到有的学生好，有的学生差。教育学家Fu Danling有一本叫《在华侨城的英语作为第二语言课》的书里介绍了一个办法。这是我想讲的第二种教法。首先，老师按照学生的阅读能力把学生分到几个小组。然后，每一个小组都要读一个关于某个主题的书，但是每一本书的内容不一样。读完书以后，学生要准备给别的小组介绍他们书里面最重要的信息。同时要给别的学生介绍他们所看的书。最后，学生需要用他们分享的信息来完成任务，比如完成作业。就差异化教学而言，这个活动具有很大的优势。一方面，所有的学生能够把他们的书读完，而且能够从这本书里面挑出有意思的信息和他们的同学分享。这样，每一个学生都会有成就感。另一方面，学生都有机会读适合他们水平的书。他们不但能看懂书上的内容，而且能学到新的生词和语法。

除了上面的两个教学法以外，老师还可以利用学生自己做的生词字典来帮助学生学新的生词和句型。学生见到一个新的字的时候，他们可以先决定是不是值得去记。值得的话，他们可以把这个字与它的定义写在他们的字典里。爱画画的学生也可以画代表那个字的草图。接下来，他们可以给出几个同义词、近义词或者反义词。最后，学生可以把一个用到那个字的句子写在字典里。下次他们见到那个汉字或者句型的时候，就可以把新的例子写在字典里。比方说，学生见到"了解"这个词的时候要把它写在字典上，然后写下它的词义。学生也有机会画图帮他们记得这个词的意思。然后，学生可以写下同义词、近义词和反义词。就"了解"这个词而言，学生可能会写"懂"这个同义词，也写"理解"和"知道"这两个近义词。最后，学生可以写下他们能理解的例子。这样的字典有助于学生了解汉字的意思和用法。

主题单元设计、差异化教学的活动以及学生自造的字典，都有益于提高学生的阅读能力。值得注意的是，这些差异化教学的活动和学生自造的字典都很适合主题单元设计。综上所述，老师们可以利用不同的方式来提高所有的学生的阅读能力。

由于时间的关系，我的演讲到此结束。谢谢大家耐心的倾听，要是大家还有任何疑问，欢迎探讨。

附录二：讨论会模板

讨论主题：如何鼓励学生学习中文
How to Encourage Students to LEARN Chinese = Engage Students
ACC K-12项目学员：史迪雅、李丹
Shaloma Smith and Danielle Reeder

Introduction:

1. 怎么一直有效地鼓励学生？

    - Establish respect: Good student–teacher rapport is necessary to ensure engaged learning and thus the desire to learn.
    建立互相尊重的关系，良好的师生关系对于学生注意力的集中和学习积极性的调动是非常必要的
        o Show genuine interest in each student and his or her ideas.
        老师应该对学生及他们的想法给予足够的重视
        o Respect student differences. 尊重学生不一样的个性及学习特点
        o Be committed to teach every single student.
        老师应该尽自己的责任让每一个学生学好
        o Give equal time to all students. 老师需要给学生同样的注意
        o Student to student and student to teacher respect must also be maintained.
        保持生生之间的尊重和师生之间的尊重
            ▪ Nihao/Xiexie and zaijian

2. Classroom setup 课堂环境

    - comfortable, welcoming classroom environment
    令学生感到舒适的课堂气氛
    - seating arranged for maximized engagement, seated in U (半圆), preferably without desks in front
    桌椅的摆放能够让学生最大限度地参与课堂教学，比如"半圆形"（最好没有桌子，桌子放在后面）
    - visuals: maps, pictures, charts, cultural artifacts, etc.
    视觉效果包括：地图、图片、图表、文化的艺术品等

如何布置教室

    - 应该配合学生的兴趣，而且尽量创造舒服的环境
    - 如果学生的椅子太小，他们无法注意课堂上的内容

3. Class management 课堂管理

    - Have defined rules set at beginning of year, which are reasonable and fair (can be decided in class as group in younger grades).
    在学期开始的时候，给学生制定合理公平的规则（老师和学生共同制定规则）

- Clamp down on bullying and other inappropriate behavior – unacceptable.
  禁止欺凌弱小等不文明行为
    o Deflect any negative comments with a quick upbeat reply and smile to keep positive class energy – maintain a sense of humor.
      通过幽默的方式来避免负面的影响——保持课堂气氛良好
- Know when to speak out in front of class and when to speak to a student privately ("office" or after class).
  在学生犯了错误的时候，老师应该知道什么时候可以当众指出错误，什么时候需要私下指出错误
- Ways to get students back on task. 让学生回到任务上的方法
    o Give a look. 用眼神或者肢体语言引起学生注意
    o Proximity – make presence known, tap table if necessary.
      注意教师与学生之间的距离
    o Be sensitive to multi-tasking. 注意课堂任务的多样性
- Remember that you are the adult – brain research has shown that full development of the frontal lobe occurs sometime in the early to mid-20s! This means that students' reasoning abilities are heavily overshadowed by an unusually large emotion-driven response in the high school years.
  根据研究，人类的大脑在二十几岁才会得到充分的发展，所以高中生容易感情用事，老师应该注重学生的感情发展
- Encourage positive behavior – be a positive role model.
  鼓励积极的行为——做一个很好的榜样
- A teacher who takes classroom environment and management seriously is respected by students.
  只有重视课堂气氛和课堂管理的老师才能得到学生们的尊重
- 使用不同颜色的卡来表示老师对学生行为的感觉：绿牌，黄牌，红牌。
- 分小组讨论：面临这些不同学生所带来的困难和挑战，你们会怎么办？
    o 第一组例子：大卫是一种愤怒感/叛逆性很强的学生，总是有会影响他学习的问题，或者会影响其他学生的学习环境
        - 一种策略是老师很快让学生知道哪种行为不会吸引老师的关注，但同时保证学生的心理健康，下课以后可以跟那个学生谈话
    o 第二组：兰兰比其他的学生慢得多，在课上很容易看得出来。老师要一边避免让她有挫败感，一边避免其他的学生笑她
        - 让学生知道无论她做得好不好，老师一直会支持她
    o 第三组：亨利和陪元的父母都是中国人，水平已经比其他的学生高一些。但上课的时候，亨利有沉默怪癖的表现，不善于流利地用中文与别人进行交流，而陪元总是随时回答问题，剥夺其他学生练习的机会
        - 有机会分配伙伴的话，应该把组织力/注意力很强的学生跟注意力/积极性稍微差一点的学生放在一起
    o 第四组：麦克天天不带课堂用具——课本、笔等等。
        - 让学生用中文解释为什么每天都会有这个问题

4. How to maintain student interest 如何保持学生对中文的兴趣
    - student vs. teacher centered 以学生为中心/以老师为中心
    - make sure students have the tools needed to succeed in studying on own: zhongwen.com; mdbg; gaojian; skritter
      给学生提供必要的工具以便自我学习
    - adjust materials to suit the pace and interest of students, as well as differentiated learning – challenging, but not threatening
      课堂节奏灵活多变，适应学生的水平和兴趣。推动学生前进而不让学生产生挫败感
    - use a variety of teaching methods and media – multiple intelligences (Howard Gardner)
      使用多样教学法和多媒体的方法——多重智力观
    - meaningful: personalized and real world – task-based to community and world
      有意义的任务——基于社会的个性化真实化的任务
    - student choices 学生的选择
    - cooperative 合作学习
    - creative 创造性的学习
    - high tech and current pop culture 高科技和现代流行的文化
    - demand 100% participation 100%地参与课堂活动
    - Panda International http://www.pandasinternational.org/
    - Peace Corps Worldwide http://www.peacecorps.gov/wws/multimedia/slideshows/chn_throndsen_mandarin.cfm

5. Error correction and assessment 错误的改正和评估
    - goal is student mastery of material 目标就是学生能掌握课上的内容
    - gauge understanding by class participation and homework
      根据课堂的参与度和作业情况来判断学生是否理解
    - if students have problems on assessments, they need more time and/or different methods to successfully cover materials
      如果学生在评估阶段问题仍未改正，老师应用更多的时间和不同的方法来有效地改正错误
    - give constant personalized and positive feedback
      持续给予个性化和积极的反馈
    - in-class corrections 课堂纠错
        - 学过的策略：直接改正，重述，要求澄清，元语言反馈，诱导，重复

6. Homework 布置合适的作业
    - 如果灵活性和机械性教学法都需要，什么时候应该用哪一个，之间的比例呢？
    - homework: try to keep between 5 and 15 minutes' worth, but never over weekends or breaks, with grading that encourages mastery
      只在工作日，而不在周末布置作业，作业应该配合学生的年龄和水平，应该控制在5–15分钟之内（这一点激发了老师们的关注和积极的讨论。对于学生应该花多长时间来写作业，老师们之间的看法还存在很大的分歧）
    - 写得比较好的学生可获得鼓励

7. 评估方式
    - testing/projects/performances 考试/小组活动/表演
    - 让学生提前做好准备
    - go over answers together and have students circle any errors or questionable parts 老师修改/学生修改
    - 老师给出学生成绩的方式，给学生改错的机会 may choose to allow students to make corrections for half credit or allow student to retake exam

8. Encourage out of school programs. Go as group or on own (extra credit?): community festivals, competitions, summer programs, travel, study abroad. 鼓励学生参加课外项目：社区节日活动、展示汉语水平的比赛，夏令营，旅游，留学
    - Startalk, Hanban, Year Abroad, Flagship 不同的汉语项目

附录三：课堂用语

STARTING CLASS	
OK, let's start class.	我们现在开始上课。
Hello everyone/Hello teacher.	各位同学好/老师好。
Let's see who's here today.	我们现在来点名。
Everybody's here.	今天大家都来了。
DOING A LISTENING COMPREHENSION ACTIVITY	
OK, I have a story for you today.	今天我要给你们讲一个故事/我要给你们念一段话。
Would you like to hear it?	你们想不想听？
Right now I just want you to listen; don't write.	请你们先听，什么都不要写。
Listen carefully.	请注意听。
If you don't understand everything, don't worry.	要是听不懂，也不必担心/紧张。
I'm going to read the story twice.	我会讲两次/我会念两次。
How much did you understand?	你听懂了多少？
OK, I'm going to read the story a second time.	我现在要讲第二次。
This time I want you to take notes.	好，这一次我讲/念的时候，请你们记笔记。
This time, if you don't understand, raise your hand.	要是有听不懂的地方，可以举手。
DOING A READING ACTIVITY	
Xiao Wang, can you pass these out, please?	小王，请你把sth.传下去给同学。
Take one and pass them on.	一人拿一classifier，然后传给下一个人。
Does everyone have a copy of the handout?	大家都有讲义了吗/大家都拿到讲义了吗？
OK, everyone please read the dialogue to yourself.	好，请你们自己念对话。
Underline any words you don't know.	请把不认识的字用横线画出来。

TEACHING NEW INFORMATION	
Has anyone heard this word/phrase before?	谁听过/知道这个字/词？
Do you know what this means?	你们知不知道它的意思是什么/你们知不知道这个字/词是什么意思？
This is important; please write it in your notebook.	这一点很重要，请做笔记。
DICTATION	
OK, time for tingxie.	好，现在（考）听写。
Please take out your tingxie notebook.	请把听写本拿出来。
Please put away … .	请把…收起来。
Put your books on the floor.	（请）把你的书放在地上。
Two more minutes.	还有两分钟。
When you're finished, please pass your tingxie notebooks to …	要是你写完了，请把听写本传给…
USING WHITE BOARDS	
Does everyone have their white board?	大家都有白板了吗/大家都拿到白板了吗？
Please take out your white boards.	请把你（们）的白板拿出来。
Xiao Zhang, you didn't bring yours? Why not?	小张，你为什么没带你的？
OK, please write _____ in characters.	好，请写XY的X。
When you've finished writing, hold up your board so I can see it.	要是你写好了，就把你的板子举起来给我看。
Any questions on stroke order?	笔顺有没有问题？
USING THE TEXTBOOK	
OK, please take out your textbook.	好，请把课本拿出来。
Turn to page 42.	（请）翻到第42页。
Look at the top of the page.	（请）看这一页的上面。
Xiao Ye, please read #1.	小叶，请念第一题。
Turn the page.	请翻到下一页。

Appendix 3   249

WRITING ON THE BOARD	
What, no chalk?! How could that be?!	咦，没有粉笔吗？怎么会没有粉笔呢？/怎么会呢？
Just a second, be right back.	等一下，我马上回来。
Please look at the board.	请看黑板。
Can everyone see this?	大家都看得到吗？
Please write this in your notebook.	请把这个字/这个sth.写在笔记本上。
Has everyone finished copying it?	都抄好了吗？
Can I erase this?	可以擦掉了吗？
TALKING ABOUT PRONUNCIATION	
How do you pronounce this?	这个字怎么发音？
What tone is it?	…几声？
Two third tones in a row, what happens to the first?	有两个三声的时候，第一个三声会怎么样？
This sound is a little difficult because it doesn't exist in English.	这个音有点难，因为英文没有这个音。
How do you spell _____ ?	怎么拼…？
Pay attention to the tones.	注意四声。
TALKING ABOUT GRAMMAR	
This grammar point is very interesting.	这个语法点/句型很有意思。
It's not hard.	…并不难。
Are English grammar and Chinese grammar the same?	英文语法/句型跟中文一样吗？
No, they're different.	不一样。
Nope.	不可以。
Can you say it this way in Chinese?	中文能这样说吗？
[Proceed with a simple grammar explanation (2–3 sentences), followed by 2–3 examples. Then drill it.]	
[Give an example of how to do this.]	先以两三句话简单地解释文法，接着举两三个例子，然后进行操练。

LANGUAGE DURING DRILL (Focus on accuracy)	
Please repeat./One more time.	再说一次。
Full sentence please.	请说整句。
Pay attention to tones.	注意四声。
Great sentence!	好句子/说得很好！
Your tones sound terrific!	你的四声很棒！
LANGUAGE DURING DRILL **(Focus on fostering interaction)**	
What did he/she say?	他说什么？
Do you agree?	你同意吗？
GETTING STUDENTS TO GUESS OR TRY	
What do you think?	你觉得怎么样？
Take a guess./Try.	猜猜看/试试看。
Good guess ... but wrong!	猜得很好，可是猜错了。
If you're wrong, there's no charge!	猜错了没有关系。
ASKING FOR VOLUNTEERS	
Who knows ... ?	谁知道…？
Who can tell me ... ?	谁能告诉我…？
TALKING ABOUT CHARACTER ANALYSIS	
OK, we're going to do character analysis.	好，我们来看看这个字/我们来分析一下这个字。
Look at this character.	请看一下这个字/请看这个字。
What's the radical in this character?	这个字的部首是什么？
Remember, "xin" has two forms ...	记住，"心"有两种写法。
How many parts (components) does this radical have?	这个部首有几个部分？
What's on the left side?/right side?	左边是什么？右边是什么？
What's on top?/under that?	上面是什么？下面呢？
___ and ___ look very similar – be careful!	A跟B看起来像，要小心。

TALKING ABOUT WRITING CHARACTERS	
How many strokes does this character have?	这个字有几画?
Any questions on the stroke order?	有没有笔顺的问题? /笔顺有没有问题?
Do you want me to write it again?	要不要我再写一次?
CLASSROOM ITEMS	

your notebook	笔记本	marker	马克笔
your binder	夹子	eraser or tissue	板擦/纸巾
a piece of paper	一张纸	pen/pencil	笔/铅笔
the textbook	课本	Please take out …	请把…拿出来
your laptop	笔记本电脑	Please put away …	请把…收起来
white board	白板	Please put _____ on the floor.	请把…放在地上

GAMES	
Face your partner.	面朝你的同伴。
Form two lines, facing the front board.	排成两队,面向白板。
Switch partners.	交换同伴。
Stand side to side.	挨着站。
Leave a little room between.	保持一点距离。
Find a partner.	找同伴。
Sit in a circle.	坐成圈。
Sit in a half-circle.	坐成半圈。
Stand in a circle.	站成圈。
Don't talk when others are talking.	别人说话的时候请保持安静。
Switch _____ (item) with another partner.	跟另一个伙伴交换你的_____。
Count off.	轮流数1、2。
Unscramble the words to make a sentence.	组词造句。
Fold once.	折一次。

Everyone, please turn to the right.	请大家向右转。
Please return to your desks/seats.	请大家回到原来的位子。
You have 5 minutes to finish the task.	你们有五分钟完成任务。
Stand back to back.	背靠背站立。
I've already paired you up.	我已经选好了同伴。
If you have a question, raise your hand.	有问题请举手。
Put … into the proper order.	应该把…进行排序。
Put … into the proper order.	把…按…排列。
Play by the rules/You should play by the rules.	按照规则玩游戏/你们玩游戏应该遵守规则。
Fold width-wise.	横着对折。
Fold lengthwise.	竖着对折。
Cut the paper into this shape.	把纸剪成这样的形状。
Choose someone.	点人。
lottery, draw lots, draw randomly	抽签。
COMPUTER TERMS	
Move the mouse up to …	把鼠标移到…上。
Press the … key.	点击…键。
Move (a computer image) up.	往上拖。
Move down.	往下移。
Move the mouse around.	移动鼠标。
Minimize (on the computer).	最小化。
Maximize (on the computer).	最大化。
Open.	点开。

附录四：专业书面表达演说范文

1. 推荐专业学术会议（格式：会议介绍与评价）
2. 邀请信（格式：正式书信）
3. 说明语言教学中的纠错反馈（格式：总结要点）
4. 讲座总结报告（格式：专业会议信息汇报）
5. 课堂观摩反馈（格式：分析与建议）
6. 主持学术会议：介绍来宾（格式：介绍来宾讲稿）
7. 主持学术会议：主持演讲后的讨论（格式：与听众交流）

推荐专业学术会议
（格式：会议介绍与评价）

  一年一度、为期三天的全美外语教师学会今年于费城举行。我有幸参加了这次大会，收获良多。
  大会报告的内容很丰富，从"主题教学设计"到"语言应用能力测试"，从"反向课程设计"到"使用目标语教学"，无所不包。每场报告时间一个小时，采用3人合作报告的形式。以"交际的三种沟通模式"的主题为例，三位主讲人分别用15分钟发表研究结果，尽管分析的角度不同，但是都以真实的教学实例为重点。最后15分钟是现场提问交流时间。这种形式不但可以让教师统一专业教学标准和原则，而且也提供了一个让专业教师分享教学经验的平台。然而，我个人认为，每位主讲人15分钟的时间稍稍有点儿紧，也许20分钟的时间可以让主讲人讲得更详细。
  我个人认为本次大会从会前的网上注册、住宿安排到会场布置都组织得很好，参会费用也不太高。大会报告形式多样，不但有学术报告、教学工作坊，也有一些小展台，展示最新的语言教学科技和媒体教材。
  综上所述，我强烈推荐专业外语教师参加全美外语教师学会年会。

邀请信
（格式：正式书信）

  尊敬的x教授：
  您好！我是ACC K-12教师培训项目协调人xx，此次来信主要是想邀请您前来担任我们语言教学工作坊的主讲者，讲授关于"以标准为本的语言教学"的题目。ACC K-12是由汉明顿大学于2008年创办的外语教师培训项目。其目的是通过为K-12的非母语中文教师提供培训机会的方式，提升美国中文教学的质量。2013年6月24日到8月3日，我们将于中央民族大学校园启动新一届的ACCK-12教师培训项目。届时为期六周的ACC K-12项目将为中文非母语者教师提供包括语言教学、教学工作坊、学校参观、文化工作坊等在内的课程。
  x教授是美国乃至全世界汉语教学界知名的专家，桃李满天下。如果此次x教授能够接受我们的邀请于百忙之中拨冗前来，将是我们本项目全体师生的无限荣幸。
  随信附上本次ACC K-12项目的活动安排和相关事宜，敬请查看。我们热切期待您的回复。
  此致
敬礼

ACC K-12教师项目协调人 xx 敬上
201x年x月x日

说明语言教学中的纠错反馈
(格式：总结要点)

为了增进学习者分辨母语与第二语言之间的差异的能力，提高自我纠错意识，教师需要采取有效的纠错反馈原则。纠错反馈可分为直接纠错反馈和间接纠错反馈两种方法。

直接纠错反馈可以在课堂中进行，主要有两种技巧，一是计划性纠错，一是随机纠错。计划性纠错又分两种，一种是直接纠错，教师先总结常见的错误，在课堂上通过举例让学生意识到目标语的结构和规则。另一种是导出错误法，也就是说，教师透过提问把学生引导到容易出错的语言点上，当导出学生的错误后，教师立刻进行纠错。

间接纠错反馈则是在自然交际中进行，技巧有三：首先是自发性纠错，这个方法并非由教师提供正确答案，而是引导学生自己找出错误，完成纠错过程；其次，在不打断学生自然交际的前提下直接改正学生的错误；最后是重复性纠错，常见的方式包括，利用上升语调重复错句暗示学生自我改正、重复错句后马上提供对的句子、先回答错句的问题再进行纠错。

上述两类纠错反馈各有各的优势，也各有各的不足。直接纠错要求教师具备充分的语言结构知识，清楚地说明语言规则。间接纠错则是在自然交际中进行，因此能建立学生表达想法的信心，但需要有丰富的教学经验才能引导学生表达得既正确又流利。

讲座总结报告
(格式：专业会议信息汇报)

上周六，我有幸在星谈项目的年会上参加了Russel教授和Zeppieri教授关于"可理解输入"的讲座，很有收获。

这场报告跟我目前教学改进的重点密切相关。两位教授的报告分为三个部分。第一部分总结了星谈项目被广泛认可的教学原则。除了"可理解输入"以外，还包括用"标准"和"主题单元"设计课程，"创造以学生为中心的课堂"等。第二部分综合前人的研究，结合具体的例子告诉参加者所谓可理解输入是指给学生提供i+1输入。在两位教授看来，可理解输入是学生进行语言习得最重要的因素。但是可理解输入只是语言习得的步骤之一。只有把可理解输入(input)、获得(intake)和输出(output)结合起来，才可能让学生真正地学会语言。最后，两位教授通过教学案例，介绍了一些教学策略，比方说：以故事为形式；控制词汇量；使用公式化语言等。

听完这场报告以后，我对自身的教学进行了反思。虽然给学生提供可理解输入对非母语教师来说是一个挑战，但我们还应尝试采取这种做法。讲座中提到了鼓励学生利用语境，我很有同感。因为语境可以提供线索，如果学生无法理解一个词汇，他可以阅读上下文或者进行语义协商。通过不断地尝试，他对这个词的理解肯定会比只靠老师讲解更加深刻。

最后，我想用会上的一句话作为这个报告的结尾：教师采用越有效的可理解输入策略，学生才越有可能真正地习得语言。

课堂观摩反馈
（格式：分析与建议）

张老师：

恭喜你完成了本学期最后一堂课。在短短的三个月中，你的教学能力有了飞跃式的进步，这实在是一件不容易的事，我代表本项目对你表达感谢和祝贺。

今天的课堂观摩是以使用目标语和提供可理解输入为重点，以下我将和你分享我所看到的优点以及可以加强之处。首先我要说明的是，这并非一项正式的教学评鉴，我希望通过这样的交流，能让教师个人的教学和我们的中文项目同时成长。

你坚持完全使用目标语教学的做法非常值得肯定，除此以外，你也应用了许多有效的可理解输入策略。其中，我认为最成功的是通过大量举例说明来让学生学习新生词。你选择例子的时候考虑了学生的年龄和生活经验，再配合图片使用，让学生同时有语音和视觉的输入，很快就掌握了意义。

语言教学理论已证明，学习者除了对语言输入进行理解诠释以外，还需要靠有效输出才能真正习得。因此，我建议你在往后的课堂中，多采用分组交流和成果汇报的任务，让学生进行人际交流和表达演说的沟通。这样一来，你也可以通过及时的反馈，巩固学生刚学习的语言结构。

我希望上述的观察能确实反映你这堂课的教学情况，如果有任何说明不够清楚之处，欢迎你随时与我讨论、切磋。

祝教学工作顺利。

项目主任 靳洪刚
2012年12月16日

主持学术会议：介绍来宾
（格式：介绍来宾讲稿）

范文1

尊敬的各位来宾：

大家下午好，首先，很感谢大家光临今天的大会，今天我们非常荣幸能邀请到来自北京语言大学的刘XX教授和我们就汉语语音教学方面的问题分享她的宝贵经验。刘教授从上个世纪50年代起就开始进行对外汉语教学，曾多次负责汉语志愿者的培训工作，并先后出版过多部颇具影响力的汉语语音教材，在汉语语音教学领域富有极高声望，是享誉国内语音教学界的知名学者。

今天能有幸聆听刘教授的教义，我们一定会受益良多。下面，请让我们以最热烈的掌声欢迎刘教授。

范文2

各位老师、各位学员：

欢迎大家参加今天的教学工作坊，在此请允许我为大家介绍今天的主讲人徐XX先生。徐先生目前就职于美国纽约州汉明顿大学，主要负责中文系一年级的教学工作，徐先生有多年汉语教学的经验，今天他将就"有效输出"这一话题跟我们分享他的教学心得，请大家热烈欢迎。

主持学术会议：主持演讲后的讨论
（格式：与听众交流）

　　感谢麦教授这场精简扼要的演讲，相信各位与会贵宾对中文阅读的策略都有了进一步的认识。作为一位语言教师，我们都希望帮助学生发展良好的阅读策略，尤其中文的学习难度又属最高级别，唯有透过正确阅读策略的使用，学习者才能在有限时间内准确理解内容，掌握最好的学习成效。

　　接下来是我们的讨论时间，今天我们难得请到麦教授拨冗莅临本项目，如果各位与会贵宾有问题，欢迎提出来一起讨论。

　　首先，让我抛砖引玉提出第一个问题。麦教授，对于您刚才提到的"自动化过程"，不知道是否有研究显示经过多少学习量，才能达到这个自动化的目标呢？

　　（麦教授回答问题）

　　感谢麦教授的回应。请问还有没有哪位老师要提问？

　　好，我们先请左手边这位老师。

　　接下来请倒数第二排那位老师。请说。

　　因为时间的关系，我们只能接受最后两个问题。

　　（结束）

　　因为时间的关系，我们的讨论不得不在这里告一段落。再次感谢麦教授，也感谢各位来宾的参与。